Human Aggression, War and Genocide

Human Aggression,
War
and
Genocide

The Psychological Roots of Violence

Vamık D. Volkan and Kevin Volkan

Pitchstone Publishing
Durham, North Carolina

Pitchstone Publishing
Durham, North Carolina
www.pitchstonebooks.com

Printed in the United States of America

Library of Congress Cataloging-in-Publication Data

Names: Volkan, Vamik D., 1932- author. | Volkan, Kevin, 1958- author.
Title: Human aggression, war and genocide : the psychological roots of violence / Vamık D. Volkan and Kevin Volkan.
Description: Durham, North Carolina : Pitchstone Publishing, [2025] | Includes bibliographical references and index. | Summary: "This book explores sociopolitical phenomena through the lens of psychoanalysis, concentrating on concepts like aggression, leadership, and the psychology of ethnic, national, religious, and ideological large groups. Drawing inspiration from the exchange between Albert Einstein and Sigmund Freud that examined the psychological roots of war and violence, this work expands that discussion to examine racism, neuropsychoanalysis, large-group dynamics, chosen traumas and chosen glories, and the relationship between leaders and their followers. The book combines historical and contemporary viewpoints, providing a comprehensive analysis of human aggression in social contexts"—Provided by publisher.
Identifiers: LCCN 2024046459 | ISBN 9781634312684 (paperback) | ISBN 9781634312677 (ebook)
Subjects: LCSH: Aggressiveness. | War—Psychological aspects. | Violence—Psychological aspects. | Genocide—Psychological aspects.
Classification: LCC BF575.A3 V63 2025 | DDC 155.2/32—dc23/eng/20241106
LC record available at https://lccn.loc.gov/2024046459

Contents

Preface

On February 24, 2022, Russia launched an invasion of Ukraine. Since then, we continue to witness horrifying events on our television screens, such as the killing of innocent children and civilians and brutality against soldiers. The invasion destroyed homes, churches, hospitals, schools, historical sites, grocery stores, and cafés. As a result of the invasion millions of Ukrainians became internally displaced persons or refugees. As of January 2024, 200,000 Russian and 130,000 Ukrainian soldiers have died, have been severely wounded, or are missing (Russia Matters 2024). By the end of July 2024, at least 11,520 civilians, including 633 children, have been killed and 23,640, including 1,551 children, have been injured (Statista 2024). In Ukraine, 9.3 million people have been displaced, roughly 21% of the population of the entire country (Russia Matters 2024; CIA 2023; United Nations n.d.). Remarks by news media, politicians, and scholars from different professions about the role of Vladimir Putin in this new human tragedy appeared worldwide. The possibility of Russia's use of tactical nuclear weapons has induced anxiety around the world. The International Criminal Court issued an arrest warrant on March 17, 2023, for the Russian president, accusing him of being responsible for war crimes. The Russia-Ukraine conflict has involved an estimated 50 million people and is the largest instance of warfare currently on planet earth. Simultaneously, a smaller conflict was also occurring in Nagorno-Karabakh. The perennial conflict between Azerbaijan and Armenia was re-inflamed in September 2023. About 8,000 Armenians, more than half of Nagorno-Karabakh's population, escaped to

Armenia. Türkiye resumed strikes against Kurdish-held northeast Syria on October 6, 2023, following a bombing in Ankara that killed 15 people. Other skirmishes, clashes and wars continue to occur throughout the world. For example, since 2019, about 10,000 people were killed, more than 4 million were internally displaced and 1.1 million became refugees due to a war between rival factions of the military government of Sudan, Sudanese Armed Forces (SAF) and the paramilitary Rapid Support Forces (RSF). Previously, in August 2017, hundreds of thousands of stateless Rohingya people, a predominantly Muslim ethnic minority, began to flee Myanmar due to increased extreme violence. Most have crossed the border to neighboring Bangladesh. Today, the Rohingya people face mounting problems in their overcrowded camps and their future looks increasingly bleak.

As of November 2023, the Council on Foreign Relations lists 27 ongoing conflicts around the world. Wars are included among these conflicts but instabilities, many of which involve intensive violence, are also listed (Council on Foreign Relations n.d.). With regard to ongoing overt warfare, there are currently 11 conflicts around the world involving an estimated 133 million people. This list includes the war in Ukraine (50 million people and refugees), the Yemeni civil war (24 million people), the Syrian civil war (17 million people), the Tigray war (6 million people), the South Sudanese war (7.8 million people), the Myanmar civil war (10 million people), the Congolese civil war (12 million people) the Burkina Faso insurgency (2 million people), the Mozambique insurgency (1 million people), the Somali civil war (3 million people), and the Nagorno-Karabakh conflict (100,000 people). This means, at the time of this writing, about 1.5% of the world's population are in need of humanitarian assistance because they live in an area of the world stricken with violent and murderous conflict. With the exception of Ukraine, most of these areas are in Africa, Asia, and the Middle East. These numbers do not include those who have been internally displaced. It is estimated that 50 million people worldwide are internally displaced persons. We can add to all these conflicts the specter of future conflicts – the potential invasion of Taiwan and ongoing threats from North Korea, to name just two. (Council on Foreign Relations n.d.; OCHA 2023; Haney et al. 1973).

The day after the Turkish bombing in Syria, on the morning of October 7, 2023, Palestinian militant groups led by Hamas carried out a horrible surprise offensive on more than 20 locations in Israel. Hamas (Ḥarakat al-Muqāwamah al-Islāmiyyah, or the Islamic Resistance Movement) formed in late 1987. In 2007, it took over from rival Fatah the Palestinian National Authority institutions in Gaza Strip and has been the *de facto* governing body of this location ever since. We can also say that the Israeli government perceived Hamas's rise as a development that created a split among Palestinians, which would be in Israel's interest. As part of its attack, Hamas fired thousands of rockets from Gaza into Israel. Hamas also sent hundreds of gunmen into Israeli territory, killing about 1,200 Israelis on the streets, in their homes and at an outdoor festival. In a short amount of time, Hamas injured about 2,000 people and took at least 242 hostages (Frankel 2023). Since the Hamas invasion, many reports of brutal sexual assault have surfaced, including murder during rape and at least one incident of gang rape (Gaveriaux 2023; Maariv 2023; Radice 2023). Many Israelis perceived the Hamas attack as an attempt to annihilate the Israeli people, akin to the way the Nazis wanted to eradicate Jews in the Holocaust.

On October 7, 2023, Israeli Prime Minister Benjamin Netanyahu declared that the country was "at war." Within a week Israel dropped approximately 6,000 bombs on Gaza. We saw incredible destruction and witnessed young and elderly people in states of helplessness, without homes, electricity and water. On October 17, 2023, the Gaza al-Ahli Arab Hospital was attacked, killing hundreds. Hamas blamed Israel, but the Israeli military and the U.S. government stated that a failed rocket launched by the Palestinian Islamic Jihad had caused this tragedy. Independent analysis of the attack reports that while a Palestinian rocket is a possible explanation, there is some doubt about whether the evidence cited for the rocket attack is plausible (Toler et al. 2023).

As of August 2024, 1.9 million Palestinians living in Gaza have been displaced from their homes, 40,435 Palestinians have been killed and

95,534 have been injured, with approximately 5,956 of those killed being women, along with 10,627 children (UN Women 2024; UNRWA 2024). More than a hundred journalists and 254 aid workers (including 188 UN personnel) have also lost their lives in Gaza (Human Rights Watch 2024; Jones, 2023; Committee to Protect Journalists 2024).

References to Iran, Russia and other countries' roles in this new human tragedy, and the idea that this is the beginning of a third world war, have emerged. Small and big gatherings began to take place in many parts of the world either supporting the Israeli position or calling attention to the plight of Palestinians. On October 28, 2023, the Israeli army entered the Gaza Strip. On the same day, hundreds of thousands of pro-Palestinians protesters got together in Istanbul, a day ahead of the centenary of Türkiye's secular republic. Turkish President Tayyip Erdoğan addressed them and stated, "*Israel has been openly committing war crimes for 22 days, but the Western leaders cannot even call on Israel for a ceasefire, let alone react to it*" (Toksabay & Senkaya 2023, p. 1). At the same time, horrific stories and images continued to emerge regarding the slaughter of innocent people by Hamas on kibbutzim and at the Nova Music Festival. The murder of babies and innocent children by Hamas fighters defies rational description. Hamas fighters did not just kill Israelis but also mutilated bodies of the slain and allegedly beheaded children (CBS News 2023) (though the claim about the beheading of babies has been disputed [Davison et al. 202]}). While a Hamas leader claimed that the plan "*was to target the Gaza division of the occupation army, and to fight only the occupation soldiers*" (Knipp 2023), it appears that Hamas targeted anyone in their vicinity, including Thai workers at a kibbutz (Dumas & Davies 2023).

Israel's subsequent bombardment of Gaza, while ostensibly aimed at Hamas, has been described as an indiscriminate attack by Amnesty International, whose secretary General Agnes Callamard stated,

> "*In their stated intent to use all means to destroy Hamas, Israeli forces have shown a shocking disregard for civilian lives. They have pulverized street after street of residential buildings killing civilians on a mass scale*

> *and destroying essential infrastructure, while new restrictions mean Gaza is fast running out of water, medicine, fuel and electricity. Testimonies from eyewitness and survivors highlighted, again and again, how Israeli attacks decimated Palestinian families, causing such destruction that surviving relatives have little but rubble to remember their loved ones by*" (Amnesty International 2023).

The Palestinian journalist Aseel Mafarjeh described what he saw in Gaza:

> "*I saw hard things in the field. How does a mother bury her martyred son with a smile? Where does she get that strength? In these moments, I break into tears. I am conflicted because I am supposed to be strong, but at that moment I am the one who needs to be consoled. Interviewing the families of martyrs after their burial is more difficult than the funeral itself. This is when his family remembers all the good things about him. Some wish they had died in their place, while others remain steadfast. You can never forget what a mother or father say about their martyred son*" (Elmalky & Nasser 2023).

The son-in-law of an Israeli friend of Vamık Volkan was killed in battle on October 7 in the Hamas terrorist attack, leaving behind his daughter, her three small children, and other family members. The next day Vamık Volkan heard from his friend informing him about this terrible unexpected loss. Vamık Volkan himself started to experience a combination of deep sadness, shock, and helplessness. To deal with this he asked Kevin Volkan to join him and begin to write this book.

Kevin Volkan received a message from a Palestinian student attending his university courses in California. She asked if she could postpone her midterm exams. Eight members of her family had been killed in the initial Israeli bombing and five others were missing. Even though she was distraught, she refused an offer to permit her to withdraw from classes, saying that if she was not attending the university she would be forced to go back to Gaza.

We began writing this book weeks after these shocking events. We aim to focus on the "hidden" psychological aspects that underlie human violence, genocide and war, including the Russia-Ukraine and Israel-Gaza conflicts. This does not mean that we minimize visible factors such as political, legal, military, economic and criminal events. Solutions to or the continuation of horrible international events are based on dealing with such factors. An examination of less obvious psychological aspects of massive human aggressions, however, is very much related to the visible factors and are necessary for having a deeper understanding of such events as well for addressing the resistance to finding peaceful solutions.

After graduating from medical school in Türkiye, Vamık Volkan came to the United States in 1957. He became a citizen of the United States in 1968 and slowly evolved a sense of biculturalism. In 2006, Vamık, who is the son of Turkish parents on the Mediterranean island of Cyprus, had the honor of being a Fulbright/Sigmund Freud-Privatstiftung Visiting Scholar of Psychoanalysis in Austria. He and his wife settled in Vienna for five months at a location not too far away from Berggasse 19, where Freud's house, now a museum, is located. Freud lived at Berggasse 19 with his wife Martha and their children. Freud also saw his patients at this location. While in Vienna, Vamık had his office in Freud's house and wondered why Freud thought that wars waged by Turks brought "nothing but evil" (1933, p. 207).

Vienna was besieged by the Ottoman Turks twice, in 1529 and 1683. Both times the Ottomans failed to capture the city. In 1683 they were defeated by the combined forces of the Holy Roman Empire and the Polish-Lithuanian Commonwealth under the leadership of King John III Sobieski. This defeat was perceived as a triumph of Christians over Muslims. Anyone walking in Vienna today sees many reminders of the Ottomans' failed attempts and the suffering that took place during these historical events. Freud lived in such a surrounding.

When Vamık was a child in Cyprus, at that time a British colony, there was an expectation that the Nazis would come to the island after they conquered the island Crete on May 31, 1941, following an 11-day parachute invasion. Whenever German or Italian war planes would fly over Cyprus, he and his family members would rush to an underground bunker in the garden of their house. Sometimes he would hear bombs dropping.

World War II changed his childhood environment. During this time, the streets of Nicosia, the capital city of the island, were filled with Indian Sikh soldiers wearing turbans. Once, while playing with other children in the garden of his elementary school, he witnessed a British Spitfire shoot down an Italian war plane and the Italian pilot come down in a parachute. People went to the place where the Italian plane crashed and collected items from it. Someone then gave Vamık a small piece of glass taken from the crushed Italian plane. He kept this piece of glass and always knew where it was. He even brought this piece of glass to the United States. After he became a psychiatrist, he realized that "controlling" this piece of glass was in the service of controlling his war anxiety, which he had developed in his childhood. As an adult and a psychoanalyst in the United States, after spending decades bringing together enemy representatives of opposing large groups, such as Israelis-Egyptians/Palestinians, Russian-Estonians, Serbian-Croats and Georgians-South Ossetians, for unofficial dialogues, and after studying people who lived during wars or war-like situations, such as Cypriot Turks, Bosnians and Kuwaitis, he concluded that all human large groups everywhere, including Mongols, Turks, Russians, Ukrainians, Israelis and Palestinians are the same in wanting to kill or love the Other.[1] Sometimes, under certain

1. "The Other" was introduced by Hegel as a concept related to intersubjectivity that is necessary and complementary to one's concept of one's Self. (Hegel 1807). The concept was expounded upon by other philosophers including Husserl (1961, 1992), Jean-Paul Sartre (Grene 1971) and Simone de Beauvoir (1971). The concept of "the Other" occurs early in psychoanalysis since it is somewhat synonymous with the idea of the "object." For instance, in "Psycho-Analytic Notes on an Autobiographical Account of a Case of Paranoia (Dementia Paranoides)," Freud explained, "There comes a time in the development of the individual at which he unifies his sexual instincts (which have hitherto been engaged in auto-erotic activities) in order to obtain a love-object; and he begins by taking himself, his own body, as his love-object, and only subsequently proceeds from this to the choice of some person other than himself as his object." (1911, pp. 59–60).

circumstances, it is true that these large groups bring "nothing but evil." (Volkan, V. D. 1988, 1997, 2006, 2013a, 2020).

One of the themes of this book is that genocide, racism, and war have deep psychological connections. Kevin Volkan grew up on the coast of California amidst a melting pot of immigrants, mostly from Latin America and Asia. California history is rife with the maltreatment of these immigrants, as well as the slow-motion genocide of indigenous Californians (Madley 2017). He is writing this section from a part of California that is unceded from the Chumash people. Beginning in the late 1700s, the Spanish under the Franciscan Father Junipero Serra began building missions along the cost of California. Ostensibly, the missions were established to convert the indigenous population, but they also served as a colonizing force, preparing the way for Spanish and later Mexican settlers. The indigenous people were not just converted but were also used as forced labor. Even before the missions were established, indigenous Californians were decimated by new diseases brought by the Spanish. As Edward Castillo writes,

> *"Despite romantic portraits of California missions, they were essentially coercive religious, labor camps organized primarily to benefit the colonizers. The overall plan was to first militarily intimidate the local Indians with armed Spanish soldiers who always accompanied the Franciscans in their missionary efforts. At the same time, the newcomers introduced domestic stock animals that gobbled up native foods and undermined the free or "gentile" tribe's efforts to remain economically independent. A well-established pattern of bribes, intimidation and the expected onslaught of European diseases insured experienced missionaries that eventually desperate parents of sick and dying children and many elders would prompt frightened Indian families to seek assistance from the newcomers who seemed to be immune to the horrible diseases that overwhelmed Indians. The missions were authorized by the crown to "convert" the Indians in a ten-year period. Thereafter they were supposed to surrender their control over the mission's livestock, fields, orchards and building to the Indians. But the padres never achieved this goal and the lands and wealth was stolen from the Indians."* (Castillo n.d.).

The war between the United States and Mexico, fomented by the United States' sense of Manifest Destiny, began in 1846 when Mexico refused the United States' offer to purchase Texas as well as California and territory that stretched as far north as Oregon. Eventually, this war ended with the Treaty of Guadalupe Hidalgo. Mexico gave up Texas, California, Nevada and Utah in whole, as well as parts of Arizona, Colorado, New Mexico and Wyoming, a loss of over 50% of its territory.

The United States-Mexico war ended in California with the Treaty of Cahuenga, signed in what is now North Hollywood, near the famous Hollywood sign. Some question whether this war ever really ended. For those growing up in California, its effects are apparent to this day. After the war, most Mexicans living in California became U.S. citizens, however they were also subject to a good deal of violence, including lynching, loss of property, and racial discrimination (Alcaraz et al. 1850; J. H. Smith 1919).

Kevin grew up in a society where Mexican Americans were systematically disadvantaged, racially profiled, and denied access to housing, education and healthcare and where immigrants from Mexico, as well as other parts of Latin America, were, and continue to be, exploited for cheap labor, mostly as farmworkers. (Barajas 2012, 2021). Kevin lives in Ventura County, California. Like most counties in the United States, the county's real property records contain examples of archaic discriminatory racial covenants. These are restrictions in deeds, promoted by the Federal Housing Administration and enforced by the courts until 1948, which were intended to promote segregation by prohibiting persons of marginalized or ethnic backgrounds from owning homes in certain residential areas, or even living in such homes, unless they were servants. For example, David García in his book *Strategies of Segregation* (2018) gives an example of a racial covenant applied to a subdivision in Ventura County, California in 1946:

> *"No persons of any race other than the White or Caucasian race, nor any Mexican, Indian, or East Indian, nor any person who is a lineal descendant of the first or second degree of a person born in the Republic of Mexico,*

> *shall use or occupy any building, or any lot, except that this covenant shall not prevent occupancy by domestic servants of a different race domiciled with an owner or tenant.*" (p. 44)

Only in 2022 did the California legislature require property sellers with knowledge of an illegal restrictive covenant to provide new owners with a "Restrictive Covenant Modification" form, which – if the new owner elects to submit such a form – permits the county recorder to remove offensive language from the deed.[2]

Kevin grew up around other immigrants to California, including Americans of Chinese descent. The first wave of Chinese people began immigrating to California during the time of the Gold Rush, and by 1860, one in ten Californians had Chinese heritage. Like the descendants of Mexicans native to California, Chinese immigrants faced exploitation and violence, including lynching. To appease white laborers, California legislators put discriminatory anti-Coolie laws into effect. Shockingly, California state politicians actively opposed the 14th and 15th Amendments to the federal constitution, which would have granted citizenship and voting rights to people of Chinese descent. To restrict Chinese laborers from entering the United States, Congress passed the Chinese Exclusion Act of 1882, which was extended in 1892 and permanently enforced in 1902. The Act was not completely repealed until 1965. This law became the blueprint for immigrant and border regulation in the United States, contributing to the numerous abuses that immigrants face when attempting to enter the country today (Chinese Exclusion Act [1882] 2021; Lee 2003; Lew-Williams 2018; Sandmeyer & Daniels 1991). During the COVID pandemic, hate crimes against Asians in general and Chinese specifically have increased. It is possible that anti-Asian crimes may now be on the decline, or it may be that there is an increased reluctance to report these crimes (Park 2023).

Before the Second World War, about 120,000 Japanese Americans lived in the U.S. mainland, mostly in California and the Pacific Coast.

---

2. California Government Code section 12956.2(a)(2), as amended (2021).

After the attack on Pearl Harbor, virtually all of these people (about two-thirds of whom were born in the United States) were incarcerated without due process in internment camps for up to four years by the U.S. government under Executive Order 9066. These individuals lost their property, livelihood and, to some extent, their dignity (Charles River Editors 2019; Gruenewald 2005; Wakida & Hohri 2014). Kevin has known many Japanese Americans who survived this traumatic experience. It is painfully obvious how long the effects of genocide, racism and war can persist.

Kevin missed the Vietnam War draft by a matter of months but has close friends who served in Vietnam. He heard many first-person accounts of the horrors his friends experienced and saw some traumatized not only by the psychological experience of serving in Vietnam but also by the physical effects of exposure to Agent Orange (Martini 2012; Sills 2014). At the time of this writing, a friend who served as a medic in Vietnam is dying of cancer that may have been induced by toxic exposure during his service. Lastly, as a professor, Kevin has had numerous students in his classes who served in the Gulf War and in Afghanistan. The experiences of these students and their desire to go into the field of psychology in order to help other veterans has affected and inspired him deeply.

The life experience of both authors of this book speaks to the scope and depth of the effects of human aggression and war as well as the pathological large-group processes that accompany it. We take as a point of departure Sigmund Freud's response to Albert Einstein's 1932 letter, in which the physicist essentially asks the psychiatrist, "Why war?" We will then begin to update the answers to this question with findings from present-day psychological knowledge related to object relations theory and large-group psychology, including the inflammation of the shared images of ancestors' traumatic as well as glorified pasts, the appearance of a shared sense of entitlement to dehumanize the Other and the role of the personality organizations of political leaders in massive aggressive events.[3] Further, we will focus on the shared psychological elements, including aspects of personality, that are behind Vladimir Putin's February 24, 2022, invasion of Ukraine and Hamas's October 7, 2023, attack on Israel, which Hamas refers to as Al-Aqsa Storm.

---

3. Here, the term "personality" refers to the observable and predictable patterns that a person consciously and unconsciously uses in everyday situations to maintain a stable and positive relationship with their surroundings. Personality is closely connected to the way individuals regulate themselves and adapt to their environment, both internally and in their interactions with others. Within the concept of personality, there are two additional elements: temperament and character. Temperament encompasses the genetically and constitutionally determined emotional and behavioral tendencies of a person. Character, on the other hand, is shaped by the ways in which individuals navigate internal conflicts during their formative years. When combined, temperament and character give rise to the unique personality traits of an adult.

1

Correspondence Between Albert Einstein and Sigmund Freud

When we watch the news from Ukraine and Russia, Israel and Gaza, and other places where wars or war-like situations are taking place, as psychoanalytically informed thinkers, we are reminded again and again of the correspondence between Albert Einstein and Sigmund Freud that was later published under the title "*Warum Krieg?*" ("Why War?") (Freud 1933).

In 1932, four months before Vamık Volkan was born, Albert Einstein sent a letter from Berlin to Sigmund Freud in Vienna. The questions Einstein asked in his letter (Freud 1933) reflect our present-day concerns. The same questions remain today.

> "*Is there any way of delivering mankind from the menace of war?*" (p. 199)

> "*How is it possible*" *for a small group of people craving for political power* "*to bend the will of the majority, who stand to lose and suffer by a state of war, to the service of their ambitions?*" (p. 200)

> "*Is it possible to control man's mental evolution so as to make him proof against the psychoses of hate and destructiveness?*" (p. 201)

Freud, in his response to Einstein, was pessimistic about human nature and the idea of psychoanalysis having an influence on preventing wars. He stated that "conflicts of interest between men are settled by the use of violence" and added that this is true of the whole animal kingdom to which humans also belong. Freud wrote:

> *"a glance of the of the history human race reveals an endless series of conflicts between one community and another or several others, between larger and smaller units –between cities, provinces, races, nations, empires – which have almost always been settled by force of arms.*" (p. 206–207)

In his letter to Einstein, Freud also described some behavior patterns of *large groups*. In the psychological literature the term "large group" often refers to 30 to 150 members who meet to deal with a given issue. The term "large group" sometimes also stands for "crowds" or "masses." Otto Kernberg (2003 a, b) uses the term "crowds" when referring to spectators at a big sports event or large theatrical performance. He also mentions disorganization in crowds after natural disasters, "mass movements" and "societal and cultural processes" and points at the emergence of aggression in "small groups," "crowds" and "societies" when regression and disorganization set in.

In this book the term "*large group*" defines thousands or millions of individuals who are linked by a persistent sense of linguistic, cultural, and historical sameness even, though most of them will never meet each other. We are referring to tribal, ethnic, national, religious, or ideological large groups. In everyday language we often refer to these types of large groups when, for example, we declare, "We are Apaches," "We are Spanish," "We are the Jewish community in Lithuania," We are Sunni Muslims," "We are Communists," "We are white supremacists," etc. Revising Erik Erikson's description of individual identity, we define core *large-group identity*—whether it refers to ethnicity, nationality, religion, or ideology—as the subjective experience of thousands or millions of people who are linked by a persistent sense of sameness and who define themselves as being distinct from other groups.

Freud stated that some large groups, such as the Romans and the French, have contributed to the transformation of violence into law "by establishing larger units within which the use of violence was made impossible and in which a fresh system of law led to the solution of conflicts" (p. 207). He also reminded Einstein that the Romans gave the conquered places round the Mediterranean "the priceless *pax Romana*," the Roman peace due to the absence of war, and the French kings extended their dominions by creating a united France that was peaceful. Freud followed up this thought with the idea that wars waged by Mongols and Turks produced "only evil."

In *Civilization and Its Discontents*, Freud (1930) wrote that civilization, like a garrison of a conquered city, obtains mastery over individuals' dangerous desire for aggression. But he added that sometimes large groups can have the opposite effect on individuals, releasing moral constraints and unleashing the horrors of war. In his response to Einstein, Freud informed him of two types of human instincts. The first type is called *the erotic instinct*, "exactly in the sense in which Plato uses the word 'Eros' in his *Symposium*, or 'sexual,' with a deliberate extension of the popular conception of 'sexuality'" (p. 209). Erotic instinct seeks to preserve and unite. He described how the second type of instinct, *the death instinct*, is the predilection for aggression and violence. He added that an instinct scarcely ever operates in isolation. For example, "the instinct of self-preservation is certainly of an erotic kind, but it must nevertheless have aggressiveness at its disposal if it is to fulfil its purpose" (p. 209). He also wrote, "If willingness to engage in a war is an effect of the destructive instinct, the most obvious plan will be to bring Eros, its antagonist, into play against it" (p. 212). Freud also focused on another psychological concept, "identification," and reminded Einstein that we need to keep in mind this concept when we think of the structure of a human society.

Referring to Einstein's remarks about how a small group of people who crave political power can abuse their authority, Freud suggested that "more care should be taken than hitherto to educate an upper stratum of men with independent minds, not open to intimidation and eager to pursuit of truth, whose business it would be to give direction to the dependent masses" (p. 212).

At the end of his letter, Freud expressed a tinge of optimism. He wondered how long we must wait before the rest of mankind became pacifists like himself and Albert Einstein. He did not know the answer but wrote that two factors,

> "... *the cultural attitude and the justified dread to the consequences of a future war, may result within a measurable time in putting an end to the waging of war. By what paths or by what side-tracks this will come about we cannot guess. But one thing we can say: whatever fosters the growth of civilization works at the same time against war.*" (p. 215)

Today, the growth of civilization is supported by incredible advances in technology and the appearance of artificial intelligence in human affairs. But wars still are taking place. In fact, we now experience more anxiety related to technological advances that have resulted in ever deadlier armaments as well as the existence of nuclear weapons that could annihilate all life on earth.

Shortly after this exchange, Adolf Hitler became the Chancellor of Germany on January 30, 1933, leading Einstein to flee Germany and immigrate to the United States. Freud would leave his home five years later in 1938. After the German takeover of Austria in March of that year, 82-year-old Sigmund Freud, his wife, Martha, and their daughter, Anna, fled Vienna on June 4, 1938. As Jews, they knew their lives were in immediate danger. In fact, just after Freud had made the difficult decision to leave Vienna forever, Anna was arrested by the Gestapo. She carried with her a secret vial of deadly poison in case she was tortured. Previously, Freud, who was suffering from cancer, had his home searched and his passport confiscated. It took considerable international and diplomatic pressure for Freud and his family that remained in Austria to be allowed to leave (Cohen 2012). Sigmund Freud died in London on September 23, 1939, at the age of 83.

Ernest Jones (1961), one of the well-known early psychoanalysts, later wrote that Freud was disappointed with his exchange with Einstein and also with the League of Nations. One may speculate that Freud initially perceived the League of Nations as analogous to a collective integrating ego, but after some observations, he saw that it was more like a collective superego, and as such was subject to regression. As Jacob Arlow (1973), another well-known psychoanalyst of his time, stated, the demands of the superego, especially in cases of regression, may reflect the ideals and strictures of a subculture, even amoral ones, rather than the purely moral values of the entire culture.

Freud felt that whatever fosters the growth of civilization opposes war at the same time. The growth of civilization appears to be different from culture to culture and from large group to large group. Such differences are a matter of degree, however, since more civilized large groups can also regress and indulge in destructive activities in an attempt to sustain large-group bonding, self-esteem, and support for the large group's leader. (We will describe signs of large-group regression later in this book.) Certain technological advances should not be considered as a measuring stick for progress in civilization. Real progress would also include socio-political systems that inhibit explosions of aggressive movements, a more effective harmony between people and nature, and a tilt in thinking toward humane and peaceful goals.

When Greek astronomers were elated by new discoveries, Plato criticized their preoccupation with the cosmos and their neglect of those conditions that might enhance human life. A similar criticism might be directed to modern people with nuclear weapons and now with the ability to utilize artificial intelligence. Star Wars technology may amaze us and excite us, but collections of human beings continue to burn, cripple, bury alive and kill other humans and destroy nature and wildlife in wars, just as our ancestors did.

2

Human Violence and Aggression

We are inclined towards violence. This is an inherent characteristic of our human nature. It is not necessary to embark on an extensive search to observe this phenomenon; a mere glance at the news on television or a newspaper will suffice. At any given moment, instances of human violence are taking place all over the world. While our current focus may be on the unrest in Ukraine, as well as in Israel and Gaza, it is crucial to recognize that violence is not limited to a specific geographic area or a specific period in human history. When we look at the entirety of human history, we find that violence is common. To understand large-group conflicts such as war, it is necessary to reflect on the reasons why humans are so violent. To examine this question, the fields of evolutionary biology and evolutionary psychology, as well as psychoanalysis, can provide valuable insights. According to these perspectives, human violence is not a random phenomenon; rather, it has had survival value at some point in human evolution.

Violence and Evolution

Let us start with violence at the level of the individual where people commit acts of violence against another person or other people. This type of violence is important to understand because it is at least in part related to the roots of violence in small and large groups, including nations that engage in warfare against other nations.

A key to understanding the origins of human violence begins with our closest primate relatives, such as bonobos (*Pan paniscus*),[1] chimpanzees (*Pan troglodytes*) and gorillas (*Gorilla gorilla* and *Gorilla beringei*). In the past, violence likely played a role in ensuring the survival and propagation of a primate ancestor we had in common with bonobos, chimpanzees and gorillas.

The evolutionary perspective of human violence is also related to a psychoanalytic understanding of the human mind, specifically through how we feel and process aggression. This is associated with the death drive, which we will cover in more depth later. For now, we can think of the death drive as generally representing aggression in the service of survival. To give an example, let's think about an insect walking on the ground – imagine your least favorite insect for the sake of this example. Now, if you were to approach this bug with the intention of squashing it, what would it do in response? The bug has two possible reactions. It might decide to run away, understandably wanting to avoid being squashed. This is what biologists label a "flight" response. Even though the bug doesn't have much of a brain or cognitive capacity, it still has enough awareness to try and prevent its being killed. On the other hand, the bug could choose to defend itself, employing what biologists label a "fight" response. For example, if the insect happens to be a bee or a wasp, and it perceived that you were making a threatening gesture, it would react by stinging you, causing you to abandon your plan. This aggressive behavior would allow the insect to survive and reproduce in greater numbers than insects that didn't react aggressively. According to

1. We will not discuss bonobos in this work. Bonobos are an extremely close relative to chimpanzees, and unlike chimpanzees and humans they often defuse potentially violent conflicts with sexual interaction, at least when they are in captivity. When bonobos are observed in the wild, they are seen to be relatively more violent. However, bonobo aggressiveness includes both males and females while chimpanzees exhibit mostly male-dominated hostility. Bonobos also exhibit less intergroup hostility than chimpanzees. It may be that aggression was selected against in bonobos as part of a process of self-domestication. For more on these interesting primates, see works by Leveda Cheng and colleagues 2021; Brian Hare and colleagues 2012, 2017 and Richard Wrangham, 1993.

natural selection, this protective aggressive behavior will persist because it confers survival value or "fitness" to the insect. In other words, insects that were squashed were not able to continue propagating their DNA. As a result, the surviving insects are the ones that have successfully protected themselves from danger, ensuring their ability to have offspring. This type of aggressive behavior has become programmed into their nervous systems.

Defensive Aggression

The type of defensive aggression outlined above is just one type of aggression within the animal kingdom. The biologist and ethologist Konrad Lorenz, an intriguing figure, offers an insightful theory on aggression in the animal kingdom (1966).[2] Lorenz identified four distinct types of aggression: *defensive*, *maternal*, *predatory* and *display*. As described above, defensive aggression can be seen in an animal trying to protect itself with a fight response. This form of aggression stems from an animal's innate desire to avoid being consumed or harmed. A personal anecdote gives a sense of the concept of defensive aggression.

Kevin Volkan once lived in a place where skunks were abundant. He owned a dog that was bred for hunting small animals. One warm night, he left his backdoor open, allowing the dog to go into the backyard.

---

2. Konrad Lorenz is also noteworthy for having cooperated with the Nazi regime. The question arises as to whether one can overlook or forgive Lorenz for writing a paper that could be perceived as somewhat apologetic towards Nazism or Nazi racial principles. Nevertheless, Lorenz had an academic collaboration with Nikolaas Tinbergen, who held anti-Nazi views. It is possible that Lorenz's cooperation was a means to secure a professorship under the Nazi regime. After World War II the associations that Lorenz had with the Nazis seemed to fade or become obscured over time. Despite his connection to the Nazis, Lorenz managed to achieve a significant milestone in his career when he was awarded the Nobel Prize in 1973 with Tinbergen, for their groundbreaking contributions to the field of ethology. Ultimately, the decision to pass judgment on Lorenz is an individual decision and it is not our intention to be his apologists. While Lorenz's actions are questionable at best, his contributions to academic discourse on aggression in the animal kingdom remain important. For more on Lorenz, see Theodora J. Kalikow (1983) and Peter Marler (1991).

Unfortunately, a skunk showed up, and upon spotting the small animal, the dog instinctively pounced on it. In response, the skunk released its noxious spray directly into the dog's face. Distressed and desperate for relief, the dog rushed into the house and jumped on the bed where Kevin was sleeping. This happened around three o'clock in the morning. The stench from the skunk was so overpowering that he experienced both auditory and visual hallucinations. Luckily, the 24-hour supermarket stocked large gallon bottles of an enzymatic skunk odor neutralizer called Skunk Away. This anecdote serves as a testament to the effectiveness of skunks' defensive aggression in keeping themselves alive and not becoming a meal for potential predators.[3]

Maternal (Parental) Aggression

The next type of aggression, maternal aggression, is a phenomenon that may be familiar to many. While we often associate this concept with humans and primates who care for their young over relatively long periods of time, this type of aggression is present in other animals as well. One example that is well known in popular culture is the maternal aggression displayed by bears. There are many accounts of people encountering and then approaching what seem to be adorably cute grizzly bear cubs in the wilderness. As some have found out the hard way, this seemingly innocent act can have dire consequences. For example, grizzly bear mothers are fiercely protective of their offspring and will not hesitate to become aggressive towards even the slightest perceived threat (Bombieri et al. 2019). This hyper-aggressiveness has evolved in bears because of the propensity of male bears to attack the cubs sired by other males.

It is important to note that so-called maternal aggression also occurs in fathers. In fact, this type of aggression might better be termed parental aggression. For instance, when reflecting on competitive activities for children such as Little League or soccer, it becomes evident that aggression among parents is more common than it is among the children who are competing with each other. It is not uncommon to witness fights

3. Interestingly, one of the main predators of skunks are owls, which attack from above and have a weak sense of smell (Fisher & Stankowich, 2018).

between parents arising from a perceived unfair call by an umpire or referee. Consequently, many of the sports rules for school-age children are not directed towards the children but rather towards their parents.

A noteworthy, but somewhat twisted, human example of maternal aggression occurred in Texas several years ago. In this notorious case, a mother "protected" her daughter by orchestrating a plot to kill a rival student and her mother who posed a threat to the daughter's aspiration of earning a spot on her junior high school's cheerleading squad (Swartz 1991).

Predatory Aggression

Predatory aggression is another form of aggression that is universal in the animal kingdom. This type of aggression is used when one animal seeks out and consumes another for sustenance. In contemporary times, we have become removed from this type of aggression since acquiring meat is a relatively effortless task. We visit the local market and choose from the meat section, or order meat from an online grocery delivery service. In contrast, in the not-so-distant past, if you wanted meat, you had to catch it yourself. Back in the day acquiring meat required more effort. Thus, the ability to manifest aggression was vital to procure high-density protein.

While predatory aggression, characterized by the straightforward pursuit and capture of prey, is not a prevalent feature of first-world human society, it is perhaps represented symbolically in sports and competition as well as in recreational hunting, fishing, etc. While some individuals enjoy hunting as a recreational activity, this form of aggression has been symbolized and stylized to a significant extent. We no longer find ourselves venturing into the wilderness to hunt for our daily sustenance. The act of hunting, with its subsequent rituals of bleeding, skinning, eviscerating, cleaning and cooking the prey, is not a common occurrence during our lunchtime endeavors.

It has been argued that hunting behavior played a significant role in the evolution of the hominid brain, as well as in its intellectual and imaginal capacity (Wong 2014). We became more intelligent and develop superior hunting skills, which consequently enabled us to procure greater sources of protein and denser foods to fuel our expanding brains. This symbiotic relationship between enhanced hunting abilities and heightened intelligence may have played a pivotal role in the evolution of human intellect.

Display Aggression

The last type of aggression is display aggression. Typically, animals that exhibit display aggression exist within a social hierarchy, where individuals compete for resources, territory or access to mates, specifically in the case of male animals competing for the opportunity to mate with females. While there may be exceptions, most display aggression occurs in the pursuit of territory that contains resources such as food. As Dominic Johnson and Monica Duffy Toft (2013) write,

> *"Across animal species, territorial behavior has a number of characteristics: (1) it is most developed in adult males; (2) it operates more or less clearly delimited area within which males signal strength and agility to intruders (usually of the same species); (3) the resident male usually wins (or if not, it is the larger individual that does); (4) territorial displays are among the most elaborate of all behaviors in the species' behavioral repertoire; (5) physical or auditory displays tend to make individuals appear larger and more dangerous; and (6) the competitive exchanges are mostly bluffing and fighting does not usually result in injury or death... Territoriality, however, explains many aspects of peace as well—regulations overseas and airspace, international law, exploitation right, border security, immigration controls, negotiations and treaties over territory that remain short of war and, not least, the very division of the globe into territorially bounded nation-states in the first place. The world map – even during times of peace – is a picture of human territoriality."* (p. 21)

It is worth noting that display aggression can be exhibited by an animal seeking to move up in a dominance hierarchy, or an animal in a dominant position in the hierarchy maintaining their position against challengers, or in a spontaneous competition for dominance without any reference to a hierarchy. The behavior of dogs provides a good example of display aggression that many of us have witnessed.[4] When two dogs encounter each other, they engage in a series of behaviors to establish their relative dominance or submissiveness. This typically involves sniffing each other's hindquarters, which serves as a form of communication. When dogs try to establish which is dominant, they will growl at each other. This may escalate into a fight until one animal gives up and becomes submissive. One dog attempts to assert its dominance over the other, while the other dog chooses to challenge its dominant counterpart or submit to its authority. This can sometimes escalate into physical fights, though these fights typically do not result in injury and death. However, one of the dogs will typically display submissive behavior defusing potential aggression in the other dog.. Dominance or submission doesn't seem to be related to age or weight differences between dogs. The submissive dog recognizes the other dog's superiority and avoids confrontation. When a dog shows submission, it typically performs a lowered tail wag, rolls over and exposes its belly, licks the mouth of the other dog and/or passes under its head as a sign of deference. This display of submission is a clear indicator of the power dynamics at play and

4. It should be noted that contrary to popular belief dogs do not typically form primate-like dominance hierarchies, nor do they form family-like hierarchies such as those found in wolves. However, according to Jessica Pierce and Marc Bekoff (Bekoff 2016; Pierce & Bekoff 2021), they are competitive with each other and may form dominance hierarchies that may or may not include humans. As Joanne van der Borg and her colleagues (2015) put it, "It should be made clear that animals do not need to have a notion of the concept of dominance in order to establish a dominance relationship and with it, a hierarchy. As computer simulations have shown, rank orders may arise automatically, when a few simple rules of giving or taking precedence are followed. Self-organisation is an underestimated aspect of social organisation in animal species. It arises through repeated encounters among group members, which are opportunities to gain information on the actual strength of opponents and help to avoid losing fights in the future; thus learning plays a role in the formation of dominance relationships." For an overview of the current thinking and controversies regarding canine dominance hierarchies, see Jacob Brogan (2021).

the recognition of dominance by one dog over the other (van der Borg et. al. 2015).

In most species display aggression is not lethal, though there are many exceptions, including wolves, lions and, of course, chimpanzees. Display aggression is often intricately linked to sexual access and the pursuit of mates within various animal species and is quite common among primates, including humans, in this context. In the case of human beings, however, these behaviors are not as clearly categorized or confined to specific patterns. Instead, there is a mixture of various behavioral traits that coexist in a complex manner.

A good example of display aggression studied by Lorenz can be seen in mouthbrooding cichlid fish (*Haplochromis burtoni*), which are closely related to the more commonly known fighting fish that one may encounter at an aquarium or even purchase at a pet store. These tropical fish exhibit fascinating behaviors and employ intriguing strategies in their quest for reproduction. It is worth noting that the dominant (alpha) males of this species tend to possess vibrant and eye-catching colors and engage in fierce battles to defend their territory from any potential intruders. The alpha males will fight each other to establish control over a specific territory where the females deposit their eggs. Consequently, the alpha male will fertilize these eggs by releasing his reproductive milt across them. Interestingly, other "beta" or "bachelor" males employ a cunning strategy to avoid the display aggression of the alpha males. The beta males will mimic the appearance of females and cleverly infiltrate the territory without drawing suspicion and proceed to fertilize the eggs as well.

Naturally, such a complex reproductive system necessitates the presence of aggression, specifically display aggression, which is prominently exhibited by brightly colored alpha males. Members of the animal kingdom frequently showcase genetic fitness through displays of vibrant colors—for instance, the flamboyant display of peacocks, characterized by their elaborate feathers. Although this behavior may not be inherently aggressive in nature, it does serve as a visual display aimed at attracting potential mates.

Display aggression is also observed among primates, particularly monkeys. In these cases, display aggression typically revolves around the males' efforts to gain sexual access to the females. This parallel between the animal kingdom and human behavior suggests that human beings may exhibit similar patterns of aggression in certain contexts, particularly those related to sexual dynamics.

Kruger Park

Great examples of the types of aggression outlined by Lorenz can be seen at Kruger National Park in South Africa. Vamık Volkan visited Kruger Park and experienced firsthand each type of aggression we have listed. He wrote about the deep impression his ride around the park made in his book *Enemies on the Couch* (2013):

> "*During the ride I saw a kind of 'oedipal story' performed by elephants. While we were being driven around, the air began to smell peculiar. The guide informed us that the smell was coming from a sexually aroused young male elephant; it was the smell of testosterone. This excited elephant had spotted an older male elephant with two female companions and two very young elephants. The sexually aroused male elephant rushed to this 'family gathering' in a fury, causing the female elephants to take their 'children' and slowly moved away while the two male elephants, the younger one and the older one, pulled up some trees with their trunks and started hitting each other. We watched them for some time in amazement. Then we were driven away before we could see the end of this fantastic battle … I decided to make a list of what I observed the animals doing at Kruger Park: Searching for food, possessing a territory, having sex, making babies, protecting babies, losing a loved one, forming groups, males competing with other males in the same group, exhibiting aggression and submission, experiencing fear, developing species-oriented defenses, escaping from or fighting and killing the 'other' and being preoccupied with individualized and group survival … I amused myself by thinking that no candidate in a psychoanalytic institute should be allowed to graduate without first visiting Kruger Park and observing wild animals illustrating elements that also underlie human nature*" (pp. 141–142).

There is a famous YouTube video titled "Battle at Kruger" that highlights predatory, defensive and parental aggression (Schlosberg, 2007). The video is well worth watching, as it shows a thrilling encounter between a group of Cape buffalo, a small pack of lions and two crocodiles at the Transport Dam watering hole in Kruger National Park. The video starts off with the buffalo heading towards the water, unaware of a nearby pride of the lions. In an act of predatory aggression, the lions chase the buffalo herd. The herd panics and runs off. Unfortunately, a slower-moving buffalo calf is caught by a lion and, during the ensuing struggle, falls into the water. While the lions attempt to drag the calf out of the water, the calf is attacked by two crocodiles that lock onto its hindquarters in yet another act of predatory aggression. The lions then have a tug of war with the crocodiles for the calf. Eventually, the lions are able to pull the calf out of the water. By this time, however, the buffalo herd has regrouped and in a beautiful example of collective defensive and parental aggression, the herd launches an assault on the lions, forcing them to retreat and freeing the calf.

Human Aggression

There is a reciprocal relationship between predatory aggression and defensive aggression – an arms race if you will. Defensive aggression evolves to better protect against predatory aggression and predatory aggression evolves to overcome defensive aggression. Predatory and defensive aggression primarily occurs between different species of animals. Maternal (parental) aggression occurs between the same and different species, while display aggression occurs within a species. Human beings exhibit all four types of aggression and may demonstrate mixed combinations of these types of aggression. Among humans the complexities of aggression, specifically display aggression, extend far beyond the simple examples of aggression in the animal world.

Psychoanalytically speaking, display aggression in humans is related to the Oedipus complex. The term is used to describe a stage of psychosexual development where children develop unconscious sexual desires for their opposite-sex parent and feel a sense of competition with their same-sex parent. During this stage, boys and girls have similar and different reactions. In response to their attraction to their mothers, boys unconsciously fear that their fathers will castrate or kill them. The oedipal situation of boys resolves when they begin to identify with the father and seek out their own object of attraction – a women who is like, but not, their mother. Girls are perhaps a bit more complicated. For girls, the oedipal situation is influenced by how they react to discovering the physical differences between boys and girls. Girls develop a strong attachment to their fathers and may fixate on him as a love object, but this fixation is less repressed compared to boys, since girls do not fear castration. Girls also have a special love for their mothers but may experience a heightened aggressive aspect of ambivalence towards their mothers as they recognize genital anatomical differences with boys. This can lead to a desire to have a penis, which was termed by Freud as penis envy. But when a girl realizes that obtaining a penis is not possible, she redirects her desire towards having a baby as a replacement. Another interpretation is that girls envy the mother's power to have the father's penis inside her and therefore desire to possess one themselves in order to please the mother. Feminist psychoanalysts believe that penis envy in little girls is their realization that they are denied the power and privilege granted to males. The psychoanalyst Karen Horney proposes three causes of penis envy in girls: envy over the pleasure boys get from urinating, jealousy of male exhibitionism and the perception that boys have permission to touch themselves while urinating, while girls do not (Zepf 2015). The phenomenon of penis envy is complicated as is the male counterpart: womb envy. We cover these subjects in more detail elsewhere (K. Volkan & V. D. Volkan 2023). For boys and girls, the oedipal situation is the forerunner of display aggression. It is the first instance of facing a rival for a mate. Or it can be thought of as a practice run for being able to compete for a mate. In this specific oedipal pattern, aggression towards the same-sex parent and its resolution will determine how a boy or girl will compete for a mating partner in later life.

For humans and our closest primate cousins, as well as a few other species, display aggression can be deadly. While human beings may exhibit certain parallels to the aggression observed in animals, it is crucial to recognize the distinctiveness of human behavior, which is shaped by our advanced cognitive abilities and cultural influences, as well as our psychological development. Human defensive, maternal, predatory and display aggression possess a high level of symbolism. Interestingly, when examining human behavior, one can observe that these different forms of aggression often intertwine, making them complex and not easily categorized. One of the ways we can see the complex intertwining of types of aggression in humans is to consider cheating.

Cheating

Cheating can be defined as the act of depriving others of their resources without offering anything in return, thus creating an unfair imbalance characterized by a lack of reciprocity. It can also be seen more generally as a form of dishonesty or deception in interpersonal relationships. Cheating can range from using white lies to be polite or to manage certain kinds of social situations, to a manifestation of a personality disorder (Akhtar et al. 2009). Cheating can also include theft. For psychoanalysts like Donald Winnicott, stealing is a symbolic act. He describes in children a "hopeful stealing," whereby the stolen thing replaces something lost due to negative experiences in the environment, which typically involves a lack of parenting. These lead to two types of antisocial tendencies. As Winnicott writes,

> "*Roughly speaking there can be said to be the two types of antisocial tendency. In the one the illness presents as stealing, or claiming special attention through bed-wetting and untidiness and other minor delinquencies which do in fact give the mother extra work and worry. In the other there is destructiveness provoking firm management, that is to say firm management without the added quality of retaliation. Roughly speaking, the former type of child is deprived in the sense of losing maternal care or a 'good object', and the second type of child is deprived in terms of the father or of the quality in the mother that shows that she has a man's support behind her; this includes her*

> *strictness or perhaps her capacity to survive attack and to be able to repair damage done to clothes or to the carpet, or to the walls of the house or the windows*" (1971, p. 223).

For Winnicott, physical aggression and destructiveness related to stealing is an expression of the need for containment or help with self-regulation from the parental figures (Winnicott, 1962). This sort of aggressive acting out associated with cheating seems a mixture of predatory and defensive aggression. It is also related to neurodysregulation of affects, which will be discussed below. This brings up the question of whether large-group cheating, including taking property or territory from another large group, could have some of its origins in a similar need for containment and emotional regulation parallel to individual psychodynamics.

A simple example of cheating would be a scenario where one individual encounters another who possesses food. The first person, driven by a desire for sustenance, decides to seize the food without any consideration for the other person, the rightful owner. In this hypothetical situation, the first person might even resort to physical aggression, forcefully snatching food from the unsuspecting other. This is a form of predatory aggression, but it can be mixed with display aggression. If the predator can display overwhelming aggression, the victim may just submit instead of fighting back. This may take the form of a sudden attack, display of a weapon, etc.

The act of a person taking what does not rightfully belong to him or her is made more likely by the absence of consequences or defensive aggression (in this case an aggressive act performed by the victim to prevent the theft of their food). If the perpetrator believes that his or her ability to manifest predatory aggression surpasses the ability of the victim to mount defensive aggression of the victim, there is a greater temptation to be violent. Therefore, in humans, there is an unconscious calculation of the "return on investment" of violence to determine if it will be worthwhile. This is one of the reasons that human-to-human violence is more likely to occur when the predator clearly has an advantage over the victim. We see this manifesting in street crime where a victim will often be outnumbered by multiple assailants or where the predator possesses overwhelming force such as a firearm. This principle was recognized in ancient China by Sun Tzu, who wrote in his book *The Art of War*: "*Move not unless you see an advantage; use not your troops unless there is something to be gained*" (1910, Chapter 12, Line 17).

Human beings do not want to fall victim to predatory cheaters and so they feel compelled to enhance their defensive aggression or means of self-defense. This defense mechanism can take various forms, such as physical enhancement through increased size and strength or the acquisition of a weapon to deter potential predators. Defensive aggression also can be mixed with display aggression where the potential victim may only need to display the means to protect themselves to deter attack.

Humans (and to a lesser degree many primates and other creatures such as wolves) also possess an ability that sets them apart from many other animals – the power of cooperation. Recognizing their limitations in manifesting any of the types of aggression alone, individuals may resort to forming alliances or seeking assistance from their peers. People may band together to take resources from weaker persons. Or people may come together for mutual defense against cheaters or predators, or to safeguard their children. Display aggression, though often mixed with other types of aggression, can be performed in small and large groups. It is hard to watch something like a modern football game without thinking of the game as a symbolic mixture of predatory and display aggression. After all, as the Hollywood trope goes, it is the best players that get the cheerleaders in the end. In this context, the resources must be divided, and each person only gets a share. This is still preferable, however, to not gaining the resources altogether. Thus, this cooperative response represents yet another manifestation of human aggression within a small- and large-group dynamic.

The evolution of cooperation among humans is related to cheating. Cheaters take advantage of reciprocal cooperation to obtain what they want without contributing anything to the group. This is easier to do in large groups. A way that humans have discovered to reduce cheating, especially in large groups, is to restrict cooperation to members of the in-group while tagging others as non-group members. In a simulation study, diversity within a group along with being able to identify non-group members has been shown to keep cheating at low levels, while rates of cheating increase with group size (Czárán & Aanen 2016). There may be a dark side to this cheater-reduction strategy, however. The labeling of non-group members in this context is a way of distinguishing the "good" in-group members while perceiving non-group members as "bad." Psychoanalytically speaking, this cheater-detection strategy functions because it induces a sort of splitting. As we shall discuss below, labelling the out-group as "bad" can result in dire consequences and contribute to mass violence, such as war and genocide.

The ability to recruit allies and foster cooperation is facilitated by our advanced communication skills and language abilities. Perhaps more importantly, our ability to imagine what could happen, i.e., to think of "what if" scenarios, sets humans apart from other animals. These abilities have allowed us not only to strategize and work together when faced with challenges or threats but also to imagine what could be, and to delay gratification. To a large degree, these abilities also allow us to sublimate our immediate needs and wants to gain something greater in the future. Freud, in his work *Civilization and Its Discontents* (1930), writes about how our ability to sublimate allows humans to create civilizations. However, he was pessimistic about this, stating that not fulfilling our immediate drive-related desires makes us miserable:

> "*If civilization imposes such great sacrifices not only on man's sexuality but on his aggressivity, we can understand better why it is hard for him to be happy in that civilization.*" (p. 115)

Freud implies that sublimation is a process that is easily thwarted. This leads us to treat our fellow human beings rather poorly. As Freud puts it,

> "*Men are not gentle, friendly creatures wishing for love, who simply defend themselves if they are attacked, but that a powerful measure of desire for*

> *aggression has to be reckoned as part of their instinctual endowment. The result is that their neighbor is to them not only a possible helper or sexual object, but also a temptation to them to gratify their aggressiveness on him, to exploit his capacity for work without recompense, to use him sexually without his consent, to seize his possessions, to humiliate him, to cause him pain, to torture and to kill him.* Homo homini lupus;[5] *who has the courage to dispute it in the face of all the evidence in his own life and in history?*" (p. 111)

As we shall discuss further on, in contrast to the dissatisfaction we experience in sublimating our urges, there can be an "ugly" pleasure in acting on those urges that are aggressive or violent.

Neuropsychoanalysis

In general, human beings share more commonalities than differences. Psychologically, we experience the same developmental stages, including the emergence of psychic structures such as the ego and superego. The science of *neuropsychoanalysis* is now mapping these psychic structures to structures in the brain. Here, we present a simplified and general overview that begins by conceptualizing the brain as being organized in two primary ways (Solms 2013). The first organized system centers around the cortex, and the second is related to the limbic system and parts of the brain concerned with affect and memory. The cortex is a complicated structure that is responsible for helping us negotiate the external world in a rational way that helps keep us alive and functioning. The limbic system includes the structures of the brain that are related to both negative and positive emotional states. The cortex conducts rational functions while the limbic system motivates us to seek out things that induce pleasurable feelings and avoid things that produce negative emotions such as fear. The limbic system is connected to deeper brain structures such as the hypothalamus, which communicates whether the needs of the body are being satisfied or not. Another structure in the brain, the amygdala, signals the cortex with negative affects such as anger, anxiety, or fear.

5. Latin proverb, translated as "A man is a wolf to another man," or more tersely, "man is wolf to man."

This system lets the rational part of our brain know when something is wrong and helps us to understand what is happening, in what context and how to deal with it (Valasquez et al. 2018).

There are several affective systems in the brain that have somewhat separate functions. One function is to form attachments to others, especially caretakers in early life; another is to seek out sexual gratification associated with another person; and a third is related to the fight-flight response to danger. All these affective systems involve moving toward what is pleasurable and avoiding what is unpleasurable or dangerous in specific contexts. It is possible to think of the affects either as being the same as or motivating what Freud described as pleasure seeking and aggressive drives (Kernberg 2022a, 2022b; Moccia et al. 2018). These drives allow the rational part of the brain to make decisions about what needs to be done to successfully negotiate the external world. We can think of these affective systems as being related to the different ways humans express aggression. The attachment system could be related to parental and collective defensive aggression (such as what was exhibited by the buffalo herd in the Kruger Park video). The fight-or-flight system could be related to predatory and defensive aggression, and the pairing system could be related to display aggression. As we shall see later, these same affective systems related to dependency, fight or flight, and sexual pairing also characterize the psychodynamics of small groups as outlined by Wilfred Bion. His insights have been found to apply equally to large groups (Bion 1952, 1961; K. Volkan 1994; K. Volkan & V. D. Volkan 2023).

When the equilibrium between the cortex functions and the affective systems is out of balance, it can lead to psychopathology (Kernberg 2022b). This may be because there is too much affect for the cortex to process and it becomes overwhelmed resulting in confusion and anxiety (Dimkov, 2019). If there is too little affect signaling the cortex, it may underreact and ignore affective signaling and miss things it should pay attention to. If the cortex is overwhelmed with negative affect, this could cause a person to exhibit aggressive behaviors. As we shall discuss later, if an infant experiences too much negative affect, the infant may not be able to integrate the experiences into his or her developing sense of self. If this negative affect remains unintegrated, it can contribute to overwhelming the cortex, leading to aggressive and violent behavior.

Additionally, another brain structure, the hippocampus, is where memories correlated to affective states are stored. When we have a new experience, the hippocampus is activated and examines whether the new experience reminds us of something we experienced in the past. The cortex compares what is currently being felt to how we felt in the past to better judge how to deal with the current situation. In this way we can react appropriately in the future according to what we have experienced in the past (Carhart-Harris & Friston 2010). If the person has had a great deal of negative affective experiences as a child, this may predominate what is remembered and be used to guide the person to deal with a current situation aggressively.

In a simplistic way, we can map Freud's structural model to the neurological structures we have been discussing. The cortex corresponds to the ego, which processes and regulates affective signals. The ability of the cortex to inhibit affective signaling from the limbic system is similar to how psychoanalysis describes the function of defense mechanisms (Abbass et al. 2014; Hoşgören-Alıcı et al. 2023; Solms,2018). The superego is associated with the prefrontal cortex, as well as the amygdala, insular cortex, cingulate, orbitofrontal cortex, temporal lobes and ventromedial prefrontal cortex (Dietrich et al. 2009; Valasquez et al. 2018). Lastly, the affective systems described above are like Freud's conception of libido or unconscious impulses related to pleasure and aggression.

Neuropsychoanalysis and Violence

John Archer, in his seminal paper "The Nature of Human Aggression" (2009), outlines the origins of aggressive behavior in the human brain. Like the neuropsychoanalytic description of affective systems described above, Archer reports that aggressive behavior is rooted in neural circuits located in the forebrain, which are connected to the mid and hindbrains as well as the autonomic nervous system. The basal ganglia, which is part of the reptilian brain, controls the basic action patterns associated with aggression. Emotional behavior related to aggression is regulated by the limbic system, situated in the paleomammalian brain. Additionally, the neocortex, which is part of the neomammalian brain, plays a role in self-control and inhibiting immediate aggressive responses.

When this circuitry is damaged as in the case of orbitofrontal syndrome (OBS), aggressive behavior can emerge that seems related to defensive aggression. The receptor for advanced glycation end products (termed the RAGE system, also called AGER) is involved in helping a person seek pleasure and avoid unpleasure. It is also, however, linked to aggression through two key areas in the brain: the orbitofrontal cortex (OFC) and the ventromedial prefrontal cortex (VMPFC). This system becomes active when there are imbalances in our body's natural state, such as hunger or sexual desire, or even when we experience physical pain.

Jose Muñoz Zúñiga (2017) studied a patient who experienced damage to the orbital regions of the prefrontal cortex due to a ruptured aneurysm. As a result, the executive control of the patient's RAGE system was affected, leading to changes in the functioning of neural hierarchies involved in emotional processing. The RAGE system has a role in both pleasure seeking and avoidance of unpleasure. It is linked to aggression through two key areas in the brain: OFC and the VMPFC. This system becomes active when there are imbalances in our body's natural state, such as hunger or sexual desire, or even when we experience physical pain. If the executive control centers of the RAGE system are damaged, it can result in a condition called organic aggression syndrome. This type of aggression can bypass social context and override our drive to seek pleasure and avoid unpleasurable states. The resulting outbursts are ego-dystonic and experienced like a repetition compulsion, which will be discussed later. The patient's aggressive outbursts were thought to be caused by a fracture in inner ego boundaries.

Another study by James Blair (2001) explored the relationship between different types of aggression and antisocial personality disorders and psychopathy. This study identified two main types of aggression: reactive aggression and instrumental aggression. Reactive aggression is hypothesized to be caused by threats or frustration, whereas instrumental aggression is planned. This earlier study suggests (as in the Zúñiga study) that reactive aggression is linked to brain damage in the orbitofrontal cortex and is referred to as "acquired sociopathy." This type of aggression seems related to defensive aggression. Conversely, instrumental aggression is associated with psychopathy, which may result from early amygdala dysfunction. According to Blair, psychopathy involves a failure to connect emotional cues with the consequences of one's actions. Dysfunction of the amygdala can compromise the ability to establish connections between distress cues and recognition that one's behavior can cause harm or distress to other people. These abilities are crucial for socialization. Dysfunction of the amygdala among psychopathic individuals can manifest as reduced autonomic responses to unpleasant stimuli. The impaired functioning of the amygdala in psychopathy disrupts the formation of associations between emotional unconditioned stimuli and conditioned stimuli. This dysfunction may also affect the reflex response to visual threats, which is a characteristic observed in individuals with psychopathy. From a neuropsychoanalytic viewpoint these findings point to how amygdala damage might be related to impaired superego dysfunction. It also points out how impaired amygdala function affects unconscious processes and the expression of the drives.

Interestingly, it is now possible to use modern imaging techniques, such as magnetic resonance imaging (MRI), to visualize brain dysfunction in psychopathy. Adrian Raine, in his book *The Anatomy of Violence: The Biological Roots of Crime* (2014), explores the relationship of brain structure and function with violent behavior. In the book, Raine explains that historical perspectives on biological theories of crime and violence have fallen out of favor. This is to some degree because of the discredited work of people like Cesare Lombroso, an Italian prison doctor who created hierarchies of criminality tied to racial phenotypes and outdated systems like phrenology to postulate that some of us are "born criminals." These criminal racial hierarchies were used as justification for colonization by the British and the Belgians, to give two examples. Criminal racial hierarchies also fomented eugenics movements in the

United States and Germany, which ultimately led to Nazi racial categories resulting in an extreme form of eliminationist antisemitism. Because of this, the 20th century saw a shift towards sociological explanations of crime and violence, moving their origins to the impact of learned behaviors and negative environments—a shift from nature to nurture. (An early example of this sort of thinking can be found in the writings of Mark Twain in his 1882 novel, *The Prince and the Pauper*, which likely inspired the John Landis–directed film *Trading Places* starring Eddie Murphy and Dan Aykroyd (Landis 1983).

Raine suggests that although sociological explanations of violent behavior are popular, biological factors also play a significant role. To support this claim, he cites new scientific research in neurocriminology and especially the use of newer imaging technology such as MRI. He proposes an approach that combines both biological and social perspectives to better understand crime. We see this sort of approach as consistent with a neuropsychoanalytic understanding of aggression and violence that has the potential for preventing violence through understanding how the brain interacts with the environment.

Neuropsychoanalysis and Aggression in Small and Large Groups

It is unfortunately evident that humans excel at extending violence and aggression beyond individual acts to collective efforts. How does a neuropsychoanalytic understanding of individual violence explain both small- and large-group violence? We can see from the above studies and many other similar reports that aggression and violence among individuals stems from decreased inhibition and regulation by the structures in the brain that contain ego functions. In these individuals, neural circuitry related to superego functions is also impaired. We propose that normally functioning individuals may become dysregulated when they are members of certain specific types of groups. In other words, their normal psychic structures may respond to group membership in a way that dysregulates their brain circuitry and lessens inhibitions to violent acts and/or decreases moral prohibitions toward these acts. It is possible that certain group dynamics, such as those seen in stateless or state-sponsored terrorist groups, independent militia groups or state-sponsored military organizations that have been known to target and harm innocent people and children, can induce individuals within the group to exhibit brain functioning similar to that of someone with orbitofrontal damage or psychopathy. Interactions between group members, group members and their leaders, and group members and those outside the group can put group members under psychodynamic pressure in such a way that the ability of the ego and the superego to regulate the expression of affective circuitry in the brain related to aggression is impaired. This pressure is manifested through primitive collective defense mechanisms such as splitting and projective identification that parallel defenses used by individuals with borderline or narcissistic personality organization.

The psychological patterns we develop as children allow us to lead productive and satisfying lives. When we come together in groups, however, especially large groups, our behavior can revert to something more primitive and pathological in service of the group needs and at the expense of individual mental functioning. As Seth Allcorn (2022) states, we collectively think in black and white. We split the world into binaries, such as us and them, using projection to assign who and what is good and bad. Primitive collective defense mechanisms, the type of large group and identification with a large group, as well as other factors, come into play so that collective aggressive behaviors give rise to phenomena like war and genocide. We will discuss this further, but first it will be important to understand a bit more about primitive defenses and what motivates them.

3

The Death Drive, Projective Identification and Splitting

Sigmund Freud originally did not consider aggression as something directly motivating human behavior. However, as early as 1913, Freud wrote an analysis of a scene in the Shakespeare play *The Merchant of Venice*. This paper titled *The Theme of the Three Caskets* relates how in the play Bassanio, the suitor of Portia, must choose either a gold, silver or lead casket. The three caskets are inscribed with the following inscriptions:

> Gold: "Who chooseth me shall get as much as he deserves."
> Silver: "Who chooses me shall gain what many men desire."
> Lead: "Who chooses me must give and hazard all he hath."

Bassanio carefully considers each inscription before making his choice. He rejects the gold casket, arguing that it is too ostentatious and that its inscription suggests that the chooser will be gambling with his life. He also rejects the silver casket, arguing that it is too common and that its inscription suggests that the chooser will be materialistic. Being drawn to its simple inscription, Bassanio chooses the lead casket with the idea that he must be willing to sacrifice everything for love. When he opens the lead casket, he finds a portrait of Portia and a scroll that congratulates him on his choice and confirms that he has won her hand in marriage.

Freud relates the three caskets, a symbol of death, to the choice of three women like those found in other plays and in folklore. These three women can be understood to represent a mothering person, a sexual object, and for the lead casket, death. In the play as in other similar tales, death is the prize that is longed for, closely tied to the image of the object of love.

It is possible that Freud was influenced by Sabina Spielrein who was one of the first in psychoanalytic circles to speak directly about a "death" drive (1912). As related by Arlene Richards (2018), Spielrein was in the thrall of a romance with her analyst Carl Jung and wanted to have his baby. However, she also wanted to become a physician and psychoanalyst in her own right. Having a baby with Jung would be the death of her career ambitions and her position in a society that would severely judge her for having a child with a married man. Spielrein generalizes this idea and makes the correlation between wanting to generate new life, with the psychic death of the parent.[1]

During his experience of World War I, Freud wrote a paper "Thoughts for the Times on War and Death" (1915). In this paper, Freud concludes:

> *"With the exception of only a very few situations, there adheres to the tenderest and most intimate of our love-relations a small portion of hostility which can excite an unconscious death-wish."* (p. 298)

Like Spielrein, Freud is thinking about the ambivalence of pleasure and aggression.

---

1. Sabina Spielrein was a fascinating person who was greatly influenced by and who influenced both Sigmund Freud and Carl Jung. Freud's break with Jung was to some degree made easier by his disapproval of Jung's relationship with Spielrein (Carotenuto 1986). Jung was perhaps inspired to develop his concept of the anima by his relationship with Spielrein (Jung 1963). Tragically, Spielrein, who championed Freudian psychoanalysis in Russia, was murdered along with her two daughters by the Nazis when Einsatzgruppe D slaughtered 27,000 people, most of whom were Jews, near the Russian city Rostov-on-Don in July 1942 (Richebächer 2005).

In 1920 Freud wrote *Beyond the Pleasure Principle*, where he introduces the concept of a "death" drive. Freud did not use the term *Thanatos* for the death drive. This term was first used by Wilhelm Stekel (1909) and, as stated above, was mentioned by Spielrein in her 1912 paper. Now when we refer to Thanatos we mean the same thing as the death drive and vice versa. Freud argues that the death drive is a fundamental force in human behavior:

> *"If we are to take it as a truth that knows no exception that everything living dies for internal reasons – becomes inorganic once again – then we shall be compelled to say that 'the aim of all life is death' and, looking backwards, that 'inanimate things existed before living ones.'" (p. 38)*

As Freud recounts, his idea was that human behavior is motivated solely by the pleasure principle, or Eros. This life drive seeks to maximize pleasure and minimize pain. Nevertheless, he claimed to have observed several phenomena that could not be explained by the pleasure principle alone. To explain these phenomena, Freud proposed the existence of the death drive. The death drive is a fundamental instinct that seeks to return the organism to a state of inorganic matter.[2] It is opposed to the life drive, which seeks to preserve and expand life.[3] Freud ultimately understood that there are two main drives:

> *"We, on the other hand, dealing not with the living substance but with the forces operating in it, have been led to distinguish two kinds of instincts: those*

2. We are using the terms drive and instinct interchangeably here since the German has been translated as instinct when the term drive is probably better. See Karl Menninger (1938).

3. It is also possible that the introduction of the death drive was in part a response to Freud's break from Jung, who had postulated a multiplicity of drive-like motivating psychic forces in his concept of archetypes. In fact, Freud added two sentences about Jung to *Beyond the Pleasure Principle* in 1921, claiming that Jung's conception of libido is monistic and implying that the multitude of drives suggested by Jung are just ego derivatives of this one libido.

which seek to lead what is living to death, and others, the sexual instincts, which are perpetually attempting and achieving a renewal of life." (p. 46)

For Freud, Thanatos, or the death drive, is responsible for aggression and violence, repetition compulsion and self-destruction. The idea of repetition compulsion is important: this is a tendency to repeat or re-create traumatic experiences, even though these experiences are painful. Freud argued that repetition compulsion is a way for the organism to try to gain control and mastery over traumatic experiences. We shall see that repetition compulsion can combine with self-destruction in that the repetition of a trauma to gain control over it becomes, in some cases, more important than survival and that compulsion to repeat a trauma will often continue even if the repetition is sure to bring self-destruction.

In her paper "The Death Instinct and its Vicissitudes," Arlene Richards (2018) covers the continuity of the death drive throughout psychoanalytic thinking. Melanie Klein was a major proponent of the death drive, maintaining that it was necessary for psychic development and that the conflict between life and death drives underlies anxiety. Analysts influenced by Klein such as Herbert Rosenfeld (2017) and Hanna Segal (1993) report that working with the death drive in the analytic setting is useful. Rosenfeld explores how destructive narcissism is related to the death drive and how to manage this in the clinical situation. Segal conceptualized aggression towards others as a deflection of the death drive away from self-destruction; aggression is therefore involved in projective identification. Other analytic thinkers see the death drive as a return to an undifferentiated state of bliss, which recalls Freud's initial conceptualizing on the subject.

Object Relations and the Death Drive

Following Klein, many object relations theorists consider the death drive to be related to feeling states.[4] Most object relations theorists re-

4. Object relations is the psychoanalytic study of the early development of the personality and psychic structures and how this is related to severe psychopathology. An "object" "refers to another person or persons, especially early life caretakers. For more see V. D. Volkan (1976, 1981) and K. Volkan & V. D.

ject Freud's idea of primary narcissism where the baby starts life in an undifferentiated state. Following infant research, object relations theorists believe that the infant comes into the world with some rudimentary sense of itself and others. For writers like Otto Kernberg, the infant experiences emotional states that over time become directed towards itself and objects as drives (Kernberg 1975, 1976, 1984a, 1986). This occurs through a process of internalization and projection. In our early childhood, a key part of development is when we internalize the relationships we have with objects – initially the person who gives us mothering. What is internalized includes the feelings that the relationship with the object generates within us (V. D. Volkan 1976). For instance, if our mother loves us, we internalize that feeling and feel loved, valued and safe. The internalization sets up a reciprocal relationship wherein we then project out our love for the parent. This reciprocal internalization and projection form the basis of an attachment to those in the outside world, starting with the mothering person. Forming an attachment in this fashion is crucial for developing a healthy personality. When this reciprocal relationship fails to become established, a person can subsequently suffer from severe mental disorders like personality disorders or even psychosis (K. Volkan & V. D. Volkan 2022).

For normal development to occur, introjection and projection of positive feelings need to predominate over bad feelings. The infant will introject some negative feelings like frustration and aggression from the mothering person as well as experience internally generated bad feelings because of how he or she is treated by the caregiving objects and the environment that they are in. Genetics and epigenetics undoubtably play a role here as they help determine a temperament that may be quick to anger or easily frustrated. In normal development these negative feelings need to be outweighed by positive feelings. When the infant experiences too many negative feeling states, either internal or external, he or she will be unable to integrate the positive and negative feelings. This prevents the infant from experiencing the outside world and objects in a

---

Volkan (2022).

realistic way—i.e., the infant experiences itself and those taking care of it as having both good, and to a lesser degree, bad aspects. If too much of what the infant experiences is bad, the infant's aggressiveness, frustration and sense of valuelessness will remain unintegrated and will threaten the internalized sense of what is good. This constitutes a negative motivating force for the infant. This "death" drive is created because of the interactions of the infant's negative emotional states with a predominately unfriendly, frustrating and oftentimes violent external world. In the face of this death drive, the infant will attempt to preserve the good by keeping it split off from the bad. This sort of splitting occurs during normal development but is no longer necessary once the infant can hold the sense of good and bad internally together. This internalized sense of the Other becomes ambivalent and provides the scaffolding for the infant to develop a sense of itself and a realistic consistent understanding of other people and the world outside itself (Kernberg 1975, 1976, 1986; V. D. Volkan 1976).

If there is too much negative that is internalized, the infant will try and preserve the good that it has internalized by projecting the bad out onto an Other. The good and bad will remain split and internal ambivalence will not be achieved. People suffering from personality disorders have personalities that do not develop beyond this stage, and they continue to use splitting and projection as their primary defense mechanisms in adulthood.

Projective Identification

Projection is a primitive defensive operation of the human mind. By primitive we mean that it develops early in infancy and is a primary defense mechanism in severe mental pathologies like personality disorders along with other related defenses such as splitting.

A further elaboration of this type of projection is projective identification. It is related to projection but adds the attribution of aspects of ourselves that we can't accept or tolerate to objects in the external world that then experience these aspects.

Projective identification has a relationship to the death drive. One way to think about it that we try to introject what is good and project out what is bad. Introjection is associated with the life drive while the death drive can be seen extensively in projection and by extension projective identification (Andrade 1976).

These intolerable aspects may be something the person doing the projecting (the projector) is experiencing but can't tolerate. Nevertheless, the projector may have some empathy for what is projected. In projective identification the projector is trying to induce in the Other the feelings or behaviors he or she cannot tolerate. This is also an attempt to control the object. This control prevents the object from attacking the projector.

While projection and projective identification are primitive defense mechanisms, they are used by people with all levels of personality organization. More "normal" people will use these in more subtle forms and can project positive loving feelings towards each other. This may be something that evolved to enhance social cohesion, which would have had survival value. We can still experience this sort of large and small group positive projection in religious rituals or when attending a music concert.

People with more pathology will tend to project out aggressive and hostile feelings. This type of projection is a way of distorting the Other in some way that is determined by the projector's own past history, especially his or her very early childhood. Another way of thinking about projection is that it is a way a person confuses what is going on internally with what is going on in the outside world with other people. This is the opposite of introjection.

Projective identification can also be motivated by an unconscious feeling of intense shame, which is an internal negative feeling state instigated by a reaction to an object. If through projective identification shame can be instigated in the Other, this lessens the projector's internal feeling of shame (Lansky, 2008).

With projective identification the projector subtly encourages the Other to act out, with the result that the Other experiences him or herself in the same way the projector experiences themselves. If the projected experience originates in the projector's early childhood then we can think of the projection as a transference that is replaying out a childhood relationship. This process is entirely unconscious for both the projector and the Other: the result is a replay of a repetition compulsion where the projector through the process of projective identification unconsciously sets up a recreation of an experience that can be deeply distressing. This is an unconscious attempt to replay the experience in the hopes that this time the projector will gain mastery and control over the resultant trauma. Projective identification typically involves repetition compulsion of disturbing, hostile and destructive events. This can be seen as the underlying mechanism to Freud's conceptualization of how the death drive manifests in repetition compulsions.

An example of this might be a person who was abused in some way as an infant. When this person becomes an adult, he or she projects an internalized version of the abusive parent onto people in his or her environment. If this person becomes a psychotherapy patient, he or she will likely experience the therapist as abusive. This is projection. The patient may also unconsciously encourage the therapist to feel either that the therapist is being abused, or that the therapist is an abuser. The astute therapist will recognize this as projective identification and know that this is the source of the therapist's feelings of abuse (either as a perpetrator or recipient) when the therapist is with this patient.[5]

---

5. Transference can be considered to be a specific instance of projection. It was originally defined as the projection of repressed or distressing ideas onto the analyst. Freud (1893) initially described transference thusly: "*[T]he patient is frightened at finding that she is transferring on to the figure of the physician the distressing ideas which arise from the content of the analysis. This is a frequent, and indeed in some analyses a regular, occurrence*" (p. 302). Later in his work *The Dynamics of Transference*, Freud (1912) presents transference as a replaying of an early childhood need causing a person to connect to the analyst. Transference cannot exist without projection, or as Melanie Klein put it when speaking of schizophrenia, "*the capacity for personification and for transference fails, amongst other reasons, through the defective functioning of the projection-mechanism*" (1929, p. 203). Countertransference is simply the reverse of transference. This is where the analyst or therapist projects his or her own early childhood needs onto the patient. Transference and countertransference unconsciously play out in everyday life via the mechanism of projection and projective identification. We will argue that transference and countertransfer-

Projective identification manifests essentially in three ways. The first manifestation is the act of projection. In this example, initially the patient projects his or her bad internalized aspects onto the therapist. The patient unconsciously cultivates a distorted view of his or her therapist as a bad person who is aggressive and hostile toward him or her. The patient, however, does not project perfectly. This results in the second manifestation. There remains an aspect of what the patient projected with which the patient identifies. So, the patient will to some degree act aggressively. This is an attempt to control the therapist, which inevitably causes the third manifestation: the therapist is unconsciously encouraged to aggressively act out towards the patient. Due to the use of a splitting defense, at the conclusion of this cycle of projective identification, the patient will only remember that the therapist appeared or actually was aggressive towards the patient, re-creating an early childhood pattern. The patient will be split off from the awareness that he or she had anything to do with inducing the aggressiveness in the therapist. A good example of how difficult this process can be for the therapist can be found in a paper by Robert Waska (2000).

---

ence in the guise of projection and projective identification occur at a collective level. For more on transference and countertransference, see our recent work, K. Volkan & V. D. Volkan (2023).

4

War and Psychoanalysis

Human object relations patterns and both projection and projective identification give us important tools to begin to explore the concept of war from a psychoanalytic lens. Many of the psychoanalytic theories related to war are an extension of object relations concepts from the individual to the collective. Different psychoanalytic thinkers have done this in various ways.

Since Sigmund Freud, other psychoanalysts [for example, Ernest Jones (1915), Edward Glower (1933), Roger Money-Kyrle (1951), Alix Strachey (1957), Franco Fornari (1974), Samuel Atkin (1971), Erik Erikson 1966, 1977), and V. D. Volkan (1979, 1988)] have written psychoanalytically about the *theory* of war. Most of these efforts have dealt with the collective expressions of the individual's psychic make-up, especially his or her aggressive drive.

For example, Edward Glower (1933) wrote about "curative" aspects of war and based his view on the classical psychoanalytic idea that after a regressed state such as the one found in schizophrenia there is an urge for restitution. With wars a regressed large group tries to cure itself but can accomplish only pathological adaptations. In addition to analogies with the individual mind, a comprehensive theory of war would require the application of historical, social and political elements in the interactions among large groups and the relationship between the political leader and his or her followers.

Franco Fornari's book the *Psychoanalysis of War* (1975) was written to provide a psychoanalytic perspective in order to understand and find ways of dealing with war. In addition to examining the external aspects of war, Fornari introduces the idea that war serves as a defense mechanism against internal fears and anxieties which are often the result of the grief and pain associated with some sort of loss. Individuals and societies deal with this anxiety by transforming internally terrifying fears and anxieties into an external, tangible enemy. Conversely, being deprived of war can bring about a "paranoid reaction against mourning" (p. 51) resulting in an inability to process and mourn depressive and persecutory anxieties. However, this feeds the paranoid process, and the unresolved mourning is projected onto another group, which is then perceived as the enemy. This projection serves to unite the members of a society in a common cause, which is the defense against this externalized "enemy," thus allowing them to avoid the pain of mourning by focusing on the conflict. War, in this context, is a form of acting out these unresolved psychological issues on a massive scale, avoiding the painful process of mourning by engaging in collective violence. In this sense, externally suppressing a war from occurring, such as in a *pax Romana*, only delays the conflict since the underlying unconscious pressure to go to war is unresolved. We can see this dynamic playing out in many conflicts among previously colonized people. The conflicts between Serbs and Croats, India and Pakistan, as well as Israel and Arabs states, to name a few, have this dynamic to some degree. The state, in Fornari's theory, plays an unconscious maternal-type role, where the citizens, unable to deal with their grief and loss, look to the state for comfort and security. The state then channels these collective feelings into war, which is seen as a protective and sacrificial act to preserve the safety and continuity of the nation, thus avoiding the psychological work of mourning by transferring it into a socially and ideologically sanctioned form of aggression.

The sacrificial aspects of warfare have been pointed out by Richard Koenigsberg in his book *Nations Have to Right to Kill* (2009) and other pieces (R. A. Koenigsberg, n.d.). He suggests that nations, as abstract entities, are preserved through the literal sacrifice of soldiers' bodies. In this way war functions as a ritualistic act where soldiers are sacrificial victims, maintaining the existence of the nation state. For Koenigsberg, if one believes in something enough to sacrifice their life for it, the strength of the belief makes the object or ideal real and valid. The desire to die and kill in war, genocide, revolution, and terrorism arises from an attachment to an ideology viewed as absolute. The dead and mangled bodies on the battlefield serve as proof of the validity of this ideology, reinforcing the concept that the ultimate sacrifice gives meaning to an ideological cause.

Following the ideas of Vamık Volkan (1988) and Franco Fornari (1975), Joanna Byles (2003) reminds us that psychoanalytic ideas related to superego aggression, splitting, projection, and projective identification can help us understand warfare. Byles states that war is the result of internal psychotic anxieties that must be projected into literal external dangers to gain control over them. In this way warfare can be understood as an externalization of articulated of shared unconscious fantasies. There is a correspondence between individual psychic structures and the social world. For Vamık Volkan, individuals in a society may experience a collective *state* superego as their ego ideal. This may then be projected onto a leader who can embody this state superego, shaping a society's laws and morals. These superego aspects, however, are repressed during warring conflict. It may be that individuals in a group look to the leader to manage their psychotic anxieties, which are projected onto an outside group. Through the defense of splitting the outside group is seen as all bad, preserving the good of the internal group. The leader as state superego ignores moral prohibitions and then uses the state to destroy the projected and fantasized external danger that has become real. In a war all combatant societies may be involved in this sort of collective psychic process. As Byles implies, however, genocide maybe a one-sided version of the same group psychic mechanisms. This would explain some of the stages that lead up to genocide, especially seeing the victim large group as a threat and later their process of dehumanization. Byles suggests that to control our tendency toward war:

"*What seems to be needed is for the superego to regain its developmental role of mitigating omniscient projective identification by ensuring an intact, integrated object world, a world that will be able to contain unconscious fears, hatred, and anxieties without the need for splitting and projection.*" (p. 212)

Neil Altman (2006) traces psychoanalytic thinking about war. He highlights Jessica Benjamin's idea that relationships are organized around dominance and submission and that being able to see another person's point of view is a way of resolving impasses. Clinical and political impasses are similar and can be creatively resolved if there is the mutual ability to see each other's point of view (Benjamin, 1988). Altman goes onto say that the trauma from sexual or physical abuse is related to the conflict between having a sense of safety from the same person that is the dangerous abuser. This can lead to dissociation and as such is related to war trauma:

"*Trauma deriving from war can now be thought of, in Bionian terms, as having to do with unthinkable experiences, unbearably painful experiences of torture, murder, and being witness to such events, encountering sadism and the extremes of cruelty of which human beings are capable in the context of war. These unthinkable experiences live on unmetabolizable in the psyche…*" (p. 245)

Altman relates this to the Buddhist idea that even though we feel ourselves to be permanent, we run afoul of the reality of the impermanence of everything in the world, including ourselves:

"*Herein is the paradox of the fact that death threatens to rob all earthly things of their value, while simultaneously making them precious by virtue of that very transience. The problem is denial of transience, the illusion of permanence, and that is the illusion that war, along with death itself, puts an end to… War derives from the illusions of power and pride that seek to mask the reality of death and limitation, as if death could be avoided by killing. Of course, like all neurotic and defensive behavior, war brings about precisely the outcome that it seeks to evade or deny.*" (pp. 245–246)

These are just some of the psychoanalytic ideas about war and violent conflicts. The above ideas highlight the collective object relations of a society. These psychoanalytic conceptions of war share the thought that war and other large-group violent conflicts result from unintegrated social objects relations and a need to split off the bad objects representation via projection and projective identification.

It is imperative that those entering the field of applied psychoanalysis beware the tendency toward "wild analysis". Decades ago, Alexander Mitscherlich (1971) stated that the psychoanalyst venturing into these uncharted waters needs the collaboration of other specialists. When Vamık Volkan was involved in trouble spots around the world trying to understand various international conflicts and start dialogues between opposing sides he had a historian, a sociologist, a linguist, and former diplomats on his team. While writing this book both of us have kept Mitscherlich's remarks in our minds.

5

Pseudospecies

Sigmund Freud's pessimism in his response to Albert Einstein likely played a role in the limited psychoanalytic contributions to the fields of diplomacy and peacemaking. In the previous chapter we referred to some early psychoanalysts as well as present-day psychoanalytic scholars who wrote about wars in addition to other external historical, religious, and ideological major events. Much like Freud stated in his letter to Einstein, these psychoanalysts referred to human propensity to use violence to resolve large-group conflicts. Humans, like other members of the animal kingdom, and particularly chimpanzees, are violent creatures.

Human Evolution and Imagination

Our brains' ability to imagine ideologies is an adaption that has survival value. Our brains develop in a certain way that involves a stage of early object relations where we introject and project as outlined above (Alcaro & Carta, 2019). This sequence of development had survival value in small hominid groups, because it allowed us to bond more closely, imagine, and improvise together. This made us better hunters and enhanced our ability to defend ourselves (Asma, 2017; Fuentes, 2020). The almost unlimited capacity of our imagination, however, leads us to believe that what we imagine in both small and large groups is real. In a positive sense, our imaginations function teleologically, where what we imagine pulls us forward to the point that we make what we imagine into a physical reality. We also are able to tolerate ambiguity between the real world and our imaginations, not quite knowing where to place the boundary between the two (Morley, 2003). This imaginative capacity allows us to dream up all sorts of ideologies that we believe are real (Tanggaard & Tateo, 2018). Perhaps in this sense our imaginative capacity to produce ideologies and the conviction that these ideologies are real functions as what paleontologist and zoologist Stephen J. Gould termed a *spandrel*. Gould defines a spandrel as an unexpected side effect of the evolution of a specific capacity (Gould, 2002; Gould & Lewontin, 1979). In this instance what evolved to give survival value in small isolated human groups can be both beneficial and deadly when humans form large national states.

Erikson's Pseudospecies

Erik Erikson (1966) addresses this manifestation of our imaginative capacity when he tried to answer Freud's question "Is there any way of delivering mankind from the menace of war?" He did this by coming up with the term "pseudospecies" to describe the evolution of humans into large groups such as tribes and clans. He wrote, "Man has evolved (by whatever kind of evolution and for whatever adaptive reasons) in pseudospecies, i.e., tribes, clans, classes, etc., which behave as if they were separate species, created at the beginning of time by supernatural intent" (p. 606). He theorized that primitive human sought a measure of protection for their unbearable nakedness by adopting the armor of the lower animals and wearing their skins, feathers, or claws. On the basis of these outer garments, each tribe, clan, or another large group evolved a sense of shared intra-group identity.

Erikson stated that these large groups feared the human who belonged to another subspecies of humankind, and each large group developed "a distinct sense of identity, but also a conviction of harboring the human identity" (p. 606). This attitude fortified each pseudospecies by engendering the belief that the others were "extraspecific and inimical to 'genuine' human endeavor" (p. 606).

Vamık Volkan's (2013b) expansion of Erik Erikson's supposition may further explain what happened during the course of human evolution. For centuries, neighboring tribes, due to their natural boundaries, had only each other with which to interact. Neighboring groups had to compete for territory, food, sex, and physical goods for their survival. Eventually, this level of competition assumed more psychological implications. Physical essentials, besides retaining their status as genuine necessities, absorbed mental meanings. Prestige, honor, power, envy, revenge, humiliation, loss, and submission evolved from being tokens of survival to becoming large-group symbols, cultural amplifiers, traditions, religions or shared historical memories that embedded a large group's self-esteem, narcissism, and identity.

Erikson's postulations are supported by references to the Other in many ancient documents and languages. Ancient Chinese regarded themselves as people and viewed the Other as *kuei* or "hunting spirits." The Apache Indians considered themselves to be *indeh*, the people, and all others as *indah*, the enemy (Boyer 1986). The Mundurucu in the Brazilian rainforest divided their world into Mundurucu, who were people, and non-Mundurucu, who were *pariwat* (enemies), except for certain friendly neighbors (Murphy 1957). There are other examples of large groups who consider only themselves as "people," such as the Sudanese Dinka (the name of the group translates as "people") and Nuer ("original people"), and the Arctic Yupiks ("real people") (Harari 2014). Arabs traditionally use the word *ajam* which means mumbler, to refer to non-Arabs and specifically to Persians whose first language is not Arabic. This term points out how language can play a role in defining group membership (Bosworth, 2014). Thai people borrowing from Muslim Persian and Indian traders in the past, refer to non-Thais, especially men from Western countries who come to Thailand for sex tourism as *farang*, which is possibly a derivative of the word "French" (Thompson & Smutkupt, 2016). Many more examples could be included here.

6

Racism, Otherness and Skin Color

As human large groups met and interacted with other large groups, skin color differences became psychological elements denoting group membership. A phenotypic difference in skin color often underlies the subjugation of one group of humans by another, with more lightly colored people originating in Northern climates typically subjugating darker people in more southern and warmer parts of the world. The reason why this is so remains complicated and controversial. In his book *Guns, Germs, and Steel* (2005), Jared Diamond gives a compelling account. He makes the case that lighter-skinned people in specific climates were able to cultivate grains and domesticate animals. The development of agriculture allowed these groups to have specialists who developed technologies such as weapons, and animal husbandry that promoted resistance to zoonotic diseases. This allowed these groups to establish dominance over darker-skinned groups who typically lived in places where large-scale agriculture and animal husbandry were more difficult or unnecessary. This pattern is especially apparent in the European and African/ Middle Eastern continents where racism towards people of darker skin has a long tradition.

During the Middle Ages the Spanish developed the concept of *limpieza de sangre* or purity of blood. Initially Spanish nobles promoted Christian superiority and entitlement to privilege by distinguishing themselves from semitic peoples like Jews and Muslims. As Spain expanded its territories, limpieza de sangre became a significant factor in discrimination against darker-skinned people in general and was used to justify the enslavement of Africans. Limpieza de sangre was thus used to justify social and political bigotry as well as inequity against people considered to have "impure" blood. By the time the Spanish colonized the Americas, limpieza de sangre became a social status that excluded people of non-European descent from privileges, honors, and official positions. This systemic racism was enforced through blood purity tests, which required individuals to prove their noble and pure lineage. The strict application of blood tests, however, was difficult due to there not being enough qualified individuals to fill important positions in the colonies. As a result, some privileges were extended to individuals of mixed race, and a hierarchy of racism using skin color as one of the proxies for blood purity was established (Heig, 2014; Marihuan & Aguado, 2019). As Julia Frederick (2002) writes this system was in place in Louisiana around the time of the American revolution and afterwards. There are accounts of trials enforcing limpieza de sangre laws, demonstrating obstacles to Spanish officers serving in the Louisiana colony who were required to only marry women that could prove not only pure blood but good behavior. Prospective wives were required to submit legal petitions to support their case, attesting, for example,

> *"My descendants on my mother's and father's side are all Christians from olden times and unadulterated by any inferior race, including Arabs, Jews, mulattos, Indians, or people recently converted to the religion, nor are they wanted or have they been prosecuted or convicted of crime, nor have they been sent to jail. On the contrary, we have always been of good reputation, good manners, and pure lineage"* (Frederick, 2002, p. 81).

Limpieza de sangre was not the only attempt to codify racism according to skin color. In 1685 King Louis XIV instituted *Le Code Noir* (the black code). This was the construction of a legal framework for the institution of slavery involving mostly Africans and an attempt to end the so-called "illegal" slave trade (Daykin, 2006; "The Horrors of San

Domingo," 1863). It was primarily targeted towards French colonies in Guyana, Louisiana, Reunion, and the West Indies. Le Code Noir defined the conditions of slavery in the French colonies, including edicts on sex, marriage, assembly, religions (all slaves were to be baptized as Catholics), the buying and selling of slaves, and the relationship between slave and master. The code specified limitations for freed slaves, banned all non-Catholic religions, and called for the removal of all Jewish individuals from French colonies. The code had the effect of intensifying existing racist attitudes towards people of African and Jewish descent. Racist codes and civil frameworks derived from blood purity tests and the black codes made their way into the United States and became well established throughout the slave-owning states. The influence of the codes extended from the United States slave-owning period to the post-civil war reconstruction period (Daykin, 2006; U. B. Phillips, 1918; "The Horrors of San Domingo," 1863).

After the Civil War (1865), the Reconstruction Era heralded amendments to the Constitution aiming to grant Black Americans freedom, equality, and citizenship. The end of Reconstruction, however, led to the establishment of *Jim Crow* laws, which provided legal support to racial segregation in the South and across the United States.[1] Despite the efforts of African Americans and allies, these laws remained in place until the civil rights movement of the 1950s and 1960s, which brought significant legislative victories like the *Civil Rights Act of 1964* and the *Voting Rights Act of 1965*, outlawing discrimination and protecting voting rights. Nevertheless, systemic racism based on skin tone has persisted.

---

1. In 1947, in *Mendez v. Westminster*, a Mexican-American family challenged forced segregation in Orange County, California public schools in federal court. The families won, but only because the court held that Latinos were "legally white." Courts across the nation ruled again and again on whether Japanese, Chinese, Armenian, Filipino, or Syrian youth were "white enough" to enjoy the privileges of "whiteness;" i.e., to attend public schools restricted to Whites. This absurdity ended with the United States Supreme Court unanimous decision, *Brown v. Board of Education*, in which black families were represented by NAACP chief counsel, Thurgood Marshall, who later became the first black Supreme Court Justice.

African Americans with darker skin tone are more significantly affected by racism than their lighter compatriots.

An echo of limpieza de sangre and Le Code Noir may be seen in anti-miscegenation laws in the United States, which criminalized interracial marriage. As Byron Martyn (1979) reports, these laws prohibited marriage between a person considered White and (depending on the state) a person considered Native American, Filipino, Asian, East Indian, and native Hawaiian, as well as African American. Not just a phenomenon of the South, legislatures in all but nine states adopted variants of anti-miscegenation laws. In 1967, the United States Supreme Court unanimously ruled in *Loving v Virginia* that anti-miscegenation laws violated both the Equal Protection and Due Process Clauses of the Fourteenth Amendment of the U.S. Constitution.[2] Nonetheless, many states hesitated to formally repeal their laws criminalizing interracial marriage. In 2000, Alabama was the last of the states to do so.

This "colorism" has been found to have negative health impacts (Keyes et al., 2020).

Black Americans have been affected by racism in terms of economic opportunities, housing, and education. This is particularly true in the criminal justice system. Mass incarceration, especially of black males, and the so-called war on drugs have disproportionately affected Black communities (Graff, 2016, White, 2020).

Currently, we are witnessing the continuation of these racial disparities. Movements like Black Lives Matter have brought attention to police brutality and the systemic injustice faced by Black people (Lavalley & Johnson, 2022). But there has also been a rise in white supremacy and antisemitism. The current effects of white supremacy on Black Americans manifest in various systemic inequities and direct forms of racism. Structurally, Black Americans face disparities in healthcare, with lower-quality care and higher morbidity and mortality rates, linked to chronic exposure to racism and stress from structural racism, increasing

---

2. Former President Barack Obama's parents, who were married in Hawaii in 1961, couldn't have done so if they had lived in Virginia, because the Supreme Court hadn't yet struck Virginia's so-called "Racial Integrity Act."

the risk for diseases like COVID-19, diabetes, stroke, cancer, and kidney disease (Manning et al., 2023). Maternal and infant mortality rates are also significantly higher among Black Americans compared to their White counterparts, with racism-related stress contributing to poor birth outcomes (Treadwell, 2020).

Economic disparities are stark, with a substantial wealth gap between White and Black Americans, rooted in historical and systemic inequality in property ownership, employment, education opportunities, and levels of incarceration (Price, 2022). Black women, in particular, face wage gaps that result in significant lifetime earnings loss (Ortiz & Roscigno, 2009), and Black families are often targeted by predatory lenders and for-profit schools, exacerbating financial inequities (Hill & Kozup, 2007).

In the criminal justice system, Black Americans have been disproportionately surveilled, detained, and subjected to violence, a continuation of practices dating back to slavery and segregation (Warring, 2018). The justice system has been leveraged to maintain white dominance, with mass incarceration and policing practices affecting Black communities disproportionately (Jones-Brown et al., 2014). Furthermore, the militarization of the police has led to increased police violence, especially in Black communities, with police use of force being a leading cause of death for young Black men (Hoggard & Lutchman, 2023). While there have been steps towards equality, systemic racism continues to impact the Black community across various facets of American life. The conversation on race has evolved to include discussions on privilege, intersectionality, and the need for systemic change (Equal Justice Initiative, 2018; Byrd & Clayton, 2001; Cockerham et al., 2017; "The Impact of Structural Racism on Black Americans (Report),"n.d.).

These systemic issues are often underpinned by White supremacist ideologies that have been historically justified and continue to perpetuate racial hierarchies and discrimination against Blacks and other minority groups in the United States. The book *Spreading Hate: The Global Rise of White Supremacist Terrorism*, by Daniel Byman (2022) chronicles the rise of white supremacy not only in the United States but also globally. Byman examines the rise of white supremacy-related terrorism, tracing its expansion globally post-9/11. Previously underestimated, it has incited significant violence, as well as undermined confidence in democratic systems, contributing to the rise of "strong man" leaders. White supremacy groups often reflect broader societal issues, using these to intensify divisions among those they perceive as "not white." White supremacists have learned to use social media to disseminate their beliefs to great effect. Nevertheless, many white supremacy movements are fragmented, hindered by internal discord and ineffective leadership. Byman argues that a robust response from governments and international collaboration could significantly diminish danger from these groups.

African Americans are not the only non-white group of people affects by racial hierarchies and codes. Edward Murguia and Rogelio Saenz (2002) propose that there is a now a three tired racial categorization at work in the United States. In this system the three tiers are "Whites," "Honorary Whites," and "Collective Blacks." The top "White" tier includes those of European descent but also so-called assimilated Latinos (Argentinians, Chileans, and Cubans) as well as new white immigrants who are mostly from Eastern Europe (Russians, Serbians, Albanians, etc.) The second level tier "Honorary Whites" includes light- and medium-skin Latinos, Japanese, Koreans, Chinese, and some multiracial people. The bottom tier of "Collective Blacks" consists of people of African descent, darker-skin Asians (e.g. Cambodians, Hmong, Laotians), darker-skin Latinos (e.g. Puerto Ricans, Dominicans), West Indians, and reservation-based Native Americans. Many of the same negative treatment and disparities experienced by African Americans are also experienced by "Collective Blacks."

Psychoanalysis and Racism

Racism tends to be understood in terms of the external socio-structural and several psychological factors. But this approach fails to provide any understanding of the role of the emotional origins of hatred, as well as how groups of individuals can so quickly come to the point of devaluing, discriminating, dehumanizing and engaging in violence against others who are different, ultimately leading in some cases to genocide. Psychoanalysis, however, can give a deeper understanding the psychodynamics of racism.

Freud understood racism as related to narcissism (Freud, 1921, 1930). While individuals *aspire* towards their ego ideal, groups often believe they *embody* their ideal. By comparing themselves to other large groups and denigrating non-members, large groups can feed the narcissistic belief that the group has collectively achieved its ideal and is better than other groups. This ego ideal of the large group feeds down to its members, who believe that membership in the ideal large group makes them better than people in other large groups who must be devalued and denigrated. The large group, and to some degree the leader(s) of the large group determine the ego ideal for individuals in the large group, who in turn identify with the large group and its leader as the embodiment of the ego ideal. As Robert Hinshelwood (2006) states:

> "*Where narcissism takes over a dominant position, everyone becomes the ideal. It therefore offers a compelling identity. Even in groups, which function more or less well, the very processes by which a group establishes its integrity are those that ensure that 'my' group is good, and the 'other' is bad. These are projective processes, which sustain an unrealistic belief in the attributions of value to self and others. When colleagues and the authority of the leader support that unreality, it can be irrefutable. The malignant attractiveness of a group comes from this powerful offer of confirmation of the wished-for narcissism of infancy. Not being part of a particular group means forgoing a lot – in effect not only losing the supported narcissism, but also risking becoming alien and the target for the projective system*" (p. 90).

The mechanisms of projection and especially projective identification discussed earlier play a large role in this process. While projective identification can be part of the normal process of human communication, it plays an outsized role in racial discrimination and hatred. A paper written by John Bird and Simon Clark (1999) explains that projective identification gives rise to racism by causing individuals to project their own negative qualities or fears onto a racial or ethnic group, creating stereotypes and prejudices. This leads to the formation of generalized beliefs and assumptions about that large group. This in turn reinforces and determines how individuals interpret and interact with members of the targeted large group, cementing discriminatory behaviors and attitudes. The targeted large group may respond to projective identification by experiencing feelings of devaluation, marginalization, stigmatization, and discrimination, leading to the targeted group's heightened awareness of how the negative stereotypes projected onto them impact the targeted group's members' daily lives. While some members of the targeted large group may actively and consciously resist the projected stereotypes, other members will unconsciously internalize the projected stereotypes, leading to self-doubt, low self-esteem, and a sense of inferiority. This pattern of projective identification can play a role in the creation of a large-group identity both in the large group doing the projection and in the large group being targeted. This sets up a conflictual pattern of relationship which precludes either of the large groups knowing anything about the Other. We can describe this dynamic by paraphrasing Henry Smith's (2006) explanation – "*I am white precisely to the extent that I think you are black, and you are black precisely to the extent that you think I am white.*" In this way the social construction of race is rooted in intrapsychic mechanisms.

7

Freudian Group Psychology

We have written previously on Freudian group psychology (K. Volkan, 1994; K. Volkan & V. D. Volkan, 2023; V. D. Volkan 2020), but it is important to summarize these ideas again. It is important to remember that many of the general aspects of group functioning are applicable to many types of groups – small, large, ethnic, tribal, national, religious, ideological, etc. – while others are more applicable to specific groups. Some of the differences are absolute while other elements differ by degree. In this book, with its focus on mass violence, we will concentrate primarily on large-group characteristics. We will, however, also discuss some important characteristics of small groups that can be extended to larger groups. Freud's belief was that individual psychology is largely influenced by the psychology of the large group. This concept has been refined to emphasize the importance of large-group identification in the human psyche.

In psychoanalytic theory, beginning with Freud (1921), large groups are viewed as possessing a separate "collective mind" from that of the individual, where the conscious mind of the individual is submerged and replaced by the predominantly unconscious large-group mind. This unconscious large-group mind is sustained through the unconscious identification of large-group members with each other and the large-group leader, diminishing intellectual processes while intensifying emotions. This identification fosters unity and purpose but also results in a loss of individuality and potential disconnection from reality.

Individuals in large groups surrender to their unconscious instincts to become part of the large group. The power of the large group enables the individual's unconscious wishes to overcome repression by the ego. In a large group, every sentiment and emotion become highly contagious, leading the individual to prioritize the large group's interests over their own. Large-group emotions are overwhelming and possess a hypnotic power, causing the individual to lose their conscious personality and volition. These are replaced by the psychological characteristics and volition of the large group. Because of this, large groups have the potential to be constructive, but this also allows large groups to become disconnected from consensus reality and to commit atrocities that would be abhorrent to an individual. As Freud stated in *Group Psychology and the Analysis of the Ego* (1921):

> "*And finally, groups have never thirsted after truth. They demand illusions, and cannot do without them. They constantly give what is unreal precedence over what is real; they are almost as strongly influenced by what is untrue as by what is true. They have an evident tendency not to distinguish between the two.*" (p. 80)

In his work *Totem and Taboo* (1918), Freud offers a psychoanalytic perspective on large groups where the group leader is seen as a primal father figure who is replaced by totemic law after being slain by an alliance of sons, preventing rivalry and incest within the family; he also argues that the development of large groups is influenced by oedipal issues between the large-group members and the leader, resulting in the leader being either idealized as the savior of the large group or perceived as a rival or oedipal father figure.

Wilfred Bion, a British psychoanalyst, extended the understanding of Freudian group dynamics by developing a selection process for frontline officers in World War II. He characterized small psychotherapy groups as having three types of basic assumptions: *dependency*, *fight-flight*, and *pairing*, which are present in all groups but become more noticeable during crises or structural breakdowns.

The *dependency group* is characterized by members who view themselves as inadequate and weak, relying heavily on the leader to solve problems and achieve goals. Should the leader fail to meet their unrealistic expectations, members initially deny the failure. Ultimately, they devalue the leader, and seek a substitute who can fulfill their idealized image.

In the *fight-flight group*, a sense of camaraderie is established through a shared ideology and a common enemy, leading to internal conflicts and subgroup formation. The leader's role is to continue the fight against perceived external enemies and suppress any internal conflicts, resulting in a relationship marked by control.

The *pairing group* relies on the projection of desires onto a couple within the group, symbolizing procreation and maintaining group integrity, with the sexual union seen as a means to resolve conflicts and provide intimacy and protection.

The groups described by Bion had a leader who interpreted group dynamics and encouraged members to project their anxieties onto the leader, promoting collaboration and reducing unproductive behaviors. These groups were characterized by a leader who remained neutral and delivered interpretations to the group in a cryptic manner, refusing to participate in group decision making and conflict resolution. The goal was to encourage group members to project their anxieties, feelings, and past interactions with authority figures (i.e. transferences) onto the group leader. The leader then interpreted these processes to the group. It may be that a Bion-like group leader who interprets the psychodynamics of a group, or of group-to-group interaction could be useful for facilitating interaction between warring factions, though Bion's approach would likely need to be modified. While valuing Bion's work on group processes, Otto Kernberg (1984b) critiques his therapeutic technique. As Kernberg says

> *"I hasten to add, however, that, whereas Bion's method of exploring primitive defenses, object relations, and anxieties in small unstructured groups may be of great value in learning about small group psychology and group*

> *processes, even in large organizations and large unstructured groups, I find the therapeutic value of his technique questionable.*" (p. 8)

Kernberg goes on to provide a psychoanalytic perspective on processes in work groups which can be assumed to vary from smaller to larger in size. Kernberg identifies phenomena such as aggression, denial of aggression, depression, narcissistic and antisocial personalities in leadership roles, and intolerance of individual expression. He also examines the regressive pressures faced by group leaders, including isolation, decision-making uncertainty, oedipal fears and frustrations, and limited personal time, categorizing these pressures into *aggression*, *sexuality*, and *dependency*.

Group tensions can incite aggression in leaders, prompting these leaders to assert dominance and react with hostility towards the group, potentially causing long-lasting harm to the group's structure. The leader's authority can be amplified by transference dynamics within the group, making it even more challenging when the leader exhibits sadistic traits or when the group is inclined towards fight-or-flight responses. Consequently, the leader, as a symbolic parental figure, must consistently manage the projected aggression from group members, underscoring the significance of having a leader with a stable personality capable of tolerating aggression to guide the group effectively and constructively.

The group leader's sexuality is closely connected to issues of control and power. When assuming a parental role, the leader takes on responsibilities similar to a father figure, resulting in a scarcity of women in leadership positions. The leader's gender influences the perception of possessing group members of the opposite sex. These dynamics create temptation for the leader, leading to sexual acting out at higher levels of the organization. The imbalanced sexual relationship between the leader and group member can serve as a platform for sadomasochistic dynamics, with the leader exerting dominance and the group member partner experiencing guilt. This interplay extends to the entire group, affecting control and resistance. Unconscious conflicts of the leader and group members can degrade group functioning. Sexual relationships between opposite-sex group leaders act as a defense mechanism against dependency but risk eroticizing the work environment, leading to aggression and breakdown in communication. Effective control and sublimation of sexual energy can lead to productive outcomes, depending on the maturity of the leader. The group structure must adapt to accommodate any emerging sexual relationships.

Leaders face the greatest regressive pressure due to the frustration of dependency needs, which refers to the reliance on others for support or assistance. As a leader, it can be challenging to manage the demands and expectations of group members who freely express their needs, while not being able to reciprocate in the same manner. This dynamic creates a power imbalance where the leader constantly provides for the group, while receiving little in return. On the other hand, group members may receive recognition and rewards for their contributions, leading the leader to feel overlooked and underappreciated. Despite the gratification that comes from admiration and recognition, leaders often lack genuine friendships or peers with whom they can confide and seek support. This dynamic is exaggerated for narcissistic leaders who cannot or will not seek out peers or friendships with others who are perceived as equals. A psychoanalytically-informed consultant can play an important role here as a person to whom the leader can turn in order to clarify the psychology underlying his or her position.

The potential impact of aggression, sexuality, and dependency on a group leader's psychological state can lead to regression and psychopathological manifestations. Although it is conceivable for a leader to possess pre-existing psychopathological tendencies prior to assuming their leadership role, the responsibilities and expectations associated with being a group leader considerably heighten the likelihood of such regression. Regressed leaders can display four primary character structures, namely *schizoid*, *obsessive*, *paranoid*, and narcissistic.

The *schizoid* leader is distinguished by their emotional isolation and unavailability. These leaders exhibit a tendency to maintain a significant emotional distance from their group members, which can hinder the fulfillment of the group's needs and prompt them to seek solace and assistance from a subleader or others in the group. Oftentimes, a subleader will shoulder the responsibility of leading the group, as the schizoid leader fails to adequately address the requirements of the group members. This puts a good deal of pressure on group subleaders and as a result they are typically the first to depart from a group led by a schizoid leader.

Leaders with *obsessive* traits, conversely, are rather prevalent in positions of leadership. They are renowned for their inclination towards order, precision, stability, and clarity in their directives and expectations. Although these characteristics may initially appear advantageous, they also possess negative aspects. For instance, the obsessive leader may possess an excessive inclination towards order and precision, which may not necessarily align with the requisites of the organizational group task. Moreover, the obsessive leader may feel compelled to exert stringent control over all facets of the group task, thereby impeding their ability to delegate responsibilities and trust their group members with significant assignments. This inclination can dampen the independence and decision-making capabilities of the group members, ultimately inhibiting creativity and innovation within the group. Additionally, due to their inflexible bureaucratic approach, obsessive leaders often encounter difficulties in adapting to swift changes within an organization, resulting in unwarranted stress and tension during periods of transition. Furthermore, these leaders may even oppose change by resorting to sadistic acts and attempting to enforce the preservation of the current state of affairs.

Leaders who exhibit a *paranoid* disposition are characterized by their inclination to harbor suspicion and project their own anger onto the collective, their consistent perception of concealed adversaries lurking in every nook and cranny, and their all-consuming notion of exposing conspiracies within the group. This particular brand of leader thrives in large groups with intricate hierarchies, as the myriad levels and positions afford ample opportunities for potential adversaries who stand ready to mount an attack. In this context, the paranoid leaders' primary focus shifts towards suppressing and eliminating any opposition to their authority, overshadowing the actual work of the group. While paranoid leaders may successfully channel their aggression and fears towards external factions, it is important to note that their perception of these outside entities will be significantly distorted, ultimately undermining their capacity to effectively guide their group in constructively navigating the external environment in the long term. This channeling aggression and fear towards those outside of the group is accomplished through the use of projection and projective identification.

Narcissistic leaders who are destructive epitomize the most severe manifestation of leadership pathology[3]. These individuals demonstrate a sense of grandeur and self-centeredness, concealing a hidden envy towards others. They exhibit an excessive superficiality, lacking the ability to empathize and failing to recognize the capabilities of others. Furthermore, when their personal desires are obstructed, they tend to revert to a paranoid style of leadership. They also use projection and projective identification towards those outside the group. Motivated by an intense hunger for power and prestige, narcissistic leaders often possess the aptitude to realize their ambitions. However, they cultivate an unhealthy reliance among group members, resorting to extreme measures to maintain control. As a result, they diminish the individual value of group members, attributing them with inferior qualities. Group members find themselves in a position where they must be submissive and passive if they desire even the slightest forms of satisfaction. Such satisfaction is usually granted to them as a reflection of the leader, reinforcing the notion that they must imitate.

In summary, the burden of dependency requirements exerts significant pressure on leaders, resulting in potential regression into psychopathological conditions. Leaders with schizoid tendencies are unable to fulfill the emotional needs of the group, prompting group members to seek support and connection from a subordinate leader within the group or from external sources. Obsessive leaders' desire for control and narrow focus on their potentially inexplicable agenda may impede the group's ability to operate effectively. Paranoid leaders' fixation on hidden foes and conspiracies within the group obstructs the group's long-term

3. We will comment later on reparative narcissistic leaders who are able to channel their narcissistic needs into constructive leadership.

functionality, as their distorted perception of external groups prevents them from effectively guiding the group in navigating the outside world. Destructive narcissistic leaders' grandiose and self-centered nature, coupled with a subtle envy toward others, creates a toxic style of leadership that fosters dependency and undermines the individual worth of group members. This establishes an environment in which group members feel compelled to be submissive and passive to receive even the smallest forms of gratification, further perpetuating the leader's narcissistic tendencies. The characteristic traits of schizoid, obsessive, paranoid, and narcissistic leaders each present distinct challenges and dynamics within a group context. It is vital to comprehend these dynamics to adequately support and guide leaders in their roles. Furthermore, having a consultant with a psychoanalytic background can offer leaders a secure space in which to openly discuss their concerns and seek guidance in navigating the intricate dynamics of leadership. Addressing and mitigating these pathologies is essential for cultivating a healthy and thriving group culture.

Size Matters

As Kernberg mentions in the above quote (1984b), many of the insights that have been gained from observing small groups – either naturally occurring, work groups, or psychotherapy groups, also apply to large groups. As groups become larger, however, some important differences emerge. The question then arises – what are the differences between small and large groups?

Bion's groups consisted of around eight participants but could be as large as 20 people (1952, 1961). These groups were unstructured and non-directive, allowing for natural group dynamics, or the types of groups described above, to emerge. Later others such as Albert Kenneth Rice at the Tavistock Clinic extended Bion's groups to 20-50 people (1975). As reported by Mark Ettlin (2003), one of the innovators of group psychoanalysis, Siegmund Heinrich Foulkes (1975), maintained that a large analytic practice group could have from 30 up to 120 members; there has even been an analytic group of 450 members. Ettlin notes that as a group becomes larger personal contact diminishes and the group's size is experienced as a sense of strangeness by the group members. Group members cognitively simplify their experience of the group as it becomes larger. The lack of personal contact as a group gets larger will cause the group to be experienced as more uniform and imposing, while emotions connected to the group will decrease in complexity and become increasingly split into good or bad attributions.

Malcom Pines (1975) crystallizes the difference between small and large-group functioning. He states, "The problem in the large group is of how to think, as opposed to the small group's problem of how to feel" (p. 300). In small groups, ego functions including cognition and a sense of self are intact, while emotional states are variable. In the large-group emotions are established by the group while ego functions including cognition are dulled. In large groups people feel, they don't think. Pines labels large-group functioning as "psychotic" involving primitive defenses such as splitting and projective identification. We can also include delusions. As Ettlin (2003) puts it,

> *"There is an old group adage that states: 'If one member of a group tells you that you are a horse, they are obviously crazy and can be ignored. If two members tell you that you are a horse, it's likely a conspiracy that should be defended against. If three members tell you that you are a horse (though it may be a projective identification), you had better buy a saddle!'"*

This is a good summary of the differences between small and large groups. A. C. Robin Skynner (1975) implies that constructive small groups operate similarly to Melanie Klein's depressive position where "functioning can be maintained, with containment of painful affect and sharing of experience between similar but unique and separate individuals." Large groups, conversely, operate from Klein's Paranoid/Schizoid position utilizing splitting and projective defenses.

In a mathematical simulation model Rosapia Lauro Grotto, Andrea Guazzini, and Franco Bagnoli examined the effect of size on group dynamics (2014). They present a rough breakdown of human social dynamics into crowd and group dynamics. Freud's work examines crowd dynamics, or what we would term large-group dynamics while Bion's work represents group dynamics which represents small-group dynamics. The model presented in the paper suggests that when a group has over 20 members its dynamics change from small to large-group dynamics. They report that their findings are

> "*...suggestive of the existence of two different dynamic regimen in the model, the first corresponding to the classical small group dynamics and the other corresponding to the classical large group or crowd dynamics. In the small group case, the affective structure of the interpersonal links in the group remains the main determinant of the collective state of the system, while in the case of the large group, or crowd dynamics, the cognitive dimension... is dominating the collective behavior. This is reminiscent of the Freudian hypothesis that a Common Ideal or a shared Value can very easily take the place of the 'beloved' Leader in the mass condition.*" (p. 8)

While this model suggests that the leader is less important in large groups, it does not consider the impact of a destructive narcissistic or pathological leader on large-group dynamics. Reminiscent of Bion's basic assumptions, Ettlin (2003) states that ties to an idealized leader can serve to keep a larger group together. He says that,

> "*Members may trade their individuality to be part of a single-minded, incestuous, cult-like, in-group or primal horde. The psychosocial and sociocultural conditions that support group fusionary tendencies also elicit personal identity diffusion.*" (p. 45)

Large groups function in a more primitive fashion than small groups, providing members with more unified emotions while dulling thinking. Still, the characteristics of Bion's group assumptions remain and are useful for understanding large groups (Kernberg, 1984b) or as J. Stuart Whitley (1975) says "Bion's original Basic Assumptions still apply and can be identified in the large group's behaviour" (p. 193), even if the large group is more mindless or "psychotic." While Bion's basic assumptions can be found in large groups, some important aspects of large groups are not found in small groups. We will cover these unique large-group elements in detail in a further chapter.

Projection and Projective Identification in Groups

Pathological leaders of large groups will use projection and projective identification as a way to preserve themselves and to relieve pressures on themselves and their followers. Ernest Masler (1969) reports that psychotherapy group members defensively use projection and projective identification among themselves, which will often occur when the group functions as a superego. We believe that a similar mechanism is also at play in large groups. In large dependency groups members will use these sorts of defense mechanisms to reinforce feelings of weakness and inadequacy among themselves, collectively culminating in their need for an all-good omnipotent leader. Large fight-flight groups are initially much like dependency groups, though what is projected among group members is internal conflict. With the help from the leader, large-group members will project what is bad among themselves to those outside the group leaving themselves and their leader as all good. As long as those outside the large group remain bad, the group can remain cohesive. This works against a realistic view of those outside the large group, especially of another large group that is at war with the fight-flight group. It is likely that both large groups will have flight-flight dynamics and as a result the mutual projection/projective identification processes between the large groups will be extremely hard to end. The current conflict between Israel and Hamas unfortunately seems to consist of this type of dynamic.

In large pairing groups the projection/projective identification is less likely to be aggressive and more likely to be erotically tinged. This can lead to Oedipal rivalries among group members and with the leader(s). However, the organization of this type of large group is perhaps the healthiest or most constructive of Bion's group types, and is most likely to function from Klein's depressive position (Skynner, 1975). Major aspects of pairing groups can be seen in relatively stable large groups. Stable monarchies have a king and a queen. In the United States, the First

Lady of the United States is an important and usually popular figure. The relationship of the leadership couple is a very important symbol of large-group cohesiveness and provides reassurance to group members. Hence, we see the extreme interest in the British Royals or President Obama's family life. We also see concern and curiosity of a more morbid type when something seems off about leader-couple. This explains the ongoing obsession in the news media and among late night commentators on the state of Donald Trump's relationship or lack thereof with Melania Trump.

In general, large dependency and fight-flight groups operate at a borderline or narcissistic level of personality organization. These types of groups unconsciously support and create splitting, even operating at times at a psychotic level promoting fragmentations within the large group. This large-group splitting can present in different forms. Most commonly, it presents as an "us vs them" dynamic where the large group is "all good" or "great." But this is accomplished by denigrating those outside the group who are the receptacles of the projection of "badness." The other way splitting emerges in these types of large groups is through a comparison with an idealized past, which is "all good" and to which the large group seeks to return. Senem Çevik (2023) describes in detail the historical and psychological factors for a visible splitting in Türkiye. She writes,

> "*Grandiosity in politics is a recurring phenomenon that has gained prominence in recent years on a global scale. Examples such as former U.S. President Trump's rallying cry to 'Make America Great Again' or Russian President Putin's ambitions to restore Russia's past glory illustrate how a nostalgic longing for a bygone era can manifest itself through grandiose political leadership. Likewise, in Turkey, President Erdoğan capitalizes on this collective yearning for the past to instill a sense of grandeur within Turkish society, employing ambitious policies, projects, and cultural initiatives. By projecting his own grandiose self-representation onto society, he seeks to enhance the collective self-image, in other words make Turkey great again. This process is achieved through historical revisionism and symbolic per-*

> *formative actions promoting a type of magical thinking that psychologically and institutionally attempt to resurrect the Ottoman Empire in the collective mind. Historical revisionism in Turkey is successful through a very complex set of propaganda strategies that employ elements of popular culture such as television and music which in turn help mobilize the society for its political causes".* (Çevik 2023, pp. 10–11)

These splits are actualized in people as well. Imagine giving a lecture in Türkiye at a university. Also imagine that there are 100 female students in the audience listening to you. Half of them wear head coverings and the other half do not. It is as if these female students come from two different countries as if their personalities are split.

This does not mean that the members of these large groups function individually at this level of personality organization. But collectively this seems to be the case. Likewise, leaders of large dependency and fight-flight groups have a tendency toward aggression, antisocial behavior, manipulations, narcissism, obsession, paranoia, i.e. the Dark Triad traits first described by Delroy Paulhus and Kevin Williams (2002). These traits are overrepresented in totalitarian or totalitarian-leaning governments. A quick perusal of leaders of these governments, including Mohammed bin Salman, Recep Tayyip Erdoğan, Kim Jung-un, Ali Khameni, Vladimir Putin and Xi Jinping, to name a few, supports this assertion. In the next chapter we will examine the relationship between leaders and followers.

8

The Psychology of Large-Group Leaders and Followers

Next, we will discuss the psychology of neighbors and the psychology of leaders and followers. These two psychologies dovetail. We cannot really appreciate why wars and war-like situations occur without studying these psychologies in ethnic, national, religious, or ideological large groups. Sigmund Freud, in his exchange with Albert Einstein, stated that all human beings are either leaders or followers. A political leader is one who constantly updates and modifies his or her responses to the conscious and unconscious needs of his or her followers. To a large extent these needs center around three principles.

The first of these principles is *competition.* This is an historic element in the makeup of human beings. In the past, neighboring tribes competed for physical goods such as food in order to survive. As we stated earlier, physical goods primarily represent survival, but after a while they can take on a greater meaning, for example self-esteem. This representation unconsciously influences the mind so that eventually the physical goods take on an emotional meaning above and beyond the issue of survival. The threat of losing this emotional symbol – what psychoanalysts call narcissistic supplies – increases over time and, in fact, creates and sustains competition.

The second principal deals with the issue of *non-sameness* that we described earlier. Every enemy large group is real because the thought prevails that "they" can kill "us." Every enemy is also mentally created to some extent, since "they" serve as a reservoir to absorb "our" unwanted aspects.

The third principle refers to *psychologizing physical borders* that separate neighbors. In 1986 Vamık Volkan, by Israeli permission, spent half a day in the Allenby Bridge area, which separates Israel from Jordan. He observed border patrol officials and the elaborate preoccupations they took to protect the border. One could see a definite "us" and "them" attitude in that some of their precautions were most elaborate, to the point that the patrol officers would frequently sweep dirt roads to detect any footprints, or search vehicles passing through the border by stripping them down to the bare frames. While the precautions the border guards took appear rational on the surface, in view of the electronic surveillance capabilities of the Israelis it seems that their actions also resulted from an unconscious need to protect their psychological large group "skin," rather than from only a matter of security.

A political leader will consciously and unconsciously try to uphold the three principles, and the more stress there is in the environment, the more he or she will rely on them. At the time that a leader upholds the psychology of neighbors, he or she assesses its effect on his or her followers. The leader's self-esteem largely depends on his or her followers' responses to him or her. We must acknowledge that in today's world, due to incredible developments in technology, especially communication technology, all nation large groups are neighbors.

A Two-Way Street

The political leader-followers' relationship is a two-way street, and the movement of traffic on both sides of the street depends on many factors. The two-way traffic may become congested due to the psychological make-up of the leader or due to forces that influence the followers.

Historian and political science professor James MacGregor Burns (1984) identified two types of leaders: *transactional* and *transforming*. The transactional leader depends and, in fact, thrives on bargaining, manipulating, accommodating, and compromising within a given system. He or she acts according to political polls and national "climate," and follows existing societal sentiments, becoming a spokesperson for them. On the other hand, a transforming leader "transcends and even seeks to reconstruct the political system, rather than simply operating within it" (Burns, 1984, p. 16).

In a stable democracy that is not experiencing economic, political, or military stress, the personality of a transactional leader typically is not of critical importance, and even a transforming leader will not cause fundamental changes in society or initiate drastically different policies. The formal and informal systems of "checks and balances" in a well-functioning democracy prevent a leader's personality organization—his or her habitual ways of behaving and feeling due to personal emotional problems, as well as positive adaptations—from exerting undue influence over the government and the governed.

Even when many followers are excited about a transforming leader's personality, behavior, and agenda—and identify with the leader—the changes that result are typically not drastic. Under certain circumstances, however, the personality of a political leader can influence outcomes or policies, and at times can even be a major factor in creating new and drastic societal and political processes. We can say the same about leaders of political parties or organizations.

We can define transforming leaders who dedicate themselves to changing the followers' external and internal worlds to lift their individual self-esteem and to modify their large-group identity as *reparative* and *destructive* (V. D. Volkan, 2004). Reparative leaders achieve these tasks, or try to achieve them, without humiliating, hurting, or killing groups of people who are not his or her followers. By the term destructive, we refer to leaders who resort to mass humiliation—even destruction of the Other who are not his or her followers within the same country—such as putting them in jail for this or that made-up reason. Or the Other from outside the leader's group can be subject to the leader's destructiveness. This would include an exaggeration of the "badness" of another large group or even attacking another large group as an "enemy."

"Who Are We Now?" Civilization

In the 21st century change continues to take place at an unprecedented pace and scale. Incredible advances in communication, signal and photographic intelligence and travel technologies, and financial markets that transcend national borders have made people with different large-group identities interact to a greater degree and with greater speed. Meanwhile, genealogical DNA tests have become popular world-wide, sometimes surprising people who learn of their ancestry. We are also aware that the number of the number of refugees and immigrants has been skyrocketed. As reported at the beginning of this book, according to UNHCR's estimations, 133 million people are living in parts of the world that are involved in armed conflict with close to half this number being displaced. These developments, in turn, have amplified the question "who are we now?" worldwide.

Erik Erikson (1950) used the term "basic trust" to describe how a child learns to feel comfortable putting his or her own safety in a caretaker's hands. By developing basic trust, a child also discovers how to trust him or herself. In normal circumstances, adults who depend on trusting themselves and others can see the beauty of diversities in human beings without anxiety. The "who are we now civilization?" issue has influenced many individuals to develop *blind trust* (V. D. Volkan, 2004) in a political leader who has exaggerated narcissism and who attempts to protect large-group identity and often seeks to turn a political party or organization into a "new" large-group identity for his or her followers and present himself or herself as a savior.

Leaders with a Narcissistic Personality

Narcissism refers to love of self and is linked to self-preservation. In human psychological functioning, it is as normal as sex, aggression, and anxiety (Rangell 1980, V. D. Volkan & Ast 1994; Weigert 1967). Like sex, aggression, and anxiety, it is subject to variation. It can be "healthy" or exaggerated. Leaders who have exaggerated narcissistic personalities are pre-occupied with self-importance and fantasies of unbounded success to which they feel entitled. While they demand admiration from others, they are aloof and without empathy toward them. They are compelled to be "number one" in power, prestige, and fame and split off and deny their "hungry," dependent and devalued aspects.

When individuals have an exaggerated love for themselves, they often display repeated patterns of thoughts, behaviors, and feelings that are collectively known as a narcissistic personality. Such individuals think that they are unique and grand, which causes them to feel omnipotent and to act as though they are better than anyone else. But people with narcissistic personalities live in a paradox: while they love themselves too much and feel grandiose and omnipotent, they also, in the shadows so to speak, possess an aspect that is devalued and "hungry" for love. Periodically, this hunger asserts itself into awareness and creates anxiety, shame, or humiliation in the person. Accordingly, such individuals' personality organization splits between a *grandiose self* and a *hungry self.* The splitting in the personality organization reflects a lack of cohesive identity. The personality characteristics reflecting the grandiose self are *overt*, while those characteristics reflecting the hungry self are *covert* (Kernberg, 1975; Akhtar, 1992; and V. D. Volkan and Ast, 1994).

A person may be deeply involved with politics and social issues, but he or she sees them unilaterally without reference to the views of others who are perceived as "inferior." Although the narcissistic leader may appear aloof, and therefore indicate the possibility of an obsessional character, obsessional individuals are emotionally far more in tune with those around them and are often capable of sincere and passionate concern for social and political issues (Kernberg, 1970). Because obsessional individuals have difficulty tolerating loss of control, we would expect a leader with such a personality to experience internal danger and anxiety if he or she felt that a political situation or a political rival could not be controlled. He or she may then unconsciously experience loss of love or self-esteem. The obsessional leader may then respond in an exaggerated fashion and seek rules, regulations and official policies or other sources of rationalization and intellectualization to address the crisis at the expense of exploring creative and adaptive solutions. Or he or she may exhibit extreme ambivalence toward his or her "uncontrolled" opponent and behave in irrational ways.

When a narcissistic leader's superiority and power are threatened, he or she experiences shame and humiliation. Feelings of rage may follow. To stabilize or reestablish his or her narcissistic personality, the leader is then internally compelled to act, and the decisions that result may have drastic societal or political consequences.

If a leader has excessive narcissistic qualities, he or she tends to consciously or unconsciously inflames the images of past historical and other large-group identity markers of societal, religious, economic, educational practices with the aim of bringing back an old glory and increasing the shared self-esteem of members. Such a development may increase paranoid expectations and prejudice against "the Other," including people in the same country who are not followers of the leader.

Another characteristic of such leaders is their conscious or unconscious fantasy that they live by themselves in a splendid "glass bubble" (V. D. Volkan, 1979). Through the glass they watch others outside their own glorious but lonely "kingdom" and divide them into two groups: those who support their narcissism and those who are devalued. Those who are devalued may be perceived as an enemy or may be disregarded as completely insignificant. In the next chapter we will comment on how these the characteristics manifest among political leaders.

"Reparative" or "Destructive" Leaders with Narcissistic Personality Organization

"Narcissism" should not be seen as necessarily bad. In fact, a healthy level of narcissism is essential in order to survive, work, be in relationship to others, and maintain a strong sense of self. It is, however, possible for narcissism to become problematic and lead to an unhealthy obsession with oneself or an inflated sense of one's own importance.

Volkan and Ast (1994) referred to politicians with narcissistic personality organization as "successful narcissists." These leaders are skilled at manipulating their external environment and finding ways to align their internal desires with external realities. Through this manipulation, including their interactions with supporters and opponents, they strive to protect and maintain their grandiose selves. Some political leaders can maintain this "success" for many years or even their entire lifetimes, depending on historical circumstances. Others may only experience this level of success for a shorter period. This manipulation of the external environment results in leaders with exaggerated narcissism can be categorized as either "reparative" or "destructive."

The term "reparative" refers to leaders with narcissistic personality organization who are dedicated to helping their followers progress from a regressed state. These leaders aim to change their followers' internal and external worlds to boost their self-esteem and reshape their group identity. These reparative narcissistic leaders achieve their goals, or at least try to, without resorting to mass killings or violence against any particular group.

On the other hand, the term "destructive" refers to leaders with narcissistic personality organization who resort to mass destruction of an "outside" group. These leaders influence their followers to support destructive acts while keeping the followers in a regressed state. Like reparative leaders, destructive leaders also aim to boost their followers' self-esteem and alter their group identity, but they do so by comparing themselves to the group they are targeting for destruction.

Both types of leaders use "chosen glories," "chosen traumas," which we will discuss below, or both to stimulate large-group identity, depending on their desire to inflame shared mental images of recent traumas. Both make extensive use of "purification" rituals to modify the existing large-group identity. Both may destroy some of the group's old symbols or "protosymbols" (Werner and Kaplan 1963) and change cultural values and customs. The key difference between a reparative leader and a destructive leader, however, lies in how the leader targets an "outside" group for destruction. It can be challenging to distinguish between the two types of leaders with narcissistic personality organization, as a reparative leader may later become destructive. In order for leaders with narcissistic traits to be successful, they need not only intelligence but also the ability to manipulate existing realities and test them. Some individuals with narcissistic tendencies become leaders because their desire for greatness drives them. Others may not initially have narcissistic traits, but external circumstances can cause them to change. These characteristics can become internalized as they grow fond of power and the pursuit of being on top. For example, leaders who remain in power for decades, such as Cuba's Fidel Castro or Libya's Muammar Khadafi ended up behaving to one degree or another as "successful narcissists," whether they initially had typical narcissistic personality organizations or not. Examining their psychology can provide insight into how narcissistic political leaders can be both reparative and destructive.

9

Political Leaders

The personalities of political leaders, in a general sense but not necessarily a psychoanalytic sense, have always been scrutinized, especially during elections, societal crises, scandals, war-like situations and wars. Over the course of an adult individual's lifetime, he or she exhibits habitual behavior and thought patterns, emotional expressions, modes of speech and bodily gestures which can be observed by others. Because political leaders spend a great deal of time in the public eye and have little choice but to allow much of their life and personal habitual patterns to be available to everyone through the media, attempts are sometimes made to name and even analyze their personality.

The personality of a political leader plays a crucial role in his or her attempts to maintain a stable relationship both with those who are in his or her immediate "entourage" and with the much larger group of people who comprise his or her "followers." The leader-follower relationship is a "two-way" street: it is influenced and determined by the leader's personality and from the followers' shared conscious and unconscious wishes and needs.

Under certain circumstances the personality of a political leader can influence outcomes or policies, and at times even be a major factor in creating new and drastic societal and political processes. A typical instance of this phenomenon is when a leader experiences sustained anxiety or other unpleasant emotions such as depression or humiliation due to the reactivation of his or her internal mental conflicts. The societal or political arena is then utilized in an attempt to find an external solution for an internal dilemma. At such times the leader's personality plays a key role in the "choice" of what societal or political process to initiate or become involved in.

In 1926 Sigmund Freud proposed four situations that were internally dangerous and induced anxiety in an individual. The first is the fear of the loss of a love object. The second involves fear of losing the love provided by the love object. The third can be described as losing a body part and is associated with fear of castration. The fourth danger refers to the fear of not living up to the internalized expectations of important others (superego) and therefore reflects a loss of self-esteem. When an external situation is unconsciously perceived as echoing one of these threats, or a combination of them, their images become part of internal mental conflicts and the individual may experience anxiety and regress.

As an example, we can examine former U.S. President Richard Nixon's adult life. Even a cursory examination reveals that he was primarily a narcissist who used obsessional preoccupations as a support mechanism (V. D. Volkan, Itzkowitz & Dod, 1997). Nixon was known as a "collector" of leadership positions and sought out these roles in many different organizations throughout his life. He also was known to collect honors and was especially keen to be the first at doing something. Some of these roles were significant, like becoming President of the United States or normalizing relations with Communist China, but other were trivial such as being the first president to visit Hawaii, or being the first to have had four former First Ladies attend the opening of his presidential library. John Ehrlichman, one of Nixon's aides pit it this way: "there was a running gag on any campaign; everything that happened was a 'historic first' " (V. D. Volkan, Itzkowitz & Dod, 1997, p. 94). In Nixon's case he constantly needed to collect roles, honors, and firsts, to feed his narcissism. Without these, his grandiosity would be threatened, triggering shame and a sense that he might no longer exist. This type of dynamic can cause a leader to resort to extreme or unusual decisions to counteract what could be perceived as a threat.

Before looking at the role of a political leader's psychological make-up it is necessary to state an ethical issue, telling very private things about another person that can be read by others. As psychoanalytically oriented therapists when we write case reports, we very carefully find ways to protect the identities of our own patients and others whose therapeutic processes we supervised. We think that it is appropriate to write psychobiographies of political leaders who no longer were alive or are living since in the news media these individuals' life experience are discussed even when these individuals are not involved in massive deadly socio-political processes. It is also acceptable, in some instances to write about living leaders. In these cases, as in our comments on Putin, we are not using any privileged, private information, but instead, relying on what is publicly available. We also acknowledge that any diagnoses we make are speculative.

What makes a successful psychobiography? The availability of information, the more detailed the better, as well as information about the person's culture, political history, as well as information about his or her ethnic, ideological, national, religious, or other influences on identity. As psychoanalytic clinicians we can draw parallels to politically leaders based on insights gained from our patients. A good example would be our work with narcissistic or borderline patients who tend to split the world into all good and all bad. We can see similarities in political leaders who obsessively divide people into loyal followers or haters. The use of overly positive language to describe themselves or their ideas or things such as "the best," "fantastic," "wonderful," "incredible," and "excellent" on one side and negative language such as "terrible," "fake," "shithole," "failed," "loser," "lowlife," etc., to describe those they perceive as threatening. Lying in the name of inflating their grandiosity is another hallmark of narcissistic leaders and can be seen as an attempt to overcome being perceived of as average.

As we mentioned briefly in chapter 8, people with exaggerated narcissism live in a paradox: while they love themselves too much and feel grandiose and omnipotent, they also, in the shadows so to speak, possess an aspect that is devalued and "hungry" for love. Periodically, this hunger asserts itself into awareness and creates anxiety, shame, or humiliation in the person. Accordingly, such individuals' personality organization splits between a grandiose self and a hungry self. The splitting in the personality organization reflects a lack of cohesive identity. As we stated earlier the personality characteristics reflecting the grandiose self are overt, while those characteristics reflecting the hungry self are covert. Thus, narcissistic individuals are prone to expressing feelings of envy, greed, and rage, which are emotional states that stem from their "hungry" parts. They may feel envious of others whom they perceive as having greater self-esteem or more possessions, as if their own self-esteem and possessions were taken away from them. If they are unable to escape the reality of being outcompeted, especially by individuals who possess superior power, beauty, intelligence, or wealth, they may become paranoid. We have observed these patterns during our work in psychoanalysis or psychoanalytic psychotherapy with such individuals.

People with exaggerated narcissism may not experience or express certain emotions. It is common for these individuals to struggle with showing gratitude, remorse, or sorrow. These emotions are connected to empathy and caring for others, as well as valuing them as unique individuals. Due to their constant need to inflate their grandiose selves, individuals with exaggerated narcissism are unable to experience these emotional states. This is also evident in clinical settings when working with such individuals. In the next chapter we will examine how some characteristics of narcissistic political leaders manifest as psycho-physical structures.

10

Large-Group Psychology in Its Own Right

In this chapter we describe several concepts that will illuminate our description of large-group psychology in its own right:

1. Core individual identity
2. Small-group identity and large-group identity
3. Complicated large-group mourning, transgenerational transmission, chosen trauma and undigested trauma
4. Entitlement ideologies
5. Chosen glory
6. Large-group regression, time collapse, becoming like the enemy and purification

Sigmund Freud had knowledge about "war neurosis." However, his response to Albert Einstein (Freud, 1933) had a long-lasting impact on limiting the contributions of psychoanalysis in understanding the motivations behind dangerous societal and political movements in specific societies and international relations. Despite this, several decades ago, psychoanalysts like Edward Glower (1947), Robert Waelder (1960), Franco Fornari (1966), Alexander Mitscherlich, and Margarete Mitscherlich (1975) attempted to explore these areas from a psychoanalytic perspective.

As Rafael Moses (1982) and Peter Loewenberg (1991) have reminded us, certain aspects of the history of large groups can induce anxiety, often leading to unbearable unpleasant feelings among those who have been victimized, as well as guilt and shame among perpetrators. Therefore, it took time to break the "silence" in the clinical setting, allowing psychoanalysts to examine issues related to the Third Reich in the lives of their patients.

In the 1960s, William Niederland (1964, 1968) shared some clinical observations about survivors of Nazi persecution and referred to their experience as "survivor syndrome." Ilse Grubrich-Simitis (1981, 1984) conducted a psychoanalytic study on the impact of concentration camp experiences on survivors and their children, offering insights into the theoretical and technical aspects of working with the children of Holocaust survivors. Judith Kestenberg (1982) introduced the term "transposition" to describe how trauma was unconsciously transmitted from survivor parents to their children. Additionally, Harold Blum (1986) presented his concepts on reconstructing trauma in clinical practice.

Moving into the 1990s, we witnessed a rise in psychoanalysts making valuable contributions that shed light on the interconnectedness between individuals' internal psychological structures and external societal circumstances. The focus expanded beyond the Holocaust to encompass other shared traumatic events. For instance, Michael Šebek (1994) explored societal responses to living under communism in Europe, while Sudhir Kakar (1996) examined the effects of Hindu-Muslim religious conflict in Hyderabad, India. Maurice Apprey (1998) delved into the influence of transgenerational trauma on African Americans and their culture, and Nancy Hollander explored events in South America. Salman Akhtar (1999) wrote about the topics of immigration and identity.

Increased emphasis on shared external events in the offices of psychoanalysts and psychoanalytically-oriented psychotherapists was observed in the United States and other countries, particularly after the tragic events of September 11, 2001. Following the coordinated suicide attacks carried out by al-Qaeda against the United States on that day, the International Psychoanalytic Association (IPA) established the Terror and Terrorism Study Group, which was co-chaired by Norwegian psychoanalyst Sverre Varvin and Vamık Volkan. This study group lasted for several years (Varvin & Volkan, 2003). In addition, the IPA formed a committee on the United Nations, where Vamık Volkan delivered a lecture in New York attended by a large audience. It is doubtful, however, that the psychoanalytic perspective on world affairs gained significant attention at the UN.

There has been nonetheless a growing trend in psychoanalytic examination of external world affairs. Otto Kernberg (2004 a, 2004b) explored sanctioned political violence, while Mitch Elliott, Kenneth Bishop, and Paul Stokes (2004) and John Alderdice (2010) scrutinized the situation in Northern Ireland. Nancy Hollander (2010) focused on the United States after September 11, 2001, and Gerard Fromm (2011) edited a book on the transmission of trauma from one generation to another. Tomas Böhm and Suzanne Kaplan (2011) delved into the topics of revenge and reconciliation, and Schmuel Erlich (2013) explored the mindset of terrorists.

Furthermore, a group of psychoanalysts dedicated their efforts to creating a peaceful learning environment for children, aiming to prevent bullying in schools and reduce prejudice, violence, and incest in communities (Mahfouz, Twemlow & Scharff, 2007; Twemlow & Sacco, 2011; Sklarew, Twemlow & Wilkinson, 2014).

Edward Shapiro (2019) examined the journey from individuality to citizenship and analyzed autocratic leaders and societal divisions. In Italy, psychotherapist Clara Mucci (2022) skillfully integrated past and present psychoanalytic studies on trauma, exploring what victims require from their therapists and how trauma manifests in families, organizations, and society. Gerard Fromm (2022) focused on intergenerational trauma within families, the subtle erosion of awareness within organizations, and the impact of war trauma and the pandemic on cultural healing. Additionally, Finnish psychoanalyst Juhani Ihanus (2022) examined the psychology of both individuals and large groups in relation to the Russian invasion of Ukraine on February 24, 2022.

The COVID-19 pandemic has significantly transformed the practice of therapy, primarily due to the widespread use of online sessions. It has also prompted psychoanalysts and psychoanalytic psychotherapists to pay greater attention to and analyze massive external events, considering not only their impact on individuals but also on larger groups. In Hungary, Tihamér Bakó and Katalin Zana (2023) discussed how the COVID-19 outbreak heightened psychoanalysts' awareness of the interconnectedness between shared external events and the human psyche's responses (Bakó & Zana, 2023).

Nevertheless, generally speaking, topics referring to the human history and shared external events were avoided by most classical psychoanalysts while they were sitting behind their analysands (Bowlby 1988). Even in 2002 Ira Brenner wrote that a number of analysts in the United States challenged him by arguing that "analysis deals with the realm of psychic reality only" and that Brenner's and his colleagues' focus on the impact of the Holocaust on affected individuals were introducing an unnecessary element that only "muddied the waters" and was unnecessary for successful treatment (Brenner, 2002, p. xiii).

Starting with Freud, psychoanalytically-oriented writers who wrote about wars primarily focused on individuals' unconscious perceptions of what the image of political leaders and the mental representations of ethnic, national, or religious groups symbolize (i.e. Oedipal father, nurturing mother, etc.), instead of on large-group *psychology in its own right.* As pointed out in previous chapters there is a relationship between the psychology of the individual and the large group. By tracing how individual psychology is related to group psychology we can better understand large-group psychology. Earlier we referred to "projective identification." Now let us focus an individuals' own identifications with others. As we shall see the concept of identification in an important element connecting individual psychology to large-group psychology. Large-group psychology in its own right means making formulations about the conscious and unconscious shared past and present historical/psychological experiences that exist within a large group. This is similar to clinicians making formulations about their patients' developmental histories associated with various conscious and unconscious fantasies in order to understand what motivates certain behavior patterns, symptoms, and habitual interpersonal relationships.

Core Individual Identity

Let us return to further examine individuals with narcissistic or borderline personality organizations, in particular, their contradictory self- and object images, and their having split interpersonal relationships (Bernstein, 2001; Klinkby et al., 2023). An analysand of Vamık Volkan, an attractive young man who we name George would look at the mirror every morning and say: "Move over Robert Redford, here I come. I am more handsome than any movie star!" Once, while walking on a beach in Greece, he felt that he was a Greek god and everyone on the beach was looking at him with adoration. Another time, while modeling nude for an artist in New York, he sensed that he would cause a huge traffic jam as everyone in the city rushed to see his handsome naked body. Yet, this man kept a hundred cans of food in his kitchen cupboard so that he would never go hungry, and if his stock became even slightly depleted, he was anxious until he replenished it (Volkan, V.D., 1976).

Because of our clinical experience with patients like George, or borderline patients who divide themselves and their intimate world into "good" and "bad" categories, we, as clinicians, frequently refer to *the concept of identity* when discussing cases with colleagues. Yet the concept of identity is relatively new in the mental health literature. Sigmund Freud seldom referred to identity, and when he did it was in a colloquial or unsophisticated sense. One of Freud's well-known references to identity is found in a speech he delivered to B'nai B'rith in which he wondered why he was bound to Jewry since, as a non-believer, he had never been instilled with ethnonational pride or religious faith. Nevertheless, Freud in relationship to being Jewish, noted a "safe privacy of a common mental construction," and a clear consciousness of his "inner identity" (Freud, 1926). It is interesting that Freud's remarks linked his individual identity with his large-group identity.

There is a consensus that the term identity refers to a subjective experience. Thus, identity can be differentiated from two other related concepts with which it is often confused: character and personality. Character and personality are often used interchangeably to describe others' impressions of an individual's emotional expression, modes of speech, and habitual way of thinking and behaving. If we observe that someone uses excessive intellectualization, controls emotional expressions, and is habitually clean, orderly, and greedy, we say that this person has an obsessional character. If we observe someone who is overtly suspicious, cautious, and constantly scans the environment for possible danger, we say that this person has a paranoid personality.

Unlike character and personality, which are observed and perceived by others, identity refers to an individual's inner working model—that this person, and not an outsider, senses and experiences. One psychoanalyst who focused on identity, Erik Erikson, first used the term "ego identity," and then dropped the word ego and used simply "identity." He described it as "a persistent sameness within oneself ... [and] a persistent sharing of some kind of essential character with others" (Erikson, 1950, p. 57).

In everyday life, an adult individual can typically identify numerous aspects of personal identity related to social or professional status. For example, one may simultaneously perceive oneself as a parent, a physician or anthropologist, or someone who enjoys specific sports or recreational activities; i.e., facets of identity that seem to fit Erikson's definition. But we do not believe that such individual manifestations of what we perceive as our unique identity truly reflect a sense of sameness within ourselves. If a person's social or career identity is threatened, the individual may or may not experience anxiety. Anxiety is more likely to occur if the threat is connected, mostly unconsciously, to an internal danger signal, for example, losing a loved one such as a mother (or her love), losing a body part (castration), or a loss of self-esteem. Imagine, for example, a man who habitually plays golf suffering a leg injury. He can no longer play golf and loses his "golfer identity." He may not experience much anxiety and may become a painter and develop a "painter identity." But if the leg injury unconsciously becomes connected with his castration anxiety, this man will feel anxious about losing his "golfer identity."

Unlike losing one's professional or social identity, losing one's core identity is always terrifying (Pao 1979; K. Volkan & Volkan, 2022; V. Volkan, V. D. 1995) To understand "core identity," let us consider an adult who decompensates and descends into schizophrenia. Such an individual's identity fragments, and this person may have an inner sensation of a star exploding into hundreds of pieces. He or she will definitely experience anxiety; in fact, this anxiety is so extreme that it is unspeakably terrifying. In order to escape from this terror, as soon as the individual is capable, he or she will create a new sense of identity, albeit a false (psychotic) one. Maybe this individual now believes that he is Jesus Christ, or she is Mother Theresa. If we see a patient after schizophrenia has crystallized, we can be far more certain of our diagnosis if we can elicit a history that outlines the fragmenting of the core identity, the experiencing of terror, and the reorganization of the new but psychotic identity. Losing one's core identity is intolerable; it is a psychological death (Volkan, K & Volkan, V. D. 2022). The experience of a person with schizophrenia helps define what we mean by core identity and differentiates it from other social or professional identities.

As mentioned above, infant research (Stern, 1985; Greenspan, 1989; Emde, 1991, Lehtonen, 2003) tells us that an infant's mind is more active than we had previously imagined, with potential for a variety of mental activities. As outlined above, utilizing such mental capacities and those which develop later, a child normally develops what is commonly called a mind. The evolution of the child's mind and sense of core identity largely depends on what the child experiences with the mother or her substitutes.

In normal mental development, the integration of opposing self- and object images begins at about six months of age and is completed in most cases at around 36 months when the child should be able to tolerate ambivalence—to love and hate the same person or himself at any given moment (Mahler, 1968). When the child possesses an integrated self-representation, there begins an experience of "persistent sameness" within the child—the foundation of a core individual identity.

This core identity is crystallized during the adolescent passage. Peter Blos (1962, 1967) has already described in detail how an individual's character forms at this time, and we would add that this period also completes the formation of core individual identity. During the adolescent passage there is a psychobiological regression and youngsters loosen up their investment in the images of important childhood others and modify—even disregard—identification with them. They also make additional identifications, this time with their peer groups or far beyond the restricted family or neighborhood environment. These new identifications overhaul the youngsters' sense of inner sameness.

Once a person's core identity crystallizes, it can be defined by looking at it from different angles. Salman Akhtar (1992) listed seven ways of looking at core identity. Briefly they are:

1. A sustained feeling of inner sameness while sharing some character traits with others (Erikson, 1956).
2. Temporal continuity in the self-experience: the past, the present, and the future are integrated into a smooth continuum of remembered, felt, and expected existence for the individual.
3. A genuineness and authenticity so that the person does not feel this inner existence "as if" he or she is this person or that person (Deutch, 1942) and/or a "chameleon" (Kernberg, 1975).
4. A realistic body image. Since the formation of a core identity involves one's experience with one's own body and its various images, to have a solid core identity means to have a realistic body image.
5. A sense of inner solidarity and the associated capacity for solitude.
6. Subjective clarity of one's gender.
7. A well-internalized inner morality and an inner solidarity with one's large group – such as an ethnic or religious group – and its ideals.

This last characteristic of an individual's identity indicates a link between one's personal identity and one's large-group identity, and Akhtar's description of it implies that the link occurs at the oedipal level when a child's "conscience" (superego) is crystallized. The child then identifies with the parents' prohibitions and ideals, and by extension, the surrounding large-group's prohibitions and ideals. To support this view, Akhtar refers to Chasseguet-Smirgel's (1984) remark that successful resolution of the Oedipus complex encourages the child's entrance into the father's universe. This is valid. We contend, however, that the foundation of the core large-group identity is created in the pre-oedipal period, and oedipal influences, however important, come later. Some scientific studies illustrate that there is a psychobiological potential of "we-ness" and bias toward one's own kind that exists in the early period of a child's life (Bloom 2010; Emde 1991; Greenspan 1989; Lehtonen 2003, Purhonen, Kilpeläinen-Lees, Valkonen-Korhonen, Karhu & Lehtonen 2005; Stern 1985).

Large Group, Large Canvas

An analogy of a *large canvas tent* (K. Volkan & V.D. Volkan, 2023; V.D. Volkan, 1997, 2004, 2006) helps explain large-group identity. Think in terms of when we learned to wear two layers of clothing as children. The first layer, the individual layer, fits us snugly. It is one's core personal identity that provides an inner sense of persistent individual sameness. The second layer, one's core large-group identity, is loose fitting, but allows us to share a sense of sameness with others under a common large-group tent. The two layers are interconnected. Some threads that are included in the formation of the individual identity and large-group identity come from the same source. While it is the tent pole—the leader—that holds the tent erect, the tent's canvas (large-group identity) protects both the leader and the group and creates a psychological border separating one's large group from other large groups.

Think of a man—let's say he is German—who is an amateur photographer. If he decides to stop practicing photography and take up carpentry, he may call himself a carpenter instead of a photographer, but he cannot stop being a German and become a Bulgarian. His Germanness is part of his core large-group identity, which is interconnected with his core individual identity. Both core identities evolve in childhood and become intertwined and crystallized during the adolescent passage

(Volkan, V. D.,1977, 1988). Only through the influence of long-lasting historical events may a group slowly evolve a new large-group identity. For example, a large section of Slavs became Bosniaks while under the rule of the Ottoman Empire.

The psychodynamics of ethnic, national, or religious and ideological large groups build upon but are different from the psychodynamics of "small groups," "larger groups" composed of 30 or 150 individuals, or "crowds." For example, a crowd in a football stadium supporting the same football team becomes a group and remains so just before, during, and perhaps soon after the sports event. On the other hand, in an ethnic or religious large group, like Hungarians or Catholics, the membership, as we already stated, begins in childhood, and endures through adulthood.

Some religious cults, and terrorist organizations represent large groups that evolve during adulthood. For members of religious cults or terrorist organizations, the investment in their core large-group identities that developed in childhood, drastically changes. These individuals exaggerate selected aspects of their childhood large-group identities by holding on to a restricted special religious or nationalistic belief. Sometimes they become believers of ideas that were not available in their childhood environments. In short, they give up sharing overall sentiments with people who had the same core childhood large group identity but who have not made specific new selections (Volkan, V. D., 2019).

In our routine lives in a peaceful environment, we are not keenly or constantly aware of our large-group identity, just as we are not usually aware of our constant breathing. If we develop pneumonia or if we are in a burning building, we quickly notice each breath we take. Likewise, if our huge tent's canvas shakes or parts of it are torn apart by Others, we become obsessed with our second garment, and our individual identity becomes secondary. We become preoccupied with the large-group identity and wish to stabilize, repair, maintain and protect it. Some individuals may become willing to tolerate extreme sadism or masochism if they think that what they are doing will help to maintain and protect their large-group identity. In the long run, such behavior may inevitably be reflected in politics and international relationships.

When the huge Yugoslav tent was gone, for example, the Serbs, Croats, Bosniaks, and others became preoccupied with establishing themselves under their specific smaller tents. When large groups such as these ask, "Who are we now?" they become preoccupied with repairing, protecting, and maintaining the canvas of their specific tent. To hold on to the large-group identity, each large group tries to illuminate specific symbols, which John Mack (1979) called "cultural amplifiers" woven into the fabric of its tent's canvas. Vamık Volkan named *two* of these significant markers *chosen trauma* and *chosen glory*.

Complicated Large-Group Mourning, Transgenerational Transmission, Chosen Trauma and Undigested Trauma

Sigmund Freud and several pioneering analysts were interested in examining history, culture, religion, arts, and other shared external events from a psychoanalytic angle. But in the clinical setting, the impact of such events on analysands' psyches was not of primary concern. As John Bowlby (1988) described, when he became an analyst in 1937, psychoanalysts in Great Britain were only interested in the internal worlds of their patients. Paying attention to historical events surrounding patients was considered inappropriate.

By the 1970s, psychoanalysts' avoidance of recalling and re-experiencing the dreadful external world of the Nazi period in the clinical setting had begun fading away, and more and more studies of the influence of the Second World War, the Third Reich, and the Holocaust on the psyche of the survivors (victims and perpetrators) surfaced. This led to a psychoanalytic focus on the influence of transgenerational transmission, also under other terms such as "transgenerational transposition" (Kestenberg, 1982), "ancestor syndrome" (Schützenberger, 1998), the telescoping of generations (Faimberg, 2005) and "transgenerational haunting" (Apprey, 2023). (Also see: Brenner, 2014, 2019; Fromm, 2012; Eckstaedt, 1989; Kogan, 1995; Laub & Auerhahn, 1993; Volkan, V. D., Ast & Greer, 2002.).

After a large group suffers a catastrophic loss, humiliation, and helplessness at the hand of an enemy the members of the victimized large group are unable to mourn such losses and reverse their humiliation and helplessness. They pass on to their offspring the images of their injured selves and psychological tasks that need to be completed. A chosen trauma (V. D. Volkan, 1987, 2004, 2006) is the shared mental representation of an event in a large group's history in which the large group suffered a catastrophic loss, humiliation, and helplessness at the hands of enemies. As decades pass, the mental representation of this event links the individuals in the large group. Thus, the event's mental representation emerges as a significant large-group identity marker on the large group.

Not all past mass tragedies at the hands of others evolve as chosen traumas. Nonetheless, the mythologizing of victimized heroes, the telling of moving stories associated with a collective trauma popularized in songs and poetry, and political leaders who create a preoccupation with a past trauma and related events, all play a role in turning a historic event into a chosen trauma.

There are firmly established chosen traumas: Russians recall the "memory" of the Tatar-Mongol invasions in the thirteen and fourteen centuries; Greeks link themselves when they share the "memory" of the fall of Constantinople (Istanbul) to the Turks in 1453; Czechs commemorate the 1620 Battle of Bila Hora, which led to their subjugation under the Hapsburg Empire for nearly 300 years; Scots keep alive the story of the battle of Culloden of 1746 and the failure of Bonnie Prince Charlie to restore a Stuart to the British throne; the Dakota people of the United States recall the anniversary of their decimation at Wounded Knee in 1890. Israelis and Jews around the globe, including those not personally affected by the Holocaust, all define their large-group identity by direct or indirect references to it. The Holocaust is still too "hot" to be considered a truly established chosen trauma as described above, but it has become a large-group marker of an "undigested trauma," even though Orthodox Jews still refer to the 586 BC destruction of the Jewish temple in Jerusalem by Nebuchadnezzar II of Babylonia as the chosen trauma of the Jews.

Entitlement Ideologies

Entitlement ideology is a shared sense of entitlement to recover what has been lost in reality and fantasy during an undigested shared trauma or during a chosen trauma. Holding on to such an ideology reflects a complication in large-group mourning, an attempt both to deny losses as well as a wish to recover them. What Italians call irredentism (*advocating for the restoration of territory* formerly belonging to a country), what Greeks call the "*Megali Idea*" (Great Idea), what Serbians call *Christoslavism*, what Turks call *Pan-Turkism* and what extreme religious Islamists call "the return of an Islamic Empire" are examples of entitlement ideologies. Such ideologies may last for centuries and may disappear and reappear when historical circumstances change.

Political leaders may initiate the reactivation of chosen traumas in order to fuel entitlement ideologies. Vamık Volkan (1997) documented the story of how Slobodan Milošević allowed and supported the re-appearance of the Serbian chosen trauma—the mental representation of the June 28, 1389, Battle of Kosovo.

Chosen Glory

Many nations celebrate their Independence Day, and all large groups have ritualistic recollections of events and heroes whose mental representations include a shared feeling of success and triumph among its members. Such events and the persons appearing in them become heavily mythologized over time. These mental representations become large-group markers called *chosen glories* (Volkan, V.D. 1988, 2004, 2006), and they are passed on to succeeding generations through transgenerational transmissions made in parent/teacher-child interactions and later through participation in ritualistic ceremonies recalling past successful events.

Chosen glories link a large group's children with each other and with their large group, and the children experience increased self-esteem by their association with such glories. It is not difficult to understand why parents and other important adults pass the mental representation of chosen glories on to their children; the mental representations of chosen glories are saturated with derivatives of the libidinal drive, and it is pleasurable to share them with succeeding generations. Past victories in battle and great accomplishments of a technical or artistic nature frequently appear as chosen glories; virtually every large group has tales of grandeur associated with its creation. The shared importance of such events helps also to bind the individuals in a large group together. A good example of focusing on chosen glory in a large group has been described by Yana Nikolova (2024). She informs the reader how Bulgarians at the present time regularly use the phrase "Bulgaria on three seas" on national celebration and government election days, in populist campaigns, on television shows, on social media, at folkloric concerts and gatherings and in simple everyday conversations recalling the glorious historical times when Bulgaria reached the Black, White and Adriatic seas. Today Bulgaria only reaches the Black Sea. Niklova describes in detail how a chosen glory bolsters today's Bulgarian large-group identity.

In stressful situations or times of war, leaders also reactivate the mental representation of chosen glories and heroes associated with them to bolster large-group identity. A leader's reference to chosen glories excites his followers by simply stimulating an already existing shared large-group marker. While no complicated psychological processes are involved when chosen glories increase collective self-esteem, the role of a related concept, chosen traumas, in supporting large-group identity and its cohesiveness, is more complex. It is for this reason that a chosen trauma is a much stronger phenomenon than a chosen glory in political and international conflicts.

The Maintenance of the Non-Sameness Principle and Psychological Border

In 1917 Sigmund Freud wrote:

> "*It is always possible to bind together a considerable number of people in love, so long as there are other people left over to receive the manifestation of their aggressiveness… it is precisely communities with adjoining territories and related to each other in other ways as well, who are engaged in constant*

> *feuds and in ridiculing each other – like the Spaniards and the Portuguese, for instance, the North Germans and the South Germans, the English and Scotch, and so on. I gave this phenomenon the name of 'narcissism of minor differences,' a name which does not do much to explain it. We can now see that it is a convenient and relatively harmless satisfaction of the inclination to aggression, by means of which cohesion between the members of the community is made easier.*" (p.114)

We agree with David Werman (1988) who reminded us that in the social sphere minor differences harbor "the potential for a pernicious escalation into hostile and destructive actions on a widespread scale" (p.451). One large group cannot be the same as or even similar to a neighbor who is perceived as a dangerous enemy. When large groups regress, any signal of similarity is perceived, often unconsciously, as unacceptable; minor differences therefore become elevated to great importance to protect non-sameness.

Another unalterable principle in large-group relationships, related to the maintenance of non-sameness, reflects the need to keep a legal border, gap, or tangible space between large groups in conflict. When a danger is perceived against a large group, its physical borders become highly psychologized and begin to symbolize the canvas of the large-group tent. Leaders, official organizations, and people become preoccupied with the protection of these borders.

From 1961 to 1989 the Berlin Wall was a guarded concrete barrier that separated West Berlin of the Federal Republic of Germany (West Germany) from the German Democratic Republic (East Germany). The Berlin Wall also stood as an excellent example for a psychological wall. Donald Winnicott (1969) reminded us that, while this man-made barricade was unsightly and was completely disassociated from beauty, without the Berlin Wall, there would have been a war in the 1960s. Winnicott went on to further elucidate the beneficial aspect of the Wall. He argued that a dividing line between opposing forces, at its worst, postpones conflict and at best, separates opposing forces for long periods of time so that people may play and pursue the arts of peace. These peaceful arts belong to the temporary success of a dividing line between opposing forces, the lull between times when the wall has ceased to segregate good and bad (Winnicott, 1969, p. 224).

The reunification of Germany was not only a major political change, but was also a major psychological event, prompting a new wave of renegotiations with the Nazi past. Among these renegotiations within German society was the Nazi skinhead movement, a maladaptive manifestation of shame and guilt derivations related to the mental representation of the Third Reich (Rosenthal 1997, Streeck-Fischer 1990). Psychoanalytic considerations of the German reunification evoked questions of psychology for Germans, and the necessity of a psychohistorical reflection of German identity since 1933 (Ohlmeier 1991). When Martin D. Ohlmeier refers to "a psychology for Germans" he was considering large-group identity issues.

Large-Group Regression, Time Collapse, Becoming Like the Enemy, and Purification

Recently Stephen Frosh (2022) from University of London wrote that even though much has changed in the world during the last century, especially in relation to technology and globalization, much remains the same. He added:

> "*Wars continue; people are displaced in huge numbers; women are still attacked daily; sexual and gender pluralities still produce moral panics and deep hatred; inequality is pervasive; and racism still the most tangible, most destructive and most widespread force running through societies everywhere. Even antisemitism, which was a definite feature of Freud's time and which one might have hoped had been eradicated along with the Third Reich, has been fully resurrected and made respectable again; and antiblack racism in its various formations, the legacy of colonialism and slavery, is rife.*" (p. 327)

What Stephen Frosh described suggests that "regression" in large-group psychology exists constantly. We borrowed the term "regression" from individual psychology because we do not have a word that stands solely for large-group regression. As already implied, we can say that regression in groups often leads to a collective form of borderline or narcissistic personality disorder where hate and aggression are projected out to those external to the large group. We need to go beyond a general description of the emergence of hate and aggression in large groups including their shared paranoid or narcissistic sentiments and examine other manifestations of regression within each specific large group.

As we stated earlier, in a regressed large group, minor differences become elevated to protect non-sameness and legal borders become highly psychologized. Leaders, official organizations, and people become preoccupied with protecting legal borders. When there is in fact a realistic danger out there from an "enemy" group, or even from a non-human enemy such as COVID-19, legal borders obviously need to be protected. Because of this reality, it may become difficult to study the psychological aspects of this preoccupation. There are also invisible borders, such as those between two opposing political parties, and references to them, in the news media, becomes obvious and repetitive.

When a large group is in a regressed state, the personality and the internal world of the political leader assumes great importance. This relates to how the leader manipulates what is considered good or bad within the large-group psychology. For example, the personality organization of Slobodan Milošević was a crucial factor in what happened in the former Yugoslavia (Volkan, V. D. 1997). Besides rallying around the leader, a severe split may occur within the society itself as we mentioned earlier. The correspondence between the regressed state of the leader and the defensive "split" state of the society can currently be seen in several places around world. This dynamic exists in Hungary under Victor Orbán (Stefkovics, 2021), India under Narendra Damodardas Modi (Sahoo, 2020), and Türkiye under Recep Tayyip Erdoğan (Pew Research Center, 2014).

The term *time collapse* denotes the conscious and unconscious connections between a large group's past historical trauma and contemporary threats that typically emerge when a chosen trauma is drastically reactivated. The reactivation of shared anxieties, expectations, fantasies, and defenses associated with the chosen trauma magnifies the image of current enemies and current conflicts. If the large group is now in a powerful position, a sense of revenge may become exaggerated or even ennobled. If the large group is in a powerless position or has experienced oppression, genocide or war, a current event may reanimate a shared sense of victimization. Time collapse may lead to irrational and sadistic or masochistic decision-making by the leadership of a large group. In turn, members of the large group or at least the followers of the leader may become psychologically prepared to commit sadistic or masochistic acts. In the worst-case scenario, the large group may perpetrate monstrous cruelty against the Other.

What externalization/projection is for an individual, purification is for large ethnic, religious, national, or ideological large groups. After a nation or large group emerges from crises such as war, the break-up of a political system, or drastic revolutionary change, a period of re-stabilization typically ensues. During this time of reassessment and redefinition, when a large group collectively asks, "Who are we now," attempts at purification often occur, much like the purification rituals of the adolescent passage in individual psychology. Like a snake shedding its skin, a large group will cast off certain elements such as symbols or ideologies that no longer seem useful or appropriate, or those things that seem to impede growth and the revitalization of large-group identity. Large-group purification rituals erasing symbols of other cultures such as destroying churches, synagogues, or mosques. These are instances of a large group strengthening its identity through purification. Ethnic cleansing or genocide is an extreme form of purification.

11

Genocide

In this chapter we want to touch on the distressing subject of the use of violence against non-combatants, i.e., genocide. This is a pervasive occurrence that regrettably transcends borders, cultures, and historical time periods. It will be useful to explore common threads that can be observed in genocide, and how genocide is similar or different from other types of human violence.

We have discussed the types of large-group dynamics and elements that provide the conditions for war and violent conflict. These same dynamics come into play in fomenting genocide. Additionally, we can also think in general about two other aspects that encourage genocide – symbolic transfer across generations, and obedience to external authority within and outside one's large group. These aspects are well represented by two noteworthy approaches to understanding the Holocaust perpetrated by Nazi Germany. The debate between these two philosophical approaches is represented in two well-known books on the Holocaust: *Hitler's Willing Executioners* by Daniel Goldhagen (1996) and *Ordinary Men: Reserve Police Battalion 101 and the Final Solution in Poland* written by Christopher Browning (1992).

Intentionalist Perspectives: *Hitler's Willing Executioners* and Transgenerational Trauma

The intentionalist perspective proposes that the Holocaust was largely due to pre-World War II rampant antisemitism among the Germans. The development of this so-called "eliminationist" antisemitism is traced by Goldhagen from the time of Martin Luther (1483-1546) culminating in Hitler's plan to murder Jewish people. This intentionalist understanding of the Holocaust offers a thought-provoking and controversial analysis of the role played by ordinary Germans during the Nazi regime in perpetrating the Holocaust. Goldhagen argues that by the Nazi era, due to specific historical circumstances, Germans developed a predisposition towards anti-Semitism, culminating in an eliminationist ideology that necessitated the extermination of Jewish people. For Goldhagen, the German people under Hitler developed the intent to eliminate Jewish people as well as other groups who were thought of as undesirable.

Germans developed this intent due to their unique history of antisemitism. The intent developed into what can almost be thought of as a character flaw. Goldhagen's thesis is that collective racist hatred can be carried through symbolism and transferred from generation to generation.[1]

Goldhagen's ideas corresponds closely to Vamık Volkan's ideas related to the unconscious transfer of symbolic meaning and trauma across generations. Historical events can have a significant impact on collective psychological processes and large-group behavior. Collective psychological processes are affected by the narratives constructed around historical events. These historical events can be related to family upheaval, either privately or as the result of larger group trauma. Or the historical events may be some form of collective trauma which affects individuals directly. The effect of these traumas can then be transmitted to the next generation via unconscious symbolism. It is possible for some traumas to have

1. "Hitler's Willing Executioners" is a controversial book and there are many critics of Goldhagen's conclusions, especially among historians. The book was, however, generally well received in Germany. As David Art (2005) writes, "*the open-mindedness that Goldhagen encountered in the land of the perpetrators was 'gratifying' and something of which Germans ought to be proud, even in the context of a book which sought, according to some critics, to 'erase the distinction between Germans and Nazis'* " (p. 88-89). For a detailed discussion of the book and its controversy see Yisrael Gutman's article (1998).

effects for multiple generations (V. D. Volkan, 1988, 2006).

Functionalist Perspectives: The Milgram and Stanford Prison Experiments

The functionalist perspective proposes that the Holocaust did not arise from a plan, but rather came into existence in a roundabout fashion due to specific circumstances. This perspective is represented in the book, "Ordinary Men: Reserve Police Battalion 101 and the Final Solution in Poland" written by Christopher Browning (1992). This work provides a comprehensive examination of the actions carried out by a group of German reserve police officers ordered to the Eastern front and tasked with rounding up and executing Jewish people and other individuals deemed undesirable by the Nazi regime. Browning writes that despite not being fervent Nazis, these officers willingly participated in the atrocities committed against innocent individuals. Browning refers to these individuals as "ordinary men," highlighting the disconcerting reality that under certain circumstances, any person under the influence of large-group dynamics can be convinced to commit heinous acts.

Browning makes the argument that anyone, under the right context and situation can become a killer of innocents. Two famous psychological experiments – the Milgram Experiment and the Stanford Prison Experiment, which we discuss below, support Browning's idea that under specific circumstances, and under the influence of those in authority, seemingly normal human beings will commit atrocities. Stanley Milgram's experiment on obedience to authority is widely recognized as one of the most famous, or infamous, pieces of psychological research (Milgram, 1974; Perry, 2013; Vogels, 2014). During the experiment, subjects were given instructions to give electric shocks to a "learner" when he or she answered a question incorrectly. It is important to note that the shocks were not real, but this information was not shared with the subjects and the learners were coached to simulate the effects of being shocked. A "scientist" who functioned as an authority figure was in the room with the subject and when the subject would question the effects of the shocks (which were simulated) the scientist would tell the subject to continue the experiment in a somewhat neutral manner. The intensity of the shocks increased gradually, reaching a point where they would have been fatal if they were authentic. The results of the experiment showed that a significant majority of participants continued to follow instructions and administer shocks despite hearing the learner's increasing distress. The experiment only concluded when Dr. Milgram's assistant pleaded with him to stop what he thought of as an immoral experiment.

The Milgram Experiment demonstrated that around 65% of participants followed instructions from an authority figure to administer what the subjects believed to be lethal electric shocks to other people. This experiment was repeated by Milgram and others in various forms, and places, yielding similar results. It is possible that obedience to authority is something that is derived from early human history when human behavior was not motivated by individual needs but by voice commands, either from real authority figures or vocal hallucinations (Pavlenko, 2019). It is likely that obedience to authority conferred, and still confers, survival value to humans and is to some degree genetically determined (Bouchard, 2009). It is important to note that the Milgram Experiment can be understood to be ethically controversial and would not be allowed to be replicated by academic researchers today.[2] In fact, the Milgram Experiment contributed to the development of ethical guidelines aimed at protecting experimental subjects.

The Stanford Prison Experiment was a study conducted in 1971 by Philip Zimbardo at Stanford University (Haney et al., 1973; Zimbardo, 2007; Zimbardo, 1995). This somewhat flawed piece of research remains relevant to events such as abuse of the Abu Ghraib prisoners during the Iraq war period (Allen et al., 2006; Brown, 2005; Hersh, 2004; Smeulers & Van Niekerk, 2009). In the study, 24 male student volunteers were randomly assigned to be prisoners or guards in a simulated prison set in the basement of the Stanford psychology building. The aim was to explore how perceived power and social roles influence behavior. The study was

2. Of course, reality television producers have no such ethical constraints and one of the best and most accurate recreations of the Milgram Experiment was conducted in the UK as part of the television show *The Heist* (Caron, 2006)

initially scheduled to run for two weeks but was terminated after just six days. The decision to end the experiment early was made due to the unethical treatment of the prisoners and the potential for psychological harm. Purportedly, Zimbardo himself became so wrapped up in the experiment that he did not initially perceive the abuse that was happening. Zimbardo did not end the experiment until his girlfriend visited and reflected to him what was occurring. Over a short period of time the students assigned to be guards began to display sadistic behavior towards the students assigned to be prisoners. This caused extreme stress among the prisoners who experienced loss of personal identity, a sense of dependency on the guards, and feelings of emasculation and humiliation.

New information has come to light that questions the scientific validity of the Stanford Prison Experiment, including biased data collection and the instructions given to the guards. Over the years concerns have been voiced about the ethics and methodology of the experiment. It is known that the subjects in the Stanford Prison Experiment experienced negative psychological consequences from their involvement with the experiment. Zimbardo has claimed that these negative reactions were short lived and may have even helped the participants to gain some self-knowledge (1973), unlike the prisoners at Abu Ghraib who underwent a longer and more intense (not to mention real as opposed to simulated) prison experience, and experienced considerable trauma (Keller, 2006). Nevertheless, the Stanford Prison Experiment participants were not adequately protected and that there was insufficient oversight to prevent abuse. Despite these criticisms, the Stanford Prison Experiment has made a significant impact on the field of psychology and continues to be a topic of debate (Texier, 2019).

Depositing and Identification with the Aggressor

Despite years of debate around intentionalist versus functionalist perspectives, Goldhagen's and Browning's ideas are not mutually exclusive. A good example is related to child-rearing practices in pre-Nazi and Nazi Germany. As Lloyd deMause (2006) reports, the way German children were raised had a significant impact on the development of a generation of adults who may have been more receptive to extreme Nazi ideologies. The intentional depositing of transgenerational symbolism by adults into children and the functional experience of authoritarian-type parenting likely contributed immensely to a population of Germans willing to kill innocent people. Closely related to identification, depositing occurs during childhood.

Depositing is a variation of identification. In forming an identity, a child actively absorbs and integrates object images, as well as ego and superego functions, from another person, initially a caregiver. In depositing, it is the adult-Other who takes a more active role by introducing their own self and internalized object images, as well as ego and superego functions, into the child's developing sense of self. To put it simply, the Other unconsciously utilizes the child as a reservoir for their own self and object images, as well as tasks related to ego and superego. The child does not have access to the experiences that gave rise to the deposited images and has no accompanying experiential or contextual framework. This causes identify confusion and can be overwhelming to the child who does not have the capacity to digest the deposited images (K. Volkan & Volkan, 2023; V. D. Volkan, 1987; V. D. Volkan et al., 2002; V. D. Volkan & Ast, 1997).

Another related concept is identification with the aggressor. This concept was first proposed by the psychoanalyst Sandor Ferenczi to explain how trauma can create trance-like dissociation that causes a person's personality to become fragmented. Rather than purposeful identification, the child mimics the aggressor's role. Elizabeth Howell (2014) expands Ferenczi's idea by postulating two stages in which identification with the aggressor occurs. The first stage is automatic and triggered by trauma. When a child is abused, he or she may automatically imitate the aggressor to protect him or herself. The repeated transition from being a victim to becoming an aggressor provides a sense of stability. In the second stage this becomes a dissociative defensive process. The dissociation between victim and abuser self-states is akin to a splitting defense and provides a state of stable uncertainty that avoids the experience of terrifying traumatic memories by keeping them out of consciousness.

In this way identification with the aggressor and its alternation between the victim-self and the abuser-self is reminiscent of both dissociative identity and borderline personality disorders. We shall also see that the perpetrators of the trauma experience dissociative states and engage in splitting in order to commit atrocities.

Traumatic Entrapment and Post-Traumatic Stress Disorder (PTSD)

One concept that is related to identification with the aggressor is that of traumatic entrapment. In common parlance this is thought of as "Stockholm Syndrome," a term coined by criminologist and psychiatrist Nils Bejerot to describe a robbery that took place in August of 1973 at Kreditbanken in Stockholm, Sweden. During this event, after being held hostage for six days, bank employees developed a surprising range of positive emotions towards their captors. Even after being freed, they continued to defend the actions of the robbers (Bejerot, 1974).

A more accurate term for Stockholm Syndrome is *Traumatic Entrapment Syndrome*. This is a psychological phenomenon that occurs when individuals, usually women, find themselves in a situation where they have been forcibly taken and held against their will. Rather than succumbing to fear and despair, these individuals develop a surprising bond with their captors, characterized by feelings of loyalty, empathy, sympathy, and even love. Despite facing immediate danger, loss of freedom, and unimaginable suffering such as sexual abuse and torture, these feelings can still emerge. This remarkable response has been observed in a variety of scenarios, including other bank robberies similar to the Kreditbanken incident, child abuse, domestic violence, kidnapping, and rape. Throughout the years, Traumatic Entrapment Syndrome has been either confirmed or suspected in numerous cases including the kidnappings of Sabine Dardenne, Patty Hearst, Shawn Hornbeck, Natascha Kampusch, Katya Martynova and Lena Simakhina, Fusako Sano, Elizabeth Smart, Colleen Stan, and Steven Stayner to name a few of the most notorious cases.

Writing from an evolutionary psychiatric perspective, Chris Cantor and John Price (2007) examine the basis of Traumatic Entrapment Syndrome and Post-Traumatic Stress Disorder (PTSD). Many mammalian species, particularly primates, form positive relationships with oppressors that may endure. Mammals, including humans, exhibit various defensive behaviors when dealing with oppressors. In general, there are six mammalian defenses that are exaggerated by PTSD:

1. Threat avoidance
2. Attentive immobility (freezing and careful watching as a prelude to more definitive action)
3. Withdrawal (flight response)
4. Aggressive defense (fight response)
5. Appeasement
6. Tonic immobility - playing dead to confuse the oppressor by inhibiting attack reflexes or fooling them into thinking the victim is "contaminated" food (p. 380)

Defensive behaviors can also include things like becoming physically smaller, acting in a childlike or flirtatious manner, and even showing signs of inferiority through behaviors such as crying. Traumatic Entrapment, as discussed above, can also involve a response that involves bonding with the oppressor which is related to appeasement.

Responses that resemble Traumatic Entrapment can be seen in other mammal species, particularly primates. Interestingly, research on apes has shown that when they are attacked, sometimes they seek comfort and safety from their attackers (this is called "reverted escape"). Similarly, with respect to chimpanzees, the victim of an attack may become very anxious and try to calm the situation by hugging and kissing their former combatants. These calming behaviors let the dominant animal know that the victim is submissive. Similarly in humans, victims of domestic abuse may be coerced into accepting their lower status and may try to reconcile with his or her dominant partner. This can involve behaving submissively and even offering sexual acts to appease the oppressor. Appeasement is seen as the most important defense mechanism for mammals in situations of traumatic entrapment, and it seems to be a key aspect of complex post-traumatic stress disorder (PTSD). In both complex PTSD and Traumatic Entrapment Syndrome, victims may idealize and have positive feelings towards their abusers. Cantor and Price make the case that this form of appeasement confers a survival advantage in individuals who undergo traumatic subordination to a captor. Prisoners who appease their captors are less likely to be killed and are more likely to reproduce than captives that do not demonstrate appeasement behavior. In a situation where a person is trapped and traumatized by an oppressor, it is possible that making peace may be the only way to protect oneself.

Appeasement is associated with fear and shame. Fear provides motivation for defense. Shame on the part of the victim, however, gives the signal that he or she is of no threat to the captor. In this way, shame may be the pre-cursor to appeasement. However, shame is an extremely uncomfortable emotion and as in identification with the aggressor, victims may dissociate to avoid experiencing it. This dissociation may also help the victim to continue to appease the aggressor. When the ordeal is over, the shame returns along with the other aspects of PTSD. We are the descendants of the appeasers and so this trait persists among humans. We are also, unfortunately, the descendants of the oppressors, another set of traits that persists among us. We shall see that many of the behaviors related to traumatic entrapment have psychological correlates, such as dissociation. These are especially apparent for entrapped humans who are victims of oppression, torture, and genocide.

We have been talking about traumatic entrapment among individuals such people who are abducted and kept against their will or children abused (sexually or physically) by adults including their parents over a period of time. However, we can also see instances of what is essentially, collective traumatic entrapment. The members of cults and some religions may be experiencing what is essentially traumatic entrapment, exhibiting any of the six defensive behaviors listed above, but most often appeasement. Groups of people experiencing collective traumatic entrapment will exhibit characteristics of dependency and/or fight-flight groups. In both instances leaders of these types of groups can function as oppressors and the group members as victims. As we have discussed above, primitive psychodynamics accompanies both small and large-group dynamics and group member – leader relationships. Later we will discuss Vamık Volkan's visit to a Palestinian orphanage where the orphans had severe deficits in individual identity, instead developing an identity related to the large group and its leader.

It is easy to think of genocide victims as the ones being subject to traumatic entrapment where appeasement no longer functions to ward off violence by the oppressors. However, traumatic entrapment victims can also be perpetrators – i.e. forced or coerced to commit violent acts against others that they would not normally do in service of their oppressors. The image of Patty Hearst, renamed Tanya by the Symbionese Liberation Army that kidnapped her, holding a gun in a San Francisco bank is a good example. This sort of appeasement through violence could also be a hallmark of large groups where the leaders are narcissistic and/or psychopathic and have an eliminationist ideology, such as what happened in Germany under the Nazis.

Genocidal Tendencies among Primates

Jared Diamond, author of *The Third Chimpanzee* (1992), argues that human beings are essentially a distinct species of chimpanzee, a third type with the other two being chimpanzees proper, and bonobos. He points out the fact that we are part of a group of animals that kill members of their own species (other species includes bears, horses, lions, and wolves to name just a few). Killing members of the same species is sometimes related to cannibalism. For example, the aggressive Humbolt Squid (*Dosidicus gigas*) are known to eat members of their own kind (Knapton, 2017). According to Michael Wilson and Richard Wrangham (2003) infants killed by male chimpanzees from outside the infants' group will often be eaten. Wilson and Wrangham also report that while intergroup aggression among chimpanzees doesn't always result in death or injury when there is more display than aggression, there are many accounts of intergroup male aggression involving the castration and killing of males (Boesch et al., 2008). When there is a clear advantage by one side such as when a group of males encounter a single male from another group, injury and/or death are more likely to occur. Community extinction serves as evidence that one strategy for males to gain access to more females is to kill all males from a rival group. While is not clear whether this is common among chimpanzees it is likely that the human propensity for traumatic entrapment is related to this primate pattern. In humans this pattern manifests as rape being a correlate of war and genocide. Though often underplayed, rape is a frequent event during violent human conflicts and can occur at an absolutely massive scale such as during the Second World War when it is estimated that Soviet Soldiers raped up to two million German women as they occupied the Third Reich. Some women were reportedly raped as many as 60 or 70 times (Hitchcock, 2004; Kuwert & Freyberger, 2007; "Raped by the Red Army," 2009; Schissler, 2001)

Wilson and Wrangham write that infanticide is perhaps one of the most common forms of intraspecies killing. This typically occurs when males kill the offspring of other males. Among chimpanzees this sort of killing typically occurs when males encounter mothers with infants. When one group of males kills or drives off the males from the other group, they will then kill as well as sometimes castrate the offspring of the defeated males and mate with the females from the defeated group (Drummond-Clarke et al., 2023). This situation may allow males with limited access to females in their in-group, mating opportunities (Mogielnicki, 2023). There is evidence that under these conditions the defeated nursing females will quickly become fertile. As Kelly Rooker and Sergey Gavrilets (2020) write,

> *"Infanticide, the killing of a female's offspring prior to weaning, is extremely detrimental to a female's fitness. However, committing an act of infanticide may benefit any male who is not the father of that particular offspring, and hence infanticide is often seen when a new male takes over a group. Since many female primates have prolonged lactational amenorrhea, a male killing a female's offspring results in bringing that female back to fertility sooner*

> *by prematurely ending her lactation. The infanticidal male can then subsequently mate with this female, meaning his offspring will be able to be born sooner than would otherwise be possible had he never committed infanticide."* (p. 3)

There is also evidence for gorillas and languar monkeys (*Semnopithecus dussumieri*) that male aggression stimulated female receptivity to copulation as well as actual copulation. It has also been observed that females who have had their infants killed by attacking males will subsequently joint the attacking males' group (Nadler & Miller, 1982; M. Wilson & Wrangham, 2003) the male primarily accounts for mating that is unlikely to contribute to reproduction. However, in their natural habitat, the species-typical pattern of mating for gorillas consists of one to two days of female-initiated copulation/cycle during the periovulatory period. Whether or not this is the true for chimpanzees is not clear as there is also peaceful migration of females between groups (Boesch et al., 2008).

Among primates, and especially chimpanzees, we can also witness something that could be a precursor to torture among humans. Though strong, chimpanzees are inefficient killers due to their lack of powerful teeth and claws. Therefore, when they attack, they tend to focus on the vulnerable parts of their victim's body. Chimpanzee display aggression towards another in-group member is usually not intended to kill. However, it sometimes causes severe injury or death. As we have mentioned, attacks on members of rival groups are typically more violent. When severely injured the chimpanzee attack victim often withdraws into seclusion, succumbing to a slow and painful demise. Some scholars have speculated that the human inclination to inflict prolonged suffering on others may be a leftover trait echoing the inefficiency observed in primate or chimpanzee killings. While it is important to note that there is currently no concrete evidence to support this claim the concept remains thought-provoking and deserves further investigation. Torture in the sense of it being a slow agonizing form of killing is a prevalent occurrence within human societies. It should be remembered that the largest genocides in human history perpetrated by Joseph Stalin and Mao

Zedong mostly involved the slow tormenting death of millions through starvation (Dikötter, 2010; Naimark, 2010). Unfortunately, conflicts among human beings follow these patterns fairly closely. Nevertheless, it is important to examine the distinctions between primates such as chimpanzees and human beings.

Chimpanzees have truly remarkable cognitive abilities in terms of short-term working memory and perception (Kawai & Matsuzawa, 2001; Read et al., 2022). On the other hand, humans possess exceptional long-term memory capacities and the ability to engage in future-oriented planning. Noted primate researcher Matsuzawa Tetsuro (2013) compares what is known about chimpanzee brains, cognition, and behavior to human beings. Studies of eye-tracking, helping behavior, the increase in prefrontal white matter volume during infancy, and fetal brain development supports the "social brain hypothesis." Chimpanzees see the bodies of other chimpanzees and process these visual images in a fashion similar to how humans see other human bodies (Gao & Tomonaga, 2018). Yet, while chimpanzees excel at capturing images, humans have a greater ability to comprehend the meaning behind what they see. Chimpanzees tend to overlook social contexts and focus on the most noticeable things in their environment. Humans, however, pay special attention to other people and consistently recognize things in a social context. Humans also have an attentional bias towards emotional states which is not present in chimpanzees (Kret et al., 2018). This is likely related to the human capacity for high levels of altruism and collaboration. Our evolution has prioritized cooperation and mutual support which may have laid the foundation for the development of the human brain with its distinctive higher cortical (ego) functions. We can speculate that this uniquely human capacity is related to the process in our development of having internalized ambivalent images of others (objects). In other words, normal human object relations development results in the ability to see others in an ambivalent way which results in better recognition of social cues and meaning. Primates like chimpanzees may not go through object relations development to same extent as humans and fail to achieve fully developed psychic structures such as the ego or superego.

It may be that primates like chimpanzees' object relations development does not go beyond something akin to borderline personality organization. This could explain some of the intense displays of alternating emotional states seen in chimpanzees as well as explain why they are more likely to overlook meaning, social context, and emotions in others, living instead for the moment. It may that during evolution borderline personality organization arose first among primates and neurotic (normal) personality organization was a further development in hominids. This is an intriguing idea that deserves more research.

The human ability to ascribe meaning to things we see and to read emotional states in other people suggests that our psychic structures are related to a socially oriented imaginal capacity. We can understand and assign meaning to images that are symbolic and empathize with emotions which helps us cooperate with each other. From a neuropsychoanalytic perspective this is related to the evolution of the cortex in the brain which, as we have discussed, is related to the psychic structure of the ego. This allows us to think in more elaborate and creative ways and understand social contexts in a deeply symbolic way compared to our primate counterparts. Unfortunately, however, this same social imaginal capacity allows us to elaborate and magnify the violent traits we share with our primate cousins.

The reason behind these differences in mental capabilities between chimpanzees and humans can be traced back to the evolutionary trajectory of our primate ancestors. As primates transitioned from living in trees to living on the ground, specifically in savannah and plains environments, they faced new challenges and increased exposure to predators. To navigate this new and more dangerous context, proto-human primates needed to develop enhanced planning and cooperative abilities or as psychoanalysis understands these – psychic structures such as the ego and superego. Humans have a great capacity for abstraction and long-term planning, essentially ego functions. Unfortunately, this has influenced and amplified our ability to manifest violence within typical primate patterns. We exhibit many of the same patterns of violence as chimpanzees but with a much greater degree of creativity and intricate long-term planning. This is in stark contrast to the more immediate and instinctual nature of violence among chimpanzees.

To summarize, we can say that with regard to primate groups our closest relatives – chimpanzees as well as some other primates:

1. Identify with a specific group of members of their species.
2. Engage in non-lethal displays of aggression when they do not perceive themselves as having an advantage over another group.
3. Perform non-lethal displays of aggression that are often at the borders of a territory. These displays serve to establish the borders between territories. The clear delineation of territories through display aggression serves to keep groups from engaging in violent aggression that results in injury or death.
4. Make violent attacks that result in injury or death occur when one group has a clear advantage over another group. The advantage can be in larger numbers or bigger size when compared to another group. Many attacks are on individuals or small numbers of individuals but there is evidence of larger conflicts occurring and whole groups of males being eliminated.
5. Males from one group may attack mothers in another group, kill their infants, and quickly mate/rape these females.
6. Inefficient primate patterns of killing may be related to the human propensity to torture.

While primate societies do not exist within our definition of large groups, these observations of primate group behavior can be seen in human groups of all sizes including large groups. The main differences between primate groups and human groups are the existence of multilevel societies, language, and perhaps most importantly, the use of weapons (M. L. Wilson & Glowacki, 2017)2017. Even though within human societies our capacity for violent behavior is more symbolic we nevertheless have displays of aggression related to territorial boundaries, perpetuate individual, small-group, and large-group violent conflicts, subject females to violence in the form of rape, and commit infanticide (though probably to a lesser degree than other primates[3]). Moreover, humans tend to mimic the inefficiency displayed by their chimpanzee counterparts by using torture to inflict harm. These patterns of violence highlight the shared evolutionary history between humans and higher primates.

Unlike chimpanzees and other animals however, humans possess highly advanced tool making ability, thanks in large part to the integration of our dexterous hands with our imaginative and forward-thinking brains. This remarkable trait enables humans to create and manipulate tools, distinguishing Homo sapiens as the preeminent toolmakers among all species. Notably, one of the earliest categories of tools developed by humans were weapons, highlighting the profound impact of violence on our evolutionary trajectory. Weapons allow us to kill more efficiently and at greater and greater distances from our adversaries.

In conclusion, the contrasting cognitive abilities between chimpanzees and humans can be attributed to the evolutionary pressures faced by our primate ancestors. Despite our unique mental capacities, humans still exhibit patterns of violence that bear resemblance to those observed in primates. What distinguishes us as humans is our unparalleled ability to augment our propensity for violence through our vast intellectual capacity for toolmaking. In essence, we compensate for the inefficiency of our fingers and teeth in the act of killing by ingeniously crafting tools that serve as formidable weapons.

Definition of Genocide

All the primate derived patterns found in human beings come into play with regard to genocide. The perpetration of violence from one large group onto another large group that cannot defend itself is a hall mark

3. This is because human females evolved paternity confusion. Human females do not advertise their fertility, nor do they experience specific times when they are fertile. Instead, human females can be impregnated anytime and if they have access to many sexual partners, it is difficult to tell who has fathered their offspring. If a male thinks he could be the father of an infant, he will be much less likely to kill it.

of genocide. This is echoed in the official definitions of genocide. The *Convention on the Prevention and Punishment of the Crime of Genocide. Adopted by the General Assembly of the United Nations on 9 December 1948* signed in January of 1951 defined genocide as

> "...*any of the following acts committed with the intent to destroy in whole or part, a national, ethnical, racial, or religious group, as such:*
> *(a) Killing members of the group;*
> *(b) Causing serious bodily or mental harm to members of the group;*
> *(c) Deliberately inflicting on the group conditions of life calculated to bring about its physical destruction in whole or in part;*
> *(d) Imposing measures intended to prevent births within the group;*
> *(e) Forcibly transferring children of the group to another group.*" (United Nations, 1951, p. 280)

Other definitions include Frank Chalk and Kurt Jonassohn who state that "*Genocide is a form of one-sided mass killing in which a state or other authority intends to destroy a group, as that group and membership in it are defined by the perpetrator*" (Chalk & Jonassohn, 1990, p. 23). Genocide is described a bit more generally by Israel Charny:

> "*Genocide in the generic sense is the mass killing of substantial numbers of human beings, when not in the course of military forces of an avowed enemy, under conditions of the essential defenselessness and helplessness of the victims.*" (Charny, 1994, p. 75)

The Stages of Genocide

Gregory Stanton, formerly of the U.S. State Department and the founder of the group *Genocide Watch* (*genocidewatch.com*) has written a widely influential paper that outlines the stages of genocide. Stanton originally had seven stages of genocide but expanded this to eight stages and more recently into ten (Stanton, 1996b, 1996a, 2019, 2023). The ten stages are as follows:

1. The first stage is *Classification*, this is where perpetrators categorize the world into different groups.
2. The second stage is *Symbolization*, where perpetrators label these groups so as to begin to split them off from the perpetrating group. Sometimes, these labels are represented physically, like the Nazi yellow star or by racial characteristics such as darker skin.
3. The third stage is *Discrimination*, when laws and customs unfairly restrict victims' rights as citizens or as human beings.
4. The fourth stage is *Dehumanization*, where perpetrators devalue their victims by likening them to vermin or diseases. Names like rats, cockroaches, cancer, or bacteria are applied to the victims. By portraying the victims as non-human, the perpetrators are attempting to justify their elimination as a "cleansing" of society instead of murder.
5. The fifth stage is *Organization*, this is when hate groups, armies, and militias become systematized and structured.
6. The sixth stage is *Polarization*, where the focus is on targeting those who could potentially stop the division of the victim group from the perpetrator group. This targeting is especially directed towards moderates from the perpetrator group.
7. The seventh stage is *Preparation*, where leaders plot out the killing and deportation of the victims. Those who are designated to actually carry out the killing receive training and weapons.
8. The eighth stage is *Persecution*, where victims are identified, arrested, transported, and confined to prisons, ghettos, or concentration camps. Once removed from the larger society and placed in these places the victims are subjected to torture and murder.
9. The ninth stage is *Extermination*, which equates to the legal definition of genocide – "the intentional destruction, either in whole or in part, of a national, ethnic, racial, or religious group."
10. The tenth and last stage is *Denial*. This was added by Stanton because he realized. That the genocide continued after the victims were murdered. Denial involves ongoing attempts to destroy the victim group psychologically and culturally, denying them even the memory of their relatives' murders. This includes minimizing what

happened to the victims, or even outright denial that their murder ever occurred.[4]

David Hamburg (2010) says that genocide can have a long incubation that are marked by many aspects of the ten stages. This includes virulent propaganda campaigns by political leaders using mass media and technology as well as roundups, and deportations that lead up to killings. The public often becomes desensitized or terrified into passive complicity. Stanton (1996a, 1996b, 2019, 2023) describes the combination of the first four processes as an "othering" process as defined by James Waller (2002). We understand stages five through nine as the "action" stages where the planning and murder are physically manifested. Stage ten, denial, can be understood to be a defensive process related to denial or dissociation.

Psychoanalysis of Genocide

As Gregory Stanton and other writers provide many examples of genocide, we will not repeat these here. Suffice it to say that genocide is so common throughout human history that we suspect the existence of this phenomena must have evolutionary origins in the primate behavior discussed above, elaborated by human cognitive and imaginal capacity, and augmented by our predilection for ever increasing lethal weaponry. While this sort of explanation for genocide can help us identify and with luck, interrupt some of its stages, understanding the psychodynamic processes involved may go further in helping us see where psychological intervention can play a role in disrupting an ongoing process of genocide

4. Denial can occur over a long period of time. One of Kevin Volkan's teachers, historian Deborah Lipstadt, was sued for libel in 2000 because she publicly stated that the controversial so-called historian David Irving was a Holocaust denier. This lawsuit, which occurred 55 years after the end of the Second World War, resulted in the High Court in London labeling Irving a falsifier of history. The court noted that no objective historian would manipulate information from historical documents the way Irving did. For more on this trial see Lipstadt's book about the trial, *History on Trial: My Day in Court with David Irving* (2005). A film titled *Denial* (Jackson, 2016) was also made about the trial.

or preventing it in the first place.

Most psychoanalytic explorations of genocide focus on the Holocaust perpetrated by the Nazis. Although the Holocaust was a genocide it also had some unique features that distinguish it from other instances of genocide, such as its racial basis and the use of modern industrial technology to facilitate mass murder. This uniqueness needs to be kept in mind when considering the Holocaust in terms of genocide.

After World War II and the end of the Holocaust experienced by Jewish people under the Nazis, several psychoanalytic scholars began to try and explain the psychology of genocide. Most of this written work tries to understand the psychology and motivation of perpetrators. One of the first of these scholars was Ernst Federn, who spent seven years in Dachau and Buchenwald concentration camps. He wrote a paper (1960) discussing the psychopathology of genocide, primarily examining Adolf Eichmann who he had met in person. Federn suggests that the psychopathology of the longest-serving commandant of Auschwitz, Rudolf Höss, is not as clear cut as other Nazi leaders (such as Adolf Eichmann) who can be understood to be robotic murderous schizoids. Höss had been part of a terrorist group in his youth and involved in a political murder. He served six years in prison for this crime and suffered from severe depression during this time. However, even though he had some schizoid traits, afterwards he did not seem to have any overt mental pathology. After the war and again in prison, Höss once more suffered from depression while awaiting execution. According to Federn, Höss was not an unfeeling murderous sociopath, but instead a product of his time, conditioned to follow orders blindly and obediently. Federn diagnoses Höss as

> *"a compulsive character with an incapacity to form meaningful interpersonal relationships; or a schizoid character with a schizophrenic core; or a person with a character disturbance – such people come to our family agencies and psychiatric clinics."* (p. 547)

We are left feeling that Höss had a distinct capacity to dissociate from his duties as commander of a death camp. In modern terms he might be understood as being on the less severe spectrum of a personality disorder. Some evidence for this is that he reported that he disliked having to be present during killings, which would have made dissociating from what was going on more difficult. This dissociation was a splitting defense that allowed him to be both a 'good' person as well as a family man, and a commander supervising the murder of millions. His condition after the war, when he became severely depressed while awaiting trial and execution, is reminiscent of Melanie Klein's depressive position. It is possible that Höss' depression was due, at least in some part, to the realization of what he had done as commandant of Auschwitz.

Another paper written by Martin Wangh (1964) examined National Socialism and the Holocaust from a psychoanalytic view. According to Wangh, the challenges faced during the depression of 1930s had a profound impact on the young people of Germany. These youth experienced childhood anxiety due to the First World War. This anxiety stemmed from the separation and defeat of fathers who were soldiers, their inability to provide economic security, as well the heightened fear and anxieties experienced by German mothers. The experience of the Great Depression reactivated these anxieties. As a result, the German population became susceptible to Nazi influences. Wangh says these anxieties awakened sadistic defenses, but instead of being directed toward an external enemy these were turned inward and focused on Jewish people within German society,

> *"'The Jews are our misfortune' replaced all bothersome self-examination and justified the weakened ego's compelling need for regressive action. And through the regressive, sadistic, military re-enactment the internalized image of the glorified, protective father was restored. These, then, were some of the vicissitudes that had taken place within the ego of this generation, but its superego functions were also distorted."* (p. 394)

For the Germans, Hitler as a glorified, charismatic father figure was experienced as a defense against the supposed Jewish enemy within

Germany. This description of the large-group psychodynamics in German during this time period is highly reminiscent of Bion's dependency groups.

Charles Strozier and Deborah Mart (2017) report that the collective humiliation is part of the process whereby large groups become perpetrators of genocide. Collective personal shame of the perpetrator large group results in humiliation that serves as the underlying motivation behind acts of large-group violence. The large-group violence is made possible by a charismatic leader who translates a genuine and traumatic past large-group humiliation into a storyline of manufactured humiliation. This symbolic and paranoid story is then used to justify calls for a response of extreme violence.

Janine Chasseguet-Smirgel (1990) explores the psychoanalytic thoughts on Nazi *biocracy* and genocide. Biocracy refers to a form of governance where biological concepts are used to justify and organize societal hierarchy and policy. It is characterized by an emphasis on racial purity and the exclusion of perceived undesirable elements from the national body and is related to the Nazi ideology of "Blood and Soil." Nazi propaganda aimed to create a collective identity, with the doctrine of Blood and Soil adding a biological aspect to this sense of unity. The conditions leading to biocracy and Nazi ideology include Germany's late decision to adopt Christianity and its geographical location. The period of French occupation of Germany under Napoleon brought about new and transformative ideas, including the emancipation of the Jewish community, which had a profound impact on societal structures. The challenges related to the unification the German Empire and later, the consequences of the Treaty of Versailles further fueled nationalist sentiments. Additionally, the economic depression of 1929, along with high unemployment rates and inflation, created favorable conditions for the emergence of extremist ideologies. These elements played a significant role in shaping Nazi Germany's national identity.

Psychologically, according to Chasseguet-Smirgel, a collective fantasy rooted in the archaic matrix of the Oedipus complex set the stage for the acceptance of extremist ideologies. This archaic matrix represented a pre-symbolic stage of mental functioning where the desire for a united nation mirrors early psychic structures. For the Nazis this was a collective fantasy that in order to be whole the nation must be cleansed. This is similar to an individual's longing for parental unity. The emphasis on racial purity and Blood and Soil was a manifestation of this archaic, non-symbolic thinking. The Nazi emphasis on racial purity and the metaphor of the "body of the nation" appealed to deep-seated desires for homogeneity. The "body of the nation" symbolizes a pure and unified country as a vibrant living being. This type of collective national identity based on race and biology views foreign elements as unwelcome guests that need to be removed.

According to Sverre Varvin (1995) genocide and ethnic cleansing have a strong connection to human behavior and the characteristics of modern society. This is especially true for especially oppressive societies. The Holocaust was perpetrated by a modern state and was at least partially related to modern technology, rational organization, and 'utopian' ideas present in a so-called civilized nation. This raises questions about the relationship between society and human nature. Varvin emphasizes the dangers of disregarding the connection between the organization of modern society and such horrific acts. It is crucial to understand that genocide is not an anomaly but rather has its roots within the very structure of modern society itself. While modern societies embrace technology, have organized bureaucracies, and espouse visions of a perfect society, these elements also cause interpersonal fragmentation and the decline of traditional cultural norms. This fragmentation and erosion of traditional culture contributes to the proliferation of primitive group dynamics and violence.

It has often been noted that bystanders who are either members of the perpetrator large group, or another large group, often do nothing to prevent or stop genocide. Mark Blechner (2009) notes that this indifference is often related to unconscious prejudice, paving the way for genocide to occur. He gives the example of the contrast in intervention by the United States in genocides based on the victims' skin color, suggesting a bias in response. Psychoanalysis has had its share of prejudicial biases, such as pathologizing homosexuality and Blechner makes a case for why psychoanalysis would be more effective if was more inclusive and prejudicial biases eliminated.

Shiela Kunkle (1999) writes about the concept of "*ugly jouissance*" from a Lacanian perspective. Jouissance is the term Lacan used to designate pleasure, enjoyment or even orgasm. It indicates a condition whereby pleasure overrides a person's ability to regulate it. The pleasure can be too much to bear or is overwhelming, as well as somewhat compulsive, producing a type of suffering. In the context of genocide ugly jouissance is where perpetrators derive a perverse pleasure from acts of violence and destruction. Kunkle explores the transformation of subjects into agents of atrocity under the influence of "*the Thing*," a Lacanian concept representing deep-seated drives and passions. This is a failure of sublimation where the laws and societal norms are inadequate to address the excesses of human passion and desire. We interpret this as a failure of the function of collective ego and superego psychic structures to regulate primitive group emotions and defenses in both small and large groups. Kunkle's thesis supports the idea that the large-group experiences pleasure in the splitting and projective processes that focus on a victim large group. In this way she highlights the sadism intertwined with genocide. The sadism or ugly jouissance may especially be an aspect of genocide experienced by so-called "bystanders" who are witness to atrocities and murder, but who do nothing to prevent or stop it. Even though bystanders do not actually commit the killings, they may take a sadistic pleasure in knowing that the victim large group is being punished. This type of sadistic enjoyment, outlined by Freud in his paper *A Child is Being Beaten* (1919) can happen at a large-group level during a genocide. The bystanders deny, rationalize, or repress, the fact that genocide is occurring while unconsciously deriving sadistic pleasure from it, leading to inaction.

For Richard Koenigsberg (1999) cultural behaviors continue to exist because they serve important psychological purposes for individuals in a society. Ideas and organizations are embraced and continued because they fulfill psychological needs for members of that society. There are hidden motivations that drive the development and continuation of particular cultural expressions including genocide. Culture provides a way for large groups to externalize and confront our deepest unconscious fears and desires, offering a means to express and understand them. According to Koenigsberg, genocide is often motivated by an ideology that creates an image of an "enemy." This externalized enemy is a way to express a desire to harm or abandon one's own nation. It represents a passionate struggle to deny the wish to separate from one's nation. This results in extreme violence against this perceived "enemy." The act of genocide can be viewed as a shared fantasy, where the destruction of others serves to confirm the reality and unity of the large group or nation. It may occur as a means to reconnect abstract beliefs with the tangible world, using violence to assert the presence of the nation. The destruction of the "enemy" in genocide serves to eliminate the perceived threat and preserve an idealized self-image of the nation. This process mirrors object relations in individuals, where individuals project unwanted parts of themselves onto others, then seek to control or destroy these projections.

James Glass (2008) explores the impact of ideas and beliefs on the formation of large groups and political movements, particularly in cases of genocide. He champions the notion of the "idea as leader," which challenges Freud's view of a necessity for a charismatic leader. For Glass, large-group fantasies are an important aspect of mass killings. A culture's willingness to normalize mass murder as national policy is a necessary condition for genocide. Large-group fantasies represent shared ideologies and beliefs that bind a large group together in psychological space. Professions and knowledge shape the leadership of the large group and its ideology. Professions play a crucial role in shaping and safeguarding our cultural practices and beliefs [5]. Within a society, clusters of knowledge form an atmosphere that influences our collective mindset. The authority of professions creates psychological spaces where the collective

5. Even psychoanalysis is not immune to being used in this way. Dušan Bjelić (2010) gives an example of how the profession of psychoanalysis was used as a tool for political manipulation and perpetrating ethnic conflict in the Balkans.

dreams and ideologies of the large group thrive. These ideologies, often fostered by professional practices, impose an ego-ideal into the way of life for the large group, offering protection against anxiety and disunity. This fosters unity within the large group as well the emergence of a collective entity with a unified political voice. In this way, the large group itself, rather than a singular leader, defines and drives genocidal ideology. Professional and scientific (or pseudo-scientific) knowledge can serve to legitimize and reinforce this ideology, contributing to the large group's justification for genocidal policies. Genocidal ideology is rooted in a shared large-group fantasy or ideology that demonizes a particular large group as an "Other" that must be destroyed.

Dianne Casoni and Louis Brunet (2007) delve into the psychological inflexibility and vulnerability behind the saying "If you're not with us, you're against us" during times of conflict.

Drawing from Otto Kernberg's perspective they note how various types of leaders relate to large groups and how this impacts large-group behaviors. Ideologies can cause large groups ignore social norms and exert a regressive pull, especially when combined with factors like intergenerational trauma and a charismatic leader. This regression can result in the large group having a collective borderline personality organization that operates using splitting and projective identification as defenses. Large-group dynamics have the potential to create an environment that encourages individuals to engage in sadistic acts, even if they would not normally do so. When individuals become part of a large group, there is a shared psychic membrane that forms, allowing for the acceptance and promotion of violent actions against specific individuals or large groups. This shared psychic membrane can lead to a decrease in the capacity for moral judgment, as the projection of individual ideals onto a leader or group can create a sense of infallibility. As a result, individuals may become less able to discern right from wrong, making them more susceptible to engaging in sadistic behavior. In the context of mass violence, even ordinary citizens may find themselves acting in ways that go against their usual values. This is because they align their behavior with the regressed psychodynamics of the large group, further blurring the lines of morality and increasing the likelihood of sadistic acts.

Christopher Bollas (2015) suggests that genocide is a manifestation of human destructiveness and a failure of democracy. The failure of democracy can lead to the rise of fundamentalism, which in turn causes an "intellectual genocide" which refers to the suppression or destruction of ideas. When humanistic and critical thinking that are hallmarks of democracy, decline, the result is a society where actual genocide becomes more conceivable. This creates a mindset that more easily dehumanizes victims and rationalizes or ignores violent acts like genocide. Bollas postulates that superego function is compromised in "regular" people who participate in mass violence. This can also be affected by the unconscious effects of intergenerational trauma.

It is easy to see genocide as a form of evil. Coline Covington (2016) gives the definition of evil as actions that are morally reprehensible, deeply shocking, and a breach of social norms.

Evil also involves actions that dehumanize others as well as using others as a means to an end, denying their humanity. Evil encompasses both premeditated acts and those arising spontaneously without conscious planning. While acknowledging that evil defines simplistic understanding, Covington situates the origins of evil in the aggression that is a primary force in early psychological development. As we have explained above, the incorporation of this aggression into normal object relations is crucial for forming healthy relationships. If this innate aggression is kept split off from feelings of pleasure this results in a primitive personality organization where aggressive affect can overwhelm the ability of the ego to regulate it, resulting in dissociation. This arises as a psychodynamic defense mechanism, enabling individuals to mentally separate themselves from their actions during participation in evil acts. According to Covington, when this aggression is combined with the dehumanization of the Other, destructiveness and aggression become evil. Belief systems and ideologies can co-opt individuals into destructive acts like genocide by providing justifications for dehumanizing behavior. Ideologies can influence large-group behavior, altering social norms and enabling demonization of the Other. The observing ego's role in maintaining psychic equilibrium can be compromised by ideology, affecting the capacity to witness and participate in evil acts. Ideological influence can disrupt the observing ego's function, facilitating the denial or rationalization of evil deeds. Totalitarian regimes and fundamentalist religious groups, like the Islamic State, exploit belief systems to glorify violence and death. Genocides, such as the Holocaust, exemplify large-scale evil through systematic extermination based on racial ideologies. Evil in the context of genocide is often facilitated by ideological adherence, even to the point of self-destruction, such as the recent actions by Hamas against Israel.

We have already discussed how large-group identity is influenced by historical traumas and entitlement ideologies. As Vamık Volkan has discussed (2013a), shared psychological experiences of victimization, humiliation, and guilt can hinder a large group's ability to adapt and mourn, perpetuating conflict. Chosen traumas and entitlement ideologies can resurface and cause a "time collapse." Chosen traumas are historical events that cause enduring collective suffering and shape large-group identity. Reactivation occurs when current events trigger the memory and emotions associated with the trauma causing a "time collapse" which is a merging of past traumatic events with current conflicts, affecting perceptions and emotions. This can serve magnify perceived threats from current conflicts and lead to acts of genocide. In Vamık Volkan's tent metaphor large-group identity encompasses and overshadows individual identities during times of conflict. This concept is deeply rooted in early childhood experiences of togetherness and gradually evolves into complex societal and cultural identities. Unfortunately, when large groups dehumanize the Other, it often leads to extreme violence and conflict, giving rise to genocide.

Genocide and Projective Identification

Jyoti Rao, (2021) using India's traumatic colonization by the British as an example, writes about how colonial powers use projection and projective identification to instill inferiority in the colonized. This typically occurs through the assertion of racial inferiority and infantilization. This psychological manipulation creates a lasting sense of incapacity and subjugation within colonized populations. As a result, projective identification has the potential to create a strong feeling of inadequacy and helplessness among colonized peoples. This can lead oppressed people to experience a false-self, self-deception, and demoralization. An internalized sense of inferiority can make individuals susceptible to rigid and extremist beliefs. Projective identification plays a role whereby colonized people unconsciously identify with their colonial oppressor. This impacts the collective identity of the colonized large group as well as their sense of entitlement.

It is also possible for an oppressed large group to resist the effects of projective identification. Beverly Stoute (2021) writes about *Black Rage* as a defensive posture resisting oppression. Black Rage needs to be understood as a controlled, modulated, form of rage that is distinct from unmodulated rage that can lead to violence. Black Rage can also be understood as a form of resilience. It is a mental construct that allows people of color to adapt to trauma and oppression, they face due to their race. It serves as a compromise formation, or a functional defensive adaptation, for protection and psychic growth in reaction to racism. The concept of Black Rage includes and responds to inherited mental images of trauma caused by oppression. As a defensive adaptation, Black Rage protects against the destructive effects of projective identification in a racist society. It involves the Black racial *Other* absorbing and withstanding the toxic projections from the dominant white culture. This psychic mechanism allows for the modulation and control of rage reactions, necessary for survival within a white supremacist society. However, enduring discriminatory experiences without the ability to control and mobilize rage adaptively can result in excessive Black Rage. This can arise when people of color are left defenseless against assaults on the self, leading to internalized degradation or uncontained anger. The accumulation of racial trauma and allostatic imbalance from ongoing threats can provoke post-traumatic reactions. If internalized, it can result in pathology such as depression, substance abuse, and other psychological symptoms, such as self-destructive behaviors, and possibly suicide. If externalized without modulation, excessive Black rage can contribute transform into retaliatory aggression and violence, further perpetuating cycles of trauma.

Mojtaba Elhami Athar (2023) has reported on the concept of "Syndrome of Collective Callous-Unemotional Traits" (SCCUT) in extremist large groups. SCCUT traits describe a pattern of attitudes and behaviors marked by a lack of empathy and remorse. Individuals with SCCUT traits exhibit shallow affect and are unconcerned with others' feelings and well-being. These traits are reminiscent of "Dark Triad" traits that occur in malignantly narcissistic and antisocial personality disordered individuals. These traits are found in serial killers and are linked to severe antisocial behavior and violence. SCCUT traits also manifest in small and large groups whose members exhibit shallow or deficient affect, and a lack of guilt feelings and remorse.

Regressed large extremist groups may develop SCCUT, resulting callous attitudes and more severe and aggressive violence toward those perceived as enemies. Large groups with SCCUT may engage in dehumanization and brutal acts as part of an "us" versus "them" mentality, leading to atrocities such as genocide. Due to projective identification, victims of SCCUT large extremist groups may adopt the aggressor's lack of empathy and remorse, leading to emotional and psychological distress. This identification with the aggressor can cause a specific type of trauma for members of the victim large group, resulting in severe confusion over identity and values. The victims will struggle to incorporate the ego dystonic SCCUT traits and attitudes imposed upon them with their pre-existing identifies. Victims may lose their sense of individuality and adopt the large group's identity This may lead to an internalization of the large group's ideology and a blurring or loss of personal values.

Victims and Survivors

Many genocide victims experience a form of traumatic entrapment and may therefore, exhibit any of the six behavioral strategies we have outlined above. Nevertheless, there are also psychological underpinnings to these strategies. The psychoanalytic literature is useful in understanding the psychology that is involved when entrapped humans are oppressed, tortured, or threatened with death. In his book on treating victims of torture and violence Peter Elsass (1997) writes that genocide survivors often utilize psychological strategies such as "closing off" and "affective anesthesia" to shield themselves from overwhelming traumatic emotions. Some Holocaust survivors display regressive changes in their sense of self and their defense mechanisms. Some coping mechanisms such as illusions and self-deception can be both beneficial to one's well-being and detrimental to their health. Normal grief allows for the reintegration of internal objects, while pathological reactions may harm the ego. This is due to what Elsass calls "internal pursuers," which are destructive internalized figures or memories that haunt individuals after traumatic experiences. They symbolize the internal threats that disrupt the ego's integrity. This leads to a deficit pathology which involves a lack of primary intentionality, where self-representations fail to become a center for impulses, feelings, and actions. This is characterized by a lack of ego-differentiation, causing disorder and confusion. This loss of ego-differentiation results in a narrowing of cognitive functions, the inability to express emotions, and problems with the individual's self-perception. These symptoms may manifest in a similar fashion to borderline personality disorder including identity fragmentation. This can make psychotherapy for survivors difficult due to the loss of "basic trust." Survivors' difficulty in articulating their traumatic experiences further complicates their psychotherapeutic treatment. The experiences of genocide can create a sense of being trapped in a "psychotic universe," making it challenging for survivors to fully convey what they have been through. The lack of open discussion surrounding events like the Holocaust, often referred to as the "conspiracy of silence," can also intensify survivors' feelings of isolation and mistrust. Nevertheless, unlike people suffering from borderline personality disorder, survivors' psychological makeup is not typically due to early childhood trauma that results in pathological personality structure. In other words, survivors' conflicts may present like borderline personality dynamics, but instead stem from external trauma rather than object relations deficits. Therefore, survivors may have more potential for targeted therapeutic interventions. Psychotherapy for survivors can focus on reconstructing destroyed ego structures, which may be more straightforward than addressing long standing pathological personality organization. Establishing "basic trust" is crucial in therapy for torture survivors, and this can lead to significant treatment progress once it is established.

Survival Syndrome

Harvey and Carol Barocas (1979) describe the enduring psychological impact and symptomatology experienced by Holocaust survivors, which includes anxiety, depression, and nightmares. This "survival syndrome" involves defensive psychic structures that were initially developed to cope with trauma in concentration camps but continue to persist once the experience of genocide is over. Survival syndrome becomes a lifelong process of mourning and a struggle with guilt and terror from past persecution. The trauma expressed in survival syndrome can be transgenerationally transmitted. The children of genocide survivors can experience psychic trauma and issues such as depression, guilt, aggression, and separation-individuation conflicts that are related to their parents' experiences. These children have a tough time figuring out who they are and separating themselves from the difficult experiences their parents went through. They also develop ways to protect themselves, just like their parents did, to deal with their anxiety and feeling of helplessness. The children of survivors also go through a period of mourning for family members they've lost and feel a strong desire to find comfort being with others, presumably in both small and large-group settings.

Psychoanalytic practitioners have been searching for ways to understand and treat intergenerational trauma. Vamık Volkan, Gabriele Ast, and William Greer (2002) explore the psychological impact of the Holocaust and intergenerational trauma. The Holocaust had a tremendous impact on people's mental well-being, causing significant psychological distress such as PTSD. This distress manifested in symptoms like feeling constantly on edge and perceiving things differently. Those who survived the Holocaust had difficulty grieving, which led to them internalizing feelings of shame, humiliation, and helplessness. Moreover, the trauma they went through often affected future generations, influencing how they saw themselves and represented themselves. It's important to note that people's psychological responses to the Holocaust varied because everyone had different experiences and circumstances before the trauma. Holocaust survivors often refuse to acknowledge their deep connection to lost loved ones to avoid feeling guilt for not being able to protect them. This denial is a defense mechanism against the pain of loss and the survivor's guilt. Survivors find it difficult to express their emotions or rebel against their circumstances due to a sense of helplessness and the need for silence. The traumatic events they experienced caused them to rely on external objects or symbols, even if these were associated with their persecutors while simultaneously denying any attachment to these dangerous objects.

Survivors struggle to experience "normal" anger because of the overwhelming guilt they feel, which makes the process of mourning even more complicated. The mourning process is further complicated by external and internal factors, such as sudden deaths or unresolved past losses. The cohesion of larger groups during times of trauma makes it difficult for individuals to mourn, as disconnecting from the large group induces feelings of guilt and loneliness. The survivors hold onto memories of their losses, fearing that forgiving and forgetting could result in a repetition of the horrors they faced. The internal turmoil caused by feelings of shame and victimization prevents the survivors from going through the necessary psychological processes to come to terms with the tragedy they experienced.

In relation to intergenerational trauma, the descendants of survivors receive complex and often overwhelming expressions of sorrow and find themselves in an ongoing state of grief. The passing down of trauma, which includes memories and fantasies, is handed from one generation to the next in a dynamic manner. Individuals who come from a lineage of trauma may inherit psychological challenges that are connected to the survivor's traumatic experience, impacting their fundamental understanding of themselves. Significant historical events can transform into "chosen traumas," assuming a mythical status and becoming an integral part of a large group's identity. The experiences of survivors become intertwined with the psychological processes of their descendants, potentially resulting in symptoms of post-traumatic stress disorder (PTSD). The mental representations of trauma are inherited by the descendants, deeply ingrained in their core sense of self. The psychological consequences of the original trauma can extend across multiple generations. The fundamental identities of offspring are shaped early on through their interactions with caregivers who have experienced trauma. The transmission of trauma can vary and intersect with the core identities and self-perceptions of subsequent generations. Vamık Volkan, Ast, and Greer (2002) suggest that treatment for survivors facilitate the expression of emotions and retrospection to counteract survivor guilt and denial of attachment to lost ones. Psychoanalytic treatment should explore the main facts of historical trauma releasing patients from the need to remember their trauma through action, or to unconsciously act out. It is also important to address the mental representation of trauma within the survivors' large-group identities to lessen the trauma's malign influences. Without psychotherapeutic intervention survivors are likely to compulsively repeat their traumatic experiences in thoughts and behaviors. For the descendants of survivors, it is important to prevent the unconscious transmission of unresolved conflicts and psychological tasks by resolving the survivors' issues. Descendants of survivors need to address deposited images and associated psychological tasks that were bequeathed to them to avoid perpetuating trauma.

Gabriela Mann (2020) describes a group of 14 analysts from Germany and Israel who came together to explore their personal and analytical histories in the context of the Holocaust. Their discussions led to a transformation of Holocaust related traumas into shared experiences. These analysts established a common language based on psychoanalytic thinking, which allowed for discussions that were previously not possible. During their discussions, they introduced the concept of "radioactive identification" which metaphorically, symbolizes unwelcome intrusions of social violence into a person's psyche. This intrusion involves unknowingly internalizing harmful traces of past trauma that can appear as an unhealthy identification with the aggressor or other signs. Radioactive identification can be passed down through generations impacting the well-being of future descendants, such as the analysts in the group. Over the course of fourteen years, the analysts' group process showed a shift from seeing themselves as either "perpetrators" or "victims" to a place of mutual recognition and safety. Towards the end of their meetings, they found that writing about their experiences helped them approach the events in a more professional and less emotionally involved manner.

Summary

Perpetrator large groups operate under a collective borderline personality organization that uses splitting and projective identification to preserve itself as "good" while projecting "badness" onto the victim group. Extremist large groups may operate at the more pathological end of this spectrum. Eliminating the victim large group allows the large perpetrator group to remain "good," or "pure." The "othering" mentioned to describe the first four stages of genocide is essentially a manifestation of a collective splitting defense as well as encouraging negative projection towards the victim large group. Unlike in war, the victim large group does not necessarily collectively split and project back to the perpetrator group. Instead, victims react to the projective identification of the perpetrator groups by trying to defend against the projections as in Black rage. Or victims can be "colonized", incorporating the projection as a sense of being devalued, demeaned, and inferior. This leads to severe confusion and a blurring or loss of identity and possibly an attempt to resolve this unpleasant state by identifying with the aggressor, taking on their characteristics and attitudes.

12

Psychological Aspects of the Russia-Ukraine War

Russia and Ukraine share a heritage that goes back more than a thousand years. Both Russia and Ukraine consider the medieval kingdom of Kievan Rus as their ancestry. Kievan Rus was around from the late 9th to the mid-13th century. It was home to a diverse group of people with different backgrounds and names, like East Slavik, Norse, and Finnic. The Rurik dynasty ruled over Kievan Rus during this time. When Kiev was conquered by the Tatar-Mongols in 1240, some of the people settled in Moscow while others found themselves in the Polish-Lithuanian Commonwealth. In 1654, those who were part of the Polish-Lithuanian Commonwealth (known as Ukrainians) decided to join Russia and acknowledge the authority of the Tsar. This choice was made because they were treated as second-class citizens in the Polish-Lithuanian Commonwealth, while in Russia they could enjoy more favorable treatment. It is worth noting that they were Orthodox Christians, whereas the Poles and Lithuanians were Catholics.

During the time of the Russian Empire, from 1721 to 1917, Russians, Ukrainians, and Byelorussians were all considered as one united people. This belief was clearly shown in the Russian imperial coat-of-arms, which featured a double-headed eagle with three crowns above its heads, symbolizing the three different components of the Russian people. Following the October Revolution in 1917, the Union of Soviet Socialist Republics (USSR) was established under the leadership of Vladimir Lenin and the Bolsheviks. In December 1922, along with the Russian, Byelorussian and Transcaucasian republics, the Ukrainians became one of the founding members of the USSR. After the collapse of the Soviet Union in 1991, Ukraine would become an independent state.

After Lenin's time, Joseph Stalin, a Georgian-born man with a rather unpleasant personality, took charge of the USSR from 1924 until his death in 1953. It is interesting to note that after Stalin, the majority of Soviet leaders, such as Nikita Khrushchev, Leonid Brezhnev, and Konstantin Chernenko, were either from Ukraine or of Ukrainian descent. Even Mikhail Gorbachev, who was the last leader of the Soviet Union before its dissolution in 1991, had Ukrainian roots through his mother, and his wife Raisa Titorenko, who was also of Ukrainian ethnicity. Additionally, it is worth mentioning that out of the 41 Soviet field marshals, eleven were Ukrainian.

Mikhail Gorbachev, after assuming the role of General Secretary of the Central Committee of the Communist Party of the Soviet Union on March 11, 1985, introduced various reforms such as *perestroika* (restructuring), *glasnost* (openness), *demokratizatsiya* (democratization), and *uskoreniye* (acceleration). These changes marked a significant turning point in the history of the Soviet Union, and ultimately led to its dissolution in 1991, with Gorbachev being its final leader.

Following the collapse of the Soviet Union, Boris Yeltsin became the first president of the Russian Federation from 1991 to 1999. Throughout his presidency, Russia made attempts to regain control over the newly independent Chechnya (Chechen Republic of Ichkeria), which later resulted in the 1994-1996 Russian-Chechen war, but unfortunately, these efforts were unsuccessful. Yeltsin then turned to Vladimir Putin to handle this delicate situation. In 1999, Putin decided to reinvade Chechnya. Prior to this invasion, there were several explosions that occurred in different towns in Russia. These attacks were attributed to "Chechen terrorists," however, some independent journalists have expressed their suspicions that these explosions were caused by Russian special forces (Eckel, 2019). The victory in the Chechnya war became a defining moment for Putin, as it transformed the public's perception of him from an ordinary politician to a strong leader. It is worth noting that Putin has never been a politician in the traditional democratic sense, as he has never engaged in a public debate with another candidate seeking the same political position.

Russia's first invasion of Georgia took place at the beginning of the nineteenth century. In 1918, Georgia gained independence while Russia was preoccupied with its revolution. However, on February 25, 1921, Georgia was reinvaded and endured a totalitarian regime for 70 years. After the collapse of the Soviet Union, Georgia regained its independence, but it was soon faced with interethnic political conflicts fueled by Russia in its regions of Abkhazia and Tskhinvali (South Ossetia). These conflicts led to the declaration of independence by these two regions, resulting in the forced movement of up to 300,000 Internally Displaced People (IDP) who sought refuge in other parts of Georgia. Unfortunately, these conflicts became prolonged, and in August 2008, they escalated into a five-day Russian-Georgian war. Following this war, Russia, and its allies (Venezuela, Syria, Nicaragua, and the small island country of Nauru) recognized the independence of these breakaway regions. Since 2008, Putin has continued a gradual occupation of Georgia by progressively moving the "conflict border" (barbed wire) deeper into Georgian territory, alongside other actions constituting a hybrid war (Bolkvadze, Chachava, Ghvedashvili, Lange-Ionatamišvili, McMillan et al., 2021).

In Ukraine, just as Georgia, there was a sad occurrence of Russian annexation that began in the 1920s. To suppress the resistance of the local people, Soviet officials in 1932-1933 took away all the grain supply from the villages in the eastern and central parts of the country. They even closed the roads to limit people's movement, resulting in a terrible famine known as the *Holodomor*, which means "to kill by starvation" in Ukrainian. It is heartbreaking to know that around four and a half million lives were lost during this tragic period.

In 2013, when the pro-Russian Ukrainian President Viktor Yanukovych decided to suspend political association and free-trade agreements with the European Union, it sparked protests called the Maidan Revolution. These protests ultimately led to Yanukovych being removed from power. However, as a response to these events, Russia invaded Crimea in 2014 and initiated a war in Donbas. This led to the declaration of independence by Russian-backed separatists in Lugansk and Donetsk.

In February 2014 protesters in Ukraine overthrew President Viktor Yanukovych because he had been friendly to Russia's interests. During this revolution more than 100 protesters were killed. Following this event, during the same year, the interim Ukrainian government signed a trade agreement with the European Parliament illustrating a step toward membership in the bloc.

On January 5, 2019, Bartholomew I, the Ecumenical Patriarch of Constantinople (Istanbul), who is considered the leader of the 300-million-strong worldwide Orthodox community, signed a decree granting self-governorship to the Orthodox Church in Ukraine, ending more than 330 years of Russian religious control in Ukraine. Then Ukrainian president Petro Poroshenko was present at this ceremony in Istanbul. Poroshenko predicted that the move would open a "new era in Orthodox history." This event prompted the Russian Orthodox Church to announce days later that it was ending its relationship with the Ecumenical Patriarchate in protest.

Ukraine's gaining a religious "freedom" from Russia is a visible factor of the conflict between the two countries. While Russia is officially secular, most Russians, including Vladimir Putin himself are followers of the Orthodox Church. We will describe aspects of Putin's childhood later. Here we wish to remind the reader that Putin's mother was devout Christian and Putin is known to have worn a crucifix around his neck for most of his life.

Another visible factor of the Russia's anger towards Ukraine is Ukraine's seeking entry into the North Atlantic Treaty Organization

(NATO) which was created in 1949 to protect against Soviet aggression. But while launching an invasion of Ukraine. Russian president Vladimir Putin declared that Ukraine was governed by "neo-Nazis" and that his military operation's aim was the "denazification" and "demilitarization" of Ukraine.

In this chapter we will focus on how a war or war-like situation can occur when the personality organization of a political leader becomes intertwined with societal, religious, and political processes as well as shared historical images. Once more we wish to remind the reader that we are not suggesting that "real-world" issues and secondary process calculations related to horrible international events are not important and should be discarded in favor of psychological considerations. Once more, in this chapter our aim is to illustrate that psychoanalytic concepts can contribute to a more complete analysis of the personality organizations of political leaders, their interactions with their followers and their role in political or societal processes.

Vladimir Putin

Vladimir Putin is a fascinating subject with regards to leadership psychopathology and his family history is especially instructive with regards to his personality development[1]. Vladimir Putin's mother was married to Putin's father in 1932 when she was just 17 years old. As a newly married couple, they moved to Leningrad, which was known as St. Petersburg during the Soviet era. Shortly after, Putin's father enlisted in the Russian army's submarine fleet and completed his military service before the outbreak of World War II. However, during the war, he served in the military once again and unfortunately suffered a leg injury from a direct

1. We would like to thank Professor Jana D. Javakhishvili at Ilia State University in the Republic of Georgia, Professor Yuri Urbanovich at the University of Virginia in the United States and four colleagues in Russia, including two who appeared as supporters of Vladimir Putin's invasion of Ukraine and the other two seeing this invasion as an example of a huge human tragedy, in helping us to collect information about Putin, especially by translating into English Putin's own remarks about himself, his family, his followers (Javakhishvili, 2023; Volkan, V. D. & Javakhishvili, 2022; Volkan, V. D. 2023).

grenade attack by German soldiers. He carried shrapnel in his leg for the rest of his life. Putin's parents had limited education and lived from one paycheck to another, as Putin himself described in an interview.

Before Vladimir was born, the couple had two other children. Tragically, before World War II, one of them, Albert, passed away as an infant due to whooping cough. The other child, Viktor, died from diphtheria during the Nazi blockade of Leningrad. Experts estimate that during this blockade between September 1941 and January 1944, 600,000 to 1.5 million Russians died from starvation. Vladimir Putin was born on October 1, 1952, approximately ten years after Viktor's death, when his mother was 41 years old. He is the sole survivor among his siblings.

In January 2012, Putin shared the story of his family's experience during World War II on the anniversary of the war. He attended the annual wreath-laying ceremony at Piskaryovskoye Cemetery in St. Petersburg, where 470,000 civilians and soldiers were buried in mass graves. Putin recounted how his parents had told him about children being taken from their families in 1941. His mother had her one-year-old child, Victor, taken from her in an attempt to save him. Although they were informed that he had passed away, they were never told where he was buried. Putin has stated: "My parents told me that children were taken from their families in 1941, and my mother had a child (one year old Victor) taken from her—with the goal of saving him.... They said he had died, but they never said where he was buried" (Barry, 2012, p. 9).

In the year 2000, an organization named "We Remember Them All by Name" made an effort to locate where Victor was buried in 1942. In 2014, this organization concluded that Victor was buried in one of the mass graves. We have found no evidence to suggest that Putin instructed this organization to find his deceased brother's grave or remains. Putin himself stated in 2015 that individuals whom he did not know had independently discovered documents related to his brother.

In the book titled *First Person: An Astonishingly Frank Self-Portrait by Russia's President* (Putin, Gevorkyan, Timakova & Kolesnikov, 2000), Putin discusses his family's experience during the horrific Nazi blockade of St. Petersburg. One remarkable story recounts how Putin's mother, who was starving, lost consciousness and was placed among the deceased by government officials. She was to be transported for burial alongside the corpses. However, she groaned and was therefore not buried. Putin revealed in 2015 that his father was the person who witnessed his mother's body amongst the corpses and noticed that she was still breathing. His father had just come from the hospital where he had received medical treatment. Even after realizing that his wife was alive, the government officials still suggested that he allow them to transport her body, believing that she would die before they reached the mass grave. Putin described how his father, using his crutches, attacked the government officials and compelled them to return his wife to their family apartment. It was Putin's father who saved his mother's life. Putin's mother lived until 1999 after losing her husband in 1998. However, there are doubts regarding this version of Putin's story (Unnikrishnan, 2022). For instance, in the book *First Person*, he wrote that his father was at the front during the war and not with his mother.

Putin (2015) stated that his father had a reluctance to discuss the family's war experiences and the immense tragedies that occurred during the Nazi blockade of Saint Petersburg. However, as Putin was growing up, he would listen attentively when his parents engaged in conversations about the war and its impact on their family. On some occasions, his parents would directly involve him in these discussions. Putin recounted how his father spent several months in the hospital, and during this time, his mother would visit him daily. Seeing his mother's weakened state due to starvation, Putin's father selflessly began sharing his own food with her, concealing it from the nurses. When doctors and nurses noticed that Putin's father was fainting from hunger, they eventually discovered the reason behind it. As a result, they prohibited Putin's mother from visiting her husband for a period of time.

As a child, Putin also became aware of the losses suffered by his family during World War II. His maternal grandmother was shot by the Germans when they occupied Tver City, and it is reported that five of his father's uncles and two (or possibly five) other relatives from his mother's side also lost their lives during the war.

In his account, Putin (2015) portrays his mother as a kind-hearted individual. As previously mentioned, she was a devout Eastern Orthodox Christian and had Vladimir secretly baptized. In the book *First Person* (Putin, Gevorkyan, Timakova & Kolesnikov, 2000), Putin reveals that his father disciplined him by using a belt from preschool age through primary school. One instance when he received this kind of punishment was when young Putin ventured out on a train excursion with his friends without obtaining his parents' permission. Putin explains that after this incident, he lost his inclination to travel independently. This act of punishment from his father was not an isolated occurrence. Peter Baker and Susan Glasser (2005) describe how Putin's father frequently employed the use of a belt to discipline his son, while Putin himself always fought back, resorting to "kicking, biting, anything" (pp. 41–42). Juhani Ihanus (2022) characterizes Putin as a streetwise boy, a *gopnik* (lower class delinquent), and a hooligan. Ihanus highlights how Putin was often left to roam the violent streets, engaging in fights, and falling victim to aggression. He was consistently late for school, where he faced social exclusion from the age of 10 to 14, and he was even denied entry into the Young Pioneers organization. Putin's former teacher, Vera Gurevich, once mentioned that other classmates would lock the young Putin in the girls' restroom, where he would endure slaps from the girls. In tears, Putin vowed to his teacher that one day he would retaliate and intimidate his attackers (Ihanus 2022, p. 303). Unsurprisingly, during his early teenage years, Putin developed an interest in martial arts, and as a teenager, he became proficient in in sambo, a Russian martial art combining wrestling and judo, and judo proper.[2] Eventually, he was granted member-

2. Putin reports that he received a blackbelt in Judo at age 18 and that he still practices this martial art (Siegel, 2001). In 2012 he was awarded an 8th dan black belt, one of the highest levels in Judo, by the International Judo Federation ("Putin awarded eighth dan by international body", 2012). Putin published a book in Russian titled *Learning Judo with Vladimir Putin* (Shestakov, Levitsky, & Putin, 2000) and a little later another book *Judo: History, Theory, Practice* in English (Putin, et. al., 2004). There is also an instructional DVD with Putin teaching Judo that is now posted to YouTube (Putinery, 2012). Some martial artists have questioned whether Putin is a legitimate martial artist with Benjamin Wittes

ship in the Young Pioneers organization, later becoming a member of Komsomol (the Communist Youth League).

Putin received his education at Leningrad State University. Immediately after graduating, he joined the KGB in 1975. For a span of 16 years, he served as a KGB foreign intelligence officer. Between 1985 and 1989, he was stationed in East Germany. Following this, in 1991, Putin began working for the mayor of St. Petersburg and eventually became deputy mayor in 1994. In 1997, he was invited to be part of President Boris Yeltsin's "inner circle" and served as the deputy chief administrator of the Kremlin. Boris Yeltsin, who became the first president of Russia in 1991 after the fall of the Soviet Union, appointed Putin to this position. In March 1999, Putin assumed the role of secretary of the Security Council and provided counsel to the president on matters concerning foreign policy, national security, and military and law enforcement. Putin's involvement in the war in Chechnya significantly boosted his popularity among the citizens. He attributed numerous bombings in Moscow and other locations to Chechen terrorists while using strong language to criticize his enemies. As a result, Putin's approval ratings began to skyrocket.

Due to declining health and struggles with alcoholism, Yeltsin resigned on December 31, 1999. Putin assumed the role of acting president and four months later was elected as president for two terms. From 2008 to 2012, he served as the head of the Russian Federation's government while Dmitri Medvedev, who had strong support from Putin, served as president for a single term. In 2012, Putin was reelected as president for a third time and again in 2018 for a fourth term. Changes made to the Russian constitution in 2020 allowed him to run for reelection in 2024 as well (Belton, 2020; Myers, 2015; Roxburgh, 2013).

Following the collapse of the Soviet Union, the newly independent

---

even challenging Putin to a match (2015). Nevertheless, many martial arts experts believe that Putin possesses good Judo skills (Veltri, 2018). In any case, after the invasion of Ukraine, the International Judo Federation suspended Putin from his role as honorary president and the World Taekwondo organization stripped him of his honorary 9th degree blackbelt (Nelsen, 2022).

former Soviet states faced numerous challenges as they transitioned toward democracy. These challenges included unresolved trauma from the totalitarian regime, deeply rooted corruption, socio-economic instability, and interethnic political tensions. Many of these challenges were a result of the Soviet principle of "*Divide et Impera*" (Divide and rule), which institutionalized divisions based on identity and led to a wave of military conflicts. Since Putin came to power in 2000, democracy in Russia has been gradually deteriorating (Javakhishvili, 2014, 2018; Schmidt-Löw-Beer, Atria & Davar, 2015).

In 1983, as a young KGB agent, Putin married Lyudmila Aleksandrovna Ocheretnaya, who previously worked as a stewardess for Aeroflot. From this marriage, Putin has two daughters and two grandsons. However, Putin and his wife divorced in 2014, allegedly due to his extramarital relationship with former Olympic gymnast Alina Kabaeva, with whom he reportedly has four children. There are also claims of another "secret" love child, a daughter, attributed to Putin.

Putin's Alternate Life History

We are familiar with the book *Vova-Volodia-Volodimir* by Polish journalist Krystyna Kurczap-Redlich (2016), in which she presents a different, alternate, background for the Russian president. Krystyna claims she went to the village of Metekhi in the Georgian Republic and found Putin's mother by asking the locals for directions to her house. Kurczap-Redlich supposedly met Putin's mother, Vera Nikolaevna, who is now in her 90s on November 6, 2019. Kurczap-Redlich mentions that there used to be documentaries about Putin's mother, including a 28-minute film made by a Dutch journalist, but these films have since been removed from the internet. This account of Putin's life history derives from that interview that Kurczap-Redlich claims tells the truth about Putin's early life.

Putin had an incredibly difficult childhood. In this account, Putin, known as Vovka, was born after the Second World War near the Ural Mountains in 1950. Vera Nikolaevna disclosed that she was born in the village of Terehino. After the war, she encountered a man named Platon Privalov, engaged in a romantic relationship with him, and became pregnant. However, upon discovering that he was married, she promptly ended the affair. Consequently, she returned to her parents and gave birth to Vovka Putin on October 6th, 1950. When Vovka turned one year old, she departed for Tashkent in Uzbekistan, leaving him in the care of her parents. In Tashkent, she resided near a military base, where she crossed paths with a Georgian man named Archil Osepashvili. They quickly got married, with Osepashvili being fully aware of Nikolaevna's existing child. Together, the couple relocated to Georgia, but their financial circumstances were dire. After a year, Nikolaevna implored her mother to bring her two-year-old son Vovka to Georgia, specifically to the village of Metekhi. Little Vovka found himself amidst unfamiliar faces – a strange woman (his biological mother), an unfamiliar man (his stepfather), and a foreign language. Naturally, this strange environment left him feeling unsettled. Unfortunately, the stepfather proved to be a violent individual. When Vera Nikolaevna became pregnant with her Osepashvili's children, he developed a deep animosity towards Vovka. His drinking habits and physical abuse towards Vovka became notorious in the neighborhood. Consequently, Vovka faced was marked as a frightened and mistreated stepson. As he grew older, Vovka made the decision to learn self-defense sports, such as sambo and judo, in order to protect himself. Eventually, Vera Nikolaevna made the difficult choice to leave Vovka in the care of her parents. As she departed, Vovka cried profusely, and she claims to have never seen him since that day. Due to their advanced age, the grandparents ultimately decided to entrust Vovka to their relatives, who coincidentally shared the surname Putin. The new parents were in their forties, with the new mother being 42 years old. Prior to Vovka's arrival, this couple had two sons who unfortunately met tragic ends. The first son, Viktor, perished before World War II, while the second son succumbed to diphtheria during the Leningrad Blockade. The new father had previously served in the NKVD, the intelligence service in the Soviet Union. He had fought in Finland and had a penchant for violence. This father was an exceedingly brutal man who subjected Putin to severe beatings. Vovka spent the rest of his childhood in this family, where he was essentially a replacement for the two deceased brothers.

This biography of Vladimir (Vovka) Putin is not to be found among any official sources. It is possible that it represents a fantasy about Putin or a hagiography painting him as a victim. Professor Jana Javakhishvili, who assisted us in gathering information regarding Putin, read Kurczap-Redlich's book and observed her recent video presentation. Furthermore, we sought verification from our colleagues in Russia about this alternate account of Putin's life and arrived at the conclusion that, currently, we lack definitive evidence to substantiate Kurczap-Redlich's assertions. Nevertheless, we thought it important to include them here for completeness' sake. In the next section, our attention is directed towards elucidating Putin's role in promoting and endorsing a "time collapse" in Russia and the invasion of Ukraine, by considering him as a replacement child harboring rescue fantasies.

Replacement Children and Their Rescue Fantasies

Albert and Barbara Cain (1964) coined the term "replacement child" to refer to a child who is born following the loss of another child or significant person in the mother's life. The mother forms an internalized image of the deceased child or significant other. If she struggles to resolve her grief, she may transfer this image into the developing self-representation of her subsequent child, a phenomenon known as transgenerational transportation (Kestenberg & Brenner, 1996; Kogan, 1995; Laub & Auerhahn, 1993). The second child is then treated as a vessel to keep the memory of the deceased child "alive," thus becoming a "replacement child."

The mental health literature has extensively explored the psychology of replacement children (see, for instance: Ainslie & Solyom, 1986; Green & Solnit, 1964; Legg & Sherick, 1976; Poznanski, 1972; Volkan & Javakhishvili, 2022).

The mother, mostly unconsciously, encourages the replacement child to undertake specific ego tasks in order to safeguard and preserve what has been projected onto him or her. Replacement children are preoccupied with integrating the deposited image into their overall self-representation. The success of this integration can vary from child to child. If unsuccessful, replacement children may develop an unassimilated self-representation.

Some adults may consciously or unconsciously deposit their own traumatic experiences onto their children when forming their self-representations. In the phenomenon of the replacement child, there may also be an element of the depositor's wounded self-image being transferred to the child's self. The outcome of this process depends on how the child internalizes and handles the trauma deposited by the adult. These children often develop fantasies of being rescued.

In psychoanalytic clinical practice, we often observe the presence of rescue fantasies in patients whose families have experienced traumatic losses. Whether it is before their birth, during their childhood, or during their adolescence, these patients had mothers or other caretakers who were unable to provide adequate mothering due to depression, loss, or other factors. Additionally, they were not able to form a nurturing relationship with their fathers or father figures. As a result, their rescue fantasy is to create an illusion of having a positive mothering experience.

The content of a rescue fantasy can lead to both maladaptive and adaptive compromises in adulthood. Several scholars have written about the role of unconscious rescue fantasies in shaping individuals' career paths and leadership roles. Some individuals who have experienced the replacement child phenomenon may be driven to seek out leadership positions in order to fulfill their rescue fantasies. However, it is important to note that these leaders can either be reparative or destructive in their approach.

Vladimir Putin is an example of a leader influenced by rescue fantasies. We can speculate that his desire to have many children is linked to his unconscious need to compensate for his mother's loss. While we do not have confirmed information about his relationships with his children, his actions and policies suggest a strong attachment to the role of a protector and provider. Putin's connection of Russia to the Soviet Union and his promotion of a "time collapse" in present-day Russian life can be seen as manifestations of his rescue fantasy. This perception of historical events has played a significant role in the invasion of Ukraine, as Putin has framed it as a mission to "denazify" the country.

Time Collapse in Russia

Putin primarily ignited an unresolved trauma, namely the Nazi invasion. Additionally, he made numerous remarks that exemplified his emulation of Joseph Stalin. These types of self-made comparisons to Joseph Stalin imply that he is vying with him in some capacity and may aspire to be more renowned and significant than Stalin and other Soviet leaders in the annals of history.

An exemplification of temporal convergence in Russia is the establishment of the National Program of the Patriotic Education of Citizens of the Russian Federation in 2001.

The central objective of this program is to impart knowledge to kindergarten students of preschool age about World War II, which in the Soviet Union was termed "The Great Patriotic War". During the 70th anniversary of the victory in World War II in 2015, kindergartens and schools across the country staged ritual plays centered around this war. In many Russian towns, kindergartens and schools continue to stage and perform such ritual plays.

Typically, these plays commence with a teacher, often attired in the military uniform of the 1940s, delivering an opening speech and acquainting the participants with the notion that they will be transported back in time. Subsequently, children, also garbed in attire from the 1940s, engage in a dance accompanied by a song with the lyrics: "It's 1941 and everybody is alive." Suddenly, the music and dancing are interrupted by the voice of Yuri Levitan, the radio commentator who announced the commencement of the war, often utilizing an authentic recording of his voice. Following this, the children enact the preparations "to go to the front." This is followed by a battle scene, wherein some children "perish" while others pretend to be in graves. Those who "survive" return home, celebrating "the Great Victory," the triumph over the Nazis.

There exist variations in these plays. For instance, in some, background voices elucidate certain elements that manifest on the stage, such as the crimson blood of children on the pristine snow. In other plays, children approach their mothers and hand them papers symbolizing letters that families received during World War II, informing them of the demise of their children. Additionally, children portray the role of soldiers who did not meet their demise in battle but discover upon returning home that their mothers have passed away. At the conclusion of the plays, children often express their aversion towards war and that all they want is to live in peace. Today, these performances are available on the internet. They are proudly uploaded by performers, parents, teachers, and administrators. (See "DW Documentary", 2022 for an example of a typical ritual play).

Remembrances of the Great Patriotic War are observed constantly. There are dozens of plays by professional adults and movies "for children and their parents." A book titled *Children of War: Diaries 1941–1945* (Nikolaĭ et al., 2016) is edited by a group of journalists from the newspaper Argumenti I Fakti (Arguments and Facts), which is owned by the government. It includes stories of 35 Soviet children who experienced atrocities of war. Tragic details, particularly related to the death of family members, especially from starvation in Leningrad, are described.

Wearing 1940s-style clothing has become very fashionable in Russia. Since 2017, modern military uniforms have been replaced by military uniforms of the 1940s, now called "the winners" uniforms. There are even military outfit stores for children, and they are very popular. On May 9, Victory Day, big crowds take to the streets and march, carrying photos of their relatives who fought in WWII. We learned that Putin usually participates in a march called "Immortal Regiment" with a portrait of his father in his hands.

Preoccupation with graveyards is also observable. When the 70th anniversary of the "Great Victory" was celebrated on November 29, 2015, the Russian governmental TV channel Russia broadcasted that the grave of Emperor Alexander III (father of Nicholas II, the last tsar killed by the Bolsheviks) had been opened to authenticate the remains of Nicholas and his children.

In 2020, the Moscow Times published an article titled "Russian

Gravediggers Defy Coronavirus to Hold Speed-Digging Contest," (2020) where five teams from different areas gathered at a local cemetery to dig holes of specific dimensions. Judges evaluated their performances, and the champion was a young man from Tomsk who completed his task in 52 minutes. The readers were informed that there would be more extensive contests in the future.

After the invasion of Ukraine on March 1, 2022, Russian schools were required to conduct special social sciences lessons to educate children on how they should think and talk about the so-called "special operation" in Ukraine. The lessons focused on concepts like preventing genocide and de-Nazification. To support these efforts, a propagandistic cartoon was created and widely distributed. On Russian television, the Ukrainians are referred to as "Ukronazis," and the attack on Ukraine is associated with de-Nazification.

One of Vamık Volkan's colleagues has a firsthand understanding of the appeal of Putin's actions, especially among those residing in the breakaway regions of eastern Ukraine, namely the Donetsk People's Republic and Luhansk People's Republic, where Krasnodon is located. This colleague recalled a historical event from September 29th, 1942, when 32 Russian communist miners, who had refused to work for the invading Nazis, were buried alive near the central square. This incident led to the formation of a Komsomol underground group called the Young Guard, composed of young graduates seeking revenge for the heroic miners' martyrdom. The organization grew steadily until it was betrayed to the Nazis, resulting in the arrest and inhumane torture of its members. The Nazis and their accomplices, including local policemen, subjected the Young Guard to various brutalities like inserting needles under their nails, cutting off their ears, and carving stars on their bodies. Despite the intense torture, they remained steadfast. Enraged by their resilience, the torturers eventually threw them alive into a pit, which became their collective grave. The agonizing moans of the dying reportedly echoed from the pit for several days.

Vamık Volkan's colleague, in addition to what has been previously mentioned, took the opportunity to remind everyone that the renowned novel "*Molodaya Gvardiya*" (Young Guard) by Alexander Fadeyev (2017), which was written in the year 1946, has not only been published numerous times but has reached an impressive total of over 250 reprints. It is worth noting that during the era of the Soviet Union, this literary masterpiece was deemed so significant that it was included in the curricula of all schools within the Russian literature program. Furthermore, it is quite remarkable that in 1948, the highly esteemed Soviet director Sergei Gerasimov directed a film adaptation of this very book, a production that gained immense popularity amongst schoolchildren all across the country. The film was even screened annually in the town square of Krasnodon, captivating the attention of its citizens on a colossal display.

According to Vamık Volkan's colleague, it is crucial for us to understand that when President Putin made his commitment to extend maximum assistance to the Russian population residing in eastern Ukraine, as well as his pledge to acknowledge the existence of the Donetsk People's Republic and Luhansk People's Republic, it was not merely empty rhetoric, but rather a clear directive for action. This statement is founded upon the fact that the concept of time in Russia seems to converge, giving rise to a prevailing belief amongst Putin's followers that Ukraine still remains an integral part of the Great Russia.

Russian Entitlement Ideologies

The entitlement ideologies that are prevalent amongst contemporary Russians are commonly referred to as "*Eurasianism*" and "*Russkiy* Mir" (Russian World). The term "Eurasianism" signifies the standpoint that Russian civilization cannot be confined to the conventional classifications of "European" or "Asian," but instead belongs to the broader geopolitical concept known as Eurasia. This perspective was originally introduced by the eminent Russian historian Lev Nikolayevich Gumilyov (1912–1992). On the other hand, the concept of "Russkiy mir" was developed by a group of Russian scholars, namely Pyotr Shchedrovitsky, Yefim Ostrovsky, Valery Tishkov, Vitaly Skrinnik, and Tatyana Poloskova, during the 1990s. Their aim was to address the crisis of national ideology that Russia was facing at the time. The concept posits that the

Russian world encompasses the social totality that is united by language, traditions, and history. Furthermore, it asserts that Russia has a distinct mission to safeguard the Russkiy mir both within its own borders and among compatriots residing abroad, including not only former Soviet citizens but also Russian-speaking minorities. Russia is establishing many Russian language and culture organizations in former Soviet countries, to "plant" or reanimate Russki Mir, as younger generations in these countries often do not speak Russian (Javakhishvili, 2023).

In the year 2007, President Putin collaborated with the Russian Orthodox Church to establish the Russkiy Mir Foundation, an organization that operates under the auspices of the government. The primary objective of this foundation is to propagate the Russian language and culture on a global scale, while concurrently shaping the Russian World into a comprehensive international initiative. This initiative was outlined by Andis Kudors (2010).

"Eurasianism" has now come to define the national ideology of Putin's Russia. This concept asserts that Russian civilization possesses a distinctive and remarkable character, one that cannot be confined within the boundaries of the European or Asian categories. Gumilyov (1990) further emphasizes that the Russian ethnos represents a "super-ethnos" that must actively counter the perceived threat posed by Catholic Europe to the integrity and sovereignty of Russia. This insight was expounded upon by Charles Clover (2016).

There have been numerous reports circulating in the media, providing information that suggests that President Putin is currently experiencing some sort of illness and is currently receiving medical attention. It is important to note that these reports are not based on any concrete evidence, and therefore, we cannot claim to have any definitive knowledge regarding this matter. However, it is worth mentioning that upon observing Putin's behavior, particularly his tendency to maintain a considerable distance from others, including those within his inner circle, Jana Javakhishvili and Vamık Volkan couldn't help but wonder if this could be attributed to the potential subconscious fear of contracting COVID-19. Furthermore, they also contemplated the idea that this fear might be linked to his position as a replacement child and his role as the "First Person" (Volkan & Javakhishvili, 2022).

At the beginning of the war with Ukraine there was much talk on central TV channels within Russia that there were laboratories in Ukraine that had developed biological weapons against "Slavic nationalities". Allegedly this virus was being infected with ducks which would then fly to Russia. When the Ukrainian giant plane "Mriya" was destroyed by Russian forces, there was a fantasy about this plane on social media that the Ukrainians were planning to irrigate Russian fields with contaminated water, which would destroy crops. After a year and a half of war, the topic of Ukrainian infected mosquitoes was raised again on TV and the suggestion that "combat locust" were involved was added to this narrative (Alpatova, et. al., 2024).

It is also is plausible to consider that the threat posed by the COVID-19 pandemic may have played a significant role in influencing the timing of the invasion of Ukraine, as well as Putin's strong desire to promote and revive the sport of sambo, both within Russia and on a global scale. Interestingly, after reading Juhani Ihanus's paper on Putin in the year 2022, we discovered that he too had speculated about the potential impact of COVID-19 as a threat to Putin, which in turn could have contributed to the decision to invade Ukraine. As we delve into the writing of this paper, it is important to acknowledge that nearly two years have transpired since the commencement of this invasion, thereby emphasizing the evolving nature of the situation (Volkan & Javakhishvili, 2022; V. D. Volkan 2023).

13

Psychological Aspects of the Hamas-Israel War

The establishment of the State of Israel, after the Holocaust, was proclaimed on May 14th, 1948. In this book we will not dwell on centuries long events of the Jewish and Palestinian peoples' investment in the present location of Israel. There are a number of books on this topic, and we leave the reader to sort through the various historical viewpoints. We list some references we have found useful in understanding the history of Israel and Palestine without endorsing a simplistic or partisan view of the situation (Aly et al., 2022; Caplan, 2019; Ehrenreich, 2017; Krämer, 2011; Laqueur, 2003; Melamed & Hoffman, 2022; Oren, 2002; Sachar, 2007).

Following the establishment of Israel, four wars took place between Israel and Arabs in 1949, 1956, 1967 and in 1973. The war in 1967 is known as the *Six-Day War.* It took place between June 5 and June 10. Israel defeated Egypt, Jordan, and Syria and occupied the Sinai Peninsula, the Gaza Strip, the Golan Heights, the West Bank and the Old City of Jerusalem. Years later, between 1994 and 1999, Israel transferred security and civilian responsibility for much of the Gaza Strip and the West Bank to the Palestinian Authority.

The 1973 war is known as the *Yom Kippur War* between Israel on one side and Egypt and Syria on the other side. It was a surprise attack when the Arab coalition launched it in the Sinai and the Golan Heights on the Jewish holy day of Yom Kippur. It is also known as the *Ramadan War* since it occurred during the 10th day of the Islamic holy month of Ramadan. It is also called the *October War* since it took place between October 6 and October 25, 1973. This war ended in an Israeli victory.

On 19 November 1977, in order to advance the Arab-Israeli peace process, Egyptian President Anwar Sadat visited Jerusalem. An Egyptian born person, Ahmad Fawzi, has worked for three UN Secretaries-General: Boutros Boutros-Ghali, and Ban Ki-moon. In August 2023 Vamık Volkan, during a conversation with Ahmad Fawzi, learned that as a young person Ahmad Fawzi was in the airplane that took Sadat to Jerusalem. Ahmad Fawzi described how the Egyptians in the airplane were very concerned about their safety. They were afraid that when their airplane landed the Israelis may capture them or kill them.

Soon after the plane touched down Ahmad Fawzi was the first person to get out from the back door of the airplane and step on the Israeli soil. At this moment Ahmad Fawzi saw was an Israeli soldier holding a machine gun. He thought that he would be captured or be killed. Then he noticed two little flags, one Israeli and one Egyptian, were placed into the machine gun's barrel. This helped him to relax.

Vamık Volkan served as the first Inaugural *Yitzak Rabin Fellow Rabin Center for Israeli Studies*, Tel Aviv in 2000-2001 and lived in Israel for about 5 months. While in Israel he spoke with Israelis who were also at the Jerusalem airport with senior Israeli officials, including Prime Minister Menachem Begin. They were gathered to welcome Sadat and his companions. Vamık Volkan learned that Israelis were concerned that when the Egyptian airplane landed, Sadat would not come out. Instead, Egyptian sharp shooters would try to kill Menachem Begin and other important Israelis. Israelis had their own sharp shooters hidden locations that surrounded where the Egyptian airplane would land.

Sadat continued to find peaceful solutions despite strong opposition from most of the Arab world. United States president Jimmy Carter initiated negotiations between Sadat and Begin that resulted in the Camp David Accords (September 17, 1978). On October 6th, 1981, the courageous Sadat was assassinated by a group of Egyptian army officers at a military parade to celebrate Egypt's 1973 war against Israel.

When Sadat addressed the Knesset, the legislative body in Israel, on 20 November 1977 he referred to a "psychological wall" between the world of the Arabs and that of the Israelis. He stated that this "wall" accounted for 70 percent of the problems between them. In response, the American Psychiatric Association's Committee on Psychiatry and Foreign Affairs, of which Vamık Volkan was a member, brought influential Egyptians and Israelis once or twice per year together for unofficial dialogues for six years to find out if this "wall" could be made permeable. On the third year of these meetings Vamık Volkan became the director of the American Psychiatric Association's Committee and initiated participation of four Palestinians from Bethlehem, Ramallah, and Gaza, in these gatherings. Details of what had happened during these meetings are described Vamık Volkan's book, *Enemies on the Couch* (2013a). Here we only refer to an observation to clearly illustrates how preoccupation with large-group identity is the key conflictual psychological phenomenon between large groups in a deadly struggle.

When the American Psychiatric Association's Committee meeting took place in 1984 in Switzerland, for the first-time new members from Palestine were present. Mayor of Bethlehem Elias Freij, a Christian Palestinian who traced his family's presence in Bethlehem back 500 years, and the leader of the Palestinian participants, summarized their situation. He stated that 1,300,000 Arabs had been governed by Israel on the West Bank and in Gaza for 16 years. They lived under military occupation with all its frustrations and humiliations, and no Palestinian liked or accepted the occupation. He declared that Palestinians should challenge Israel for peace, and that Israelis and Palestinians should live as equals and neighbors within the boundaries of their own respective nations. Despite conferences held on the issue, nothing changed, and there were no serious exchanges between the two peoples. Freij stated: "Israel is here to stay, but Palestinians should have their own home and govern themselves."

One day another Palestinian participant, a psychiatrist from Gaza ended up sitting next to Israeli General Shlomo Gazit. The general had become a hero during the Six-Day War in June 1967 and later was the head of the Military Intelligence Directorate, and at the time he joined the American Psychiatric Association committee meetings, he was President of Ben Gurion University of the Negev Beersheva. He had been the first Israeli general assigned to manage the Gaza Strip. The Palestinian psychiatrist referred to the times when General Gazit was in charge managing Gaza and addressed to him:

> *"You were the first and the last Israeli general in charge of Gaza who was fair in dealing with the Arabs. I don't like living under Israeli occupation one bit. As a man, I respect you. After your tenure was over, however, none of the new military commanders assigned to Gaza have been fair to us as you were. Now, to be assigned as the Israeli military chief in Gaza is the end of a person's career. The Israelis send their unwanted military officers to us. These military officers know this, and they show their frustration by being unjust to us."*

Vamık Volkan (2013a) wrote:

> *"As the Palestinian psychiatrist spoke, his emotions overtook him. He put his right hand into the right pocket of his trousers. I could see the frantic movements of his fingers under the cloth. Since I am a psychoanalyst, I had a wild thought that sitting next to an Israeli general who was once the head of the occupiers in Gaza had induced castration anxiety in the Palestinian psychiatrist and that he was touching his penis in order to be sure he was not castrated. But then the Palestinian physician, almost screaming, declared: 'As long as I have this, you can't take my Palestinian identity from me.'"* (p. 70)

"This" turned out to be a small piece of stone on which the Palestinian colors were painted. Vamık Volkan learned that keeping his stone gave this psychiatrist an almost tangible sense of unity with other Palestinians.

Psychoanalysis understands items like this small piece of stone as something termed a *linking object.* These objects have been described by Vamık Volkan as symbolic items used by individuals to maintain a connection with a deceased loved one or a lost important object. They serve as a focal point for the mourner's self-representation to merge with that of the deceased or the lost object, allowing for the accommodation of mourning (Volkan 1972, 1981, 2007). Linking objects can include items that were worn by the deceased, objects that extend the body of the deceased, and objects with a resemblance to the deceased and personalized symbols of the lost object. Linking objects have been found among mothers mourning for son's who have died in wars (Jurcević & Urlić, 2002). Additionally, memorial shrines from many different cultures typically use linking objects, which typically include a photograph of the missing person surrounded by iconographic symbols, candles, flowers, and incense (Ng, 2013). However, linking objects can also serve to connect people with a collective sense of loss of identity.

During a time of political turmoil and shared humiliation, these little painted stones had become the shared reservoirs in which Palestinians in Gaza had, symbolically, externalized of their ethnic identity. With these reservoirs tucked away securely and secretly in their pockets, away from the sight of Israelis, their sense of ethnic identity was placed in safekeeping. For example, when they would see an Israeli soldier, they would put a hand in their pockets and touch their stones.

Vamık Volkan had another experience that taught him Palestinians' grasping on their large- group identity and how they perceived Israelis. In 1990 Vamık Volkan visited Beit Atfal al-Sumud, an orphanage in a residential district of Tunis that housed 57 Palestinian children who had lost their parents due to the Middle East conflict. He stayed in Tunis for nine days, interviewing and observing many orphans from age seven to eighteen and their Palestinian care takers. He especially noticed the behavior patterns of 5 children who had been rescued as infants from the massacres at Sabra and Shatila.

On September 15, 1982, Israeli defense forces encircled two adjacent Palestinian refugee camps, Sabra and Shatila, in West Beirut. In the late afternoon of the following day, the Lebanese Christian Phalangist militia, allies of the Israelis, attacked the camps, indiscriminately killing civilians trapped in the cramped streets. Because of this tragedy, another 1,300 Palestinian children became orphaned. Five children in Tunis had been rescued as infants from the massacres at Sabra and Shatila. Since these five children at the orphanage had never been identified, each was given an individual first name and all were called by the surname "Arafat."

Yasser Arafat was born in 1929 to Palestinian parents in Cairo Egypt. In 1967 he joined the Palestinian Liberation Organization (PLO) and in 1969 was elected chair of the Palestinian National Council. From 1994 to 2004 he would be the chairman of the Palestinian Liberation Organization (PLO). When Vamık Volkan went to Tunis in 1990 Yasser Arafat was living in Tunis.

In 1985 Israeli Air Force bombed PLO headquarters in Tunis. Because of this Arafat was staying and sleeping in different locations in Tunis to escape from other Israeli attempts to kill him. Palestinians in Tunis had a belief that Israel was sending killers by sea all the way from Israel to Tunisia and in order to assassinate important Palestinians who were at that time also were hiding in Tunisia. Arafat came to the orphanage often enough to know each child or youngster by name. The orphans called each other "brother" or "sister"; in only a few cases this reflected biological fact.

With the aid of an interpreter Vamık Volkan spoke each of five children from the Sabra and Shatila on by one. All of them then became "abnormal"—one hallucinated, and another one literally destroyed the interview room. As soon as they were placed together again, as a "team," they appeared to be "normal" once more. Vamık Volkan concluded that they must have difficulties in their sense of personal identity; on the other hand, they appeared "normal" when they were a team of "Arafats." This observation taught him a lot about replacing, to one extent or another, a person's individual identity with a "team" or large-group identity associated with ethnicity, nationality, religion, or ideology. Although the phenomenon was most pronounced in these five children, he easily noticed variations of this in the other 52 orphans, as when the orphans called one another "brother" or "sister" even when biologically most of them were unrelated. Most of these orphans also shared a fantasy of becoming pilots as adults in order to fly over Israel and bomb it.

Yasser Arafat invited Vamık Volkan for lunch when Volkan was in Tunis. Yasser Arafat's staff members and other guests sat around a long dining table. Vamık Volkan was asked to sit in front of Arafat. On the table, between Arafat and Vamık Volkan there was a roasted chicken. Arafat took a piece of this chicken and put it on his plate. When Vamık Volkan raised his left hand to take a piece of the chicken Arafat hit Vamık Volkan's hand and told him that, in Palestinian culture, using the other hand to pick up a piece chicken was necessary. Arafat was exhibiting how he was attached to his large-group identity. Not using the left hand to eat is very common in many Muslim cultures and in India among the Hindus.

October 7, 2023

Hamas' horrible surprise terrorist attack on Israel on October 7th, 2023, reminded many Israelis of the 50th anniversary of the Yom Kippur War which also took place in October. The method and ideology of Hamas also recalled the atrocities of the Holocaust. The memory of an undigested historical event became connected with a new trauma. Before the October 7th attack there were about 60000 Gaza workers every day in Israel and Israel supplied electricity and many other basic necessities to the Palestinians in Gaza. Although there were indications that Hamas was planning an attack, the Israelis were unprepared, shocked and surprised at the attack. This shock increased feelings of the Palestinians as an existential threat. Israelis could not understand why Hamas wanted to kill babies and take dozens of people including children as hostages.

We should also recall that before the October 7th Hamas terrorist attack a very noticeable division in Israel exited between those who were followers of Benjamin Netanyahu (who has been serving as the prime minister of Israel since December 2022, having previously held the office from 1996 to 1999 and again from 2009 to 2021) and other Israelis who were not supporters of the prime minister.

Hamas named the horrible October 7th 2023 attack as *Al-Aqsa Storm*. The Al-Aqsa Mosque is considered as the third holiest by the Muslims after Mecca and Medina. It was first built between 634 and 644. For several decades, Israel has been excavating under the Al-Aqsa Mosque for searching for Solomon's Temple. The Al Aqsa Mosque, the Temple Mount, the holiest site for Jews, and the Church of the Holy Sepulcher is holy for Christians are all located next to, or on top of, each other. The site has been a frequent flashpoint for violence. All three of these holy places stand for most important symbols of religious large-group identity. They also reflect the idea of entitlement ideology which we discussed previously. This location also serves as a reminder of a series of violent confrontations between Palestinians and Israelis. For example, in 2021, tensions around Al-Aqsa were followed by an 11-day Israeli assault on the Gaza Strip.

On April 5, 2023, after the evening Ramadan prayer, Palestinians barricaded themselves into Al-Aqsa Mosque. There was a belief that Jews planned to sacrifice a goat at the site (which is forbidden by Israeli law). In response, Israeli police raided the mosque in riot gear, injuring 50 people and arresting at least 400. It is reported that 12 Palestinians were injured, including three people who were transferred to the hospital and that Israeli forces banned its medics from reaching Al-Aqsa. At the end three Palestinians were transferred to the hospital. On July 27, 2023, Israel's far-right national security minister Itamar Ben-Gvir led a group of more than one thousand ultranationalist settlers to the Al-Aqsa compound, his third such entrance to the site this year.

Following the horrific Hamas attack Israel began bombing Gaza. On October 28th Israel launched the "second phase" with ground operation. We began writing this book as thousands of civilians, including babies and children, are dying. Homes, religious locations, hospitals are ruined. Some Israeli individuals are still hostages in Gaza. We decided to listen news in English not only from televisions in the United States, but also from other countries, from Israel, some Arab countries, Britain, Germany, France, Türkiye, and China. We are observing several differing explanations for the current tragedies in Israel and Gaza. Besides large-group identity, we are constantly reminded of the other psychological concepts which we described above, entitlement ideology, large-group mourning, large-group regression, projection, projective identification, splitting, time collapse, becoming like the enemy (identification with the aggressor), and purification.

We have never met the present-day Israel Prime Minister Benjamin Netanyahu and have not studied his personal background in any depth. We also do not know the life stories of Ismail Haniyeh who was assassinated in Tehran July 31, 2024, and who was widely considered Hamas' overall leader. Likewise, we do not know the life history of Yahya Sinwar, who was the leader of the Hamas movement within the Gaza Strip before being killed by an Israeli military operation on October 16, 2024. Therefore, we cannot describe how the personality characteristics of these individuals might played a significant role in the present-day situation in the Hamas-Gaza war. This is an important topic for future research.

Large-group identity investment in the Israel-Hamas war includes not only in ethnicity but also religion. Above we also referred to Ukraine's gaining a religious "freedom" from Russia as a visible factor of the conflict between the two countries. In the next chapter we will focus on the psychodynamics of religion.

14

Religion and Aggression

According to Sigmund Freud, an individual's religious commitment reflects unresolved psychological issues from childhood. The frightening feelings of helplessness during childhood create a desire for protection, which can be fulfilled through parental love. Freud concluded that the duration of one's sense of helplessness throughout life makes it necessary to seek an all-powerful father figure, an image of God, to ease the feeling of vulnerability. Therefore, religion is connected to a shared illusion (Freud 1913, 1927, 1939). In 1901, Freud even reinterpreted the well-known text of Genesis, "God created man in His own image," as "Man created God in his" (Freud 1901, p. 19). He also noticed a striking similarity between obsessive acts and religious practices, leading him to view obsessional neurosis as a distorted personal religion and religion as a form of universal obsessional neurosis.

For a long time after Freud, very few psychoanalysts explored the topic of religion or critically examined Freud's assumptions in depth. There was even a "hostility" between religion and psychoanalysis, causing most psychoanalysts to overlook the subject. However, Donald Winnicott's groundbreaking work in 1953 on "transitional objects" and "transitional phenomena" significantly expanded psychoanalytic theory by incorporating religious beliefs and emotions. In the early stages of a child's life, they choose an object to hold, and carry based on its texture, smell, and mobility. Typically, the child selects something soft like a teddy bear, which gives them a sense of control. In some cases, even the child's own hair can become a transitional object. A transitional phenomenon, such as a nursery rhyme, is an inanimate object that serves as a transitional object.

During the initial years of a child's life, the transitional object or phenomenon emerges as the very first item that distinctly represents something that is not a part of the child's own self. This initial image of "not-me" is indeed a reflection of a tangible object that exists in the tangible world surrounding the child. However, it is important to note that the transitional object is not purely "not-me" because it also serves as a substitute for the child's mother (or any other person providing mothering care). At this stage of psychological development, the child's mind hasn't fully comprehended the mother as a separate individual with her own autonomy. Instead, the toddler perceives the mother as someone under his or her absolute control.

This is precisely why engaging in play with a teddy bear or repeatedly listening to a specific melody can bring comfort and soothing to the child. Conversely, it is also why there are instances when the child can discharge aggression towards the toy (or distort the soothing melody) without any fear of retaliation from the object. The transitional object, much like the actual mother, responds to the child's need for comfort and does not abandon the child when he or she rejects it. It remains present and available, providing a sense of security and reassurance.

If one were to replace the blanket that serves as a transitional object with a different one, the child would not respond to the second blanket in the same way. The attachment and significance lie more in the transitional object itself, rather than the actual mother. The toddler firmly clings to the blanket, rubbing it, for example, to aid in falling asleep.

During his clinical practice, Vamık Volkan encountered instances where mothers displayed jealousy towards their infants' transitional objects. This highlights the importance and significance of these objects in a child's life.

Through countless repeated interactions with the teddy bear or the melody, the child gradually begins to develop an understanding of the external world. As these objects are not an inherent part of the child, they serve as a symbol of the reality that exists beyond the child's internal world. It represents the realm of "not-me" that the child discovers, creates, and ultimately relies upon. However, it is important to note that the child's perception of this reality is not grounded solely in logical thinking, as it combines elements of both reality and illusion.

Winnicott observed that the infant's experiences, throughout their life, remain deeply imprinted in the realm of intense emotions that are typically associated with the arts, religion, imaginative living, and creative scientific endeavors. The infant's experience, Winnicott observed, throughout his or her life, "is retained in the intense experiencing that belongs to the arts and to religion and to imaginative living, and to creative scientific work (Winnicott, 1953, p. 16).

In the 1960s, a number of influential figures in the field of classical psychoanalysis began to express doubts regarding some of Freud's assumptions, particularly those pertaining to religion. One such individual was Robert Waelder, who concluded that Freud's ideas "may well be correct for the father religions, the latecomers in religious history, but [they] do not offer a complete elucidation of this psychogenesis" (Waelder, 1960, p.59) In 1978 another well-known psychoanalyst, Hans Leowald, admitted that "under the weight of [Freud's] authority religion in psychoanalysis has been largely considered a sign of man's mental immaturity," an illusion "to be given up as we are able to overcome our childish needs for all-powerful parents" (Leowald 1978, p. 57). Leowald associated religion with the primary process, better known in lay terminology as illogical thinking. But he also stated that the secondary process—logical thinking in lay terminology—is nourished by the former. Leowald helped to open a way for psychoanalysts to create space to critically examine the topic of religion, challenge Freud's assumptions, and offer their own perspectives.

Among those who contributed to this conversation was William W. Meissner, a Jesuit priest and member of the Society of Jesus, who was not only a psychoanalyst but also a member of the American Psychoanalytic Association. Starting in the 1960s, Meissner dedicated numerous papers and books to exploring the relationship between psychoanalysis and religion. Eventually, he returned to the concepts introduced by Winnicott concluding: "If beliefs and belief systems facilitate psychic growth and contribute to the maintenance of psychic health and mature responsible living, they are not pathological—any more than the illusory play in the transitional space between mother and child is pathological. Or for that matter, any more than Freud's own cultural creation—psychoanalysis" (Meissner, 1990, p.114)

Furthermore, Meissner argued that individuals, in general, would find it challenging to maintain a commitment to an abstract religious belief without the presence of concrete symbols. He stated "Communion itself, the act of consuming the sacred host, is a form of concrete symbolic action" (Meissner, 1990, p. 107). Meissner reminded us that just as a transitional object can degenerate into a (pathological) fetish, "transitional religious experience can be distorted into less authentic, relatively fetishistic directions that tend to contaminate and distort the more profoundly meaningful aspects of the religious experience (Meissner 1990, p. 107). However, Meissner refrained from further exploring the connection between religion and violence. His focus was on promoting peace between religion and psychoanalysis. Psychoanalysts like Phyllis Greenacre (1970), Arnold Modell (1970), and Vamık Volkan (1976, 2013a) provided an increasingly detailed exploration of the role of transitional objects and transitional phenomena, allowing us to gain a clearer understanding of the progressive, healing, and creative aspects of religious beliefs and emotions, as well as their regressive, destructive, and limiting qualities.

J. Anderson Thomson combined information from psychoanalysis, neurosciences, cognitive science, and evolutionary psychology in an attempt to answer the question: Why do we believe in gods? He concluded: "Religion may offer comfort in a harsh world; it may foster community; it may incite conflict. In short, it may have its uses—for good and for evil. But it was created by human beings, and this will be a better world if we cease confusing it with fact" (Thomson with C. Aukofer, 2011, p. 116). Our world is a very tiny spot in the universe. On December 6, 2023,

Kelsey Johnson, Professor of Astronomy gave a lecture, "*What Caused the Big Bang*," at the University of Virginia. She reminded the listeners that still we do not know how our universe started. She said that there are some theories and added that, since she herself is a mother, she liked the theory of another universe giving birth to our universe. While listening to Professor Johnson Vamık Volkan once more thought of the human beings' need to have religious beliefs, including having a "God."

We should also need to keep in mind that religion, a mixture of illusion and reality, becomes crystallized in peoples' minds as "psychic reality" and becomes intertwined with large-group identity—or a subgroup identity—often mixed with a sense of nationalism or ethnicity and functions in a way similar to how a very special chosen glory or chosen trauma function. The "normal" range of religious beliefs and religious involvements, like the "normal" range of psychological health, is usually socially determined. The more that regression occurs in large groups, the more members of those groups will hold on to their religion. We are aware that even as scientific knowledge increased, shared and socially sanctioned "magical" beliefs did not diminish. As the president of Czech Republic Vaclav Havel stated in a speech: "By day we work with statistics; in the evening we consult astrologers" (1994). Many scientists as adults maintain their religious faiths. Maybe a more reachable wish is to feel freer to explore openly why and how "bad" and horrible things are done in the name of religion so that such research becomes routine, without the researcher experiencing hesitation or a sense of socially sanctioned opposition and rejection.

Archbishop Desmond Tutu, while attending Bill Clinton's Global Initiative meeting in September 2006, said: "Religion is like a knife. If you use it to slice bread, it is good. If you use it to slice off someone's hand, it is bad" (Duke, 2006). When studying international relations, we have no choice but to examine "bad" things done in the name of religion, since they are implicated throughout international relations and politics. Nonetheless, even though humiliating, maiming, or killing the "Other" is carried out in the name of gods, it is difficult to explore and write about the negative uses of religion; it is as if this makes one "anti-religious." Fear of this label may turn people away from joining in the needed investigation of how people use religion to sanction cutting off heads—a reality throughout human history.

15

Tunnels, Bunkers, Bubbles and Monuments[1]

After the Israel-Hamas war started we learned a great deal more about the underground tunnel network built by Hamas. In this chapter we will look at structures in the world can be seen as reflections of psychological states. Unlike other forms of human creation, architecture is rarely representational in that it does not directly report on a person's as well as a large group's psychology in the way that other creative activities might. But designed structures, while fixed in place and generally having some utilitarian value, can communicate something about the psychology of the people who were responsible for their creation and the time they were brought into being (Goodman, 1985). Protective structures, like underground tunnels, bunkers, walls, and other barriers especially seem to carry psychological meaning. This may be because these structures are intimately related to our survival and sometimes for our revenge. They can protect what is inside from external forces and prevent what is outside from breaching the interior.

This chapter will focus on the psychological meaning of protective bunker-like structures associated with individuals with narcissistic personality organization who have a leadership position.

1. Sections of this chapter are taken from a paper written by Kevin Volkan and published in the European Journal of Psychoanalysis (K. Volkan, 2021). We wish thank the journal for permission to use this material here.

Pathological Narcissism

The term narcissism and narcissistic are unfortunately overused and most often ill-defined. There are different levels or degrees of narcissism, and it is possible to find any number of works which attempt to tease out the severity of differing types of narcissistic disorders (V. D. Volkan, 2010).

Once more we wish to state that not all individuals and who have exaggerated narcissism and thus who take on leadership roles should be perceived as pathological. They may become reparative leaders and, help their followers to raise their own self-love, be proud of themselves, and feel good. We are referring to "reparative leaders" with exaggerated narcissism. Leaders like Kemal Atatürk, Nelson Mandela, Mathatma Ghandi, and Jimmy Carter could not have accomplished the reparative work they are so well known for without a high degree of narcissism and self-confidence.

Our discussion here will be focused on what has been called pathological narcissism, the narcissistic personality, or what in the official psychiatric Diagnostic and Statistical Manual (American Psychiatric Association, 2013) parlance is labeled as narcissistic personality disorder. Otto Kernberg gives a succinct and accurate description of this type of narcissism:

> *"These patients present an unusual degree of self-reference in their interactions with other people, a great need to be loved and admired by others, and a curious apparent contradiction between a very inflated concept of themselves and an inordinate need for tribute from others. Their emotional life is shallow. They experience little empathy for the feelings of others, they obtain very little enjoyment from life other than from the tributes they receive from others or from their own grandiose fantasies, and they feel restless and bored when external glitter wears off and no new sources feed their self-regard... In general, their relationships with other people are clearly exploitative and sometimes parasitic. It is as if they feel they have the right to control and possess others and to exploit them without guilt feelings – and behind a surface which very often is charming and*

engaging, one senses coldness and ruthlessness." (1975, pp. 227–228)

Earlier we described how a child integrates opposing object and self- and object images and becomes able to tolerate ambivalence. Failure to achieve this level of development occurs because the child experiences inconsistent interactions with caregivers that are tinged with aggression. The child then becomes fixated at a primitive level of unintegrated objects (as well as self-representation) using splitting to keep the good object representations from being overwhelmed by the bad/aggressive representations. This type of personality organization is typically found in people who have borderline personality disorder and results in severe diffusion of identity. Pathological narcissism has a similar etiology. It differs however, in that the inconsistent caregivers communicate to the child that there is something special about him or her.

The Grandiose Self

This sense of specialness then becomes the central focus for the formation of an identity that would otherwise be diffused. This identity, infused with a feeling of specialness and aggression, becomes the core of what is referred to as a *grandiose self* in the field of psychoanalysis. This grandiose self defends against losing coherence and reverting back to a fragmented identity associated with borderline personality organization. For individuals with pathological narcissism, this is experienced as a loss of identity, complete annihilation, or a sense of nonexistence.

During the 1960s and 1970s, American psychoanalytic circles directed their attention towards studying patients who exhibited extreme narcissistic traits. Heinz Kohut (1966, 1971, 1973) put forth a distinct developmental path from autoerotism to narcissism, leading to a more adaptive and culturally valuable form of narcissism. This process involved the child developing a grandiose and attention-seeking self-image, known as the grandiose self, as a result of deficiencies in maternal care. If these deficiencies were not too severe, the grandiose self could mature into a self with realistic aspirations and self-worth.

While Kohut was delving into his psychological understanding of narcissism, Otto Kernberg (1975, 1976) described individuals with narcissistic personality traits who relied on splitting of self and object images as their primary defense mechanism, following the work of Edith Jacobson (1964). Kernberg also employed the term "grandiose self" to describe the overtly dominant part of the self in these patients. Kernberg's concept of the grandiose self involved the merging of three elements: the *authentic self*, the *ideal self*, and the *idealized object*. The authentic self represented the child's perception of his or her own uniqueness, which was reinforced by early experiences with the mother and other influential figures fulfilling maternal roles. The ideal self was an image that compensated for the child's frustration in their environment, possessing qualities of power, beauty, or wealth. This ideal self-image also aided the child in navigating challenging emotions such as anger and envy. The idealized object referred to the imagined image of a mother figure who offered boundless support.

At the same time, the "needy" aspect of the child's self-representation, seeking psychological nurturing, merged with unacceptable aspects of the authentic self and devalued object images, but was separated from the grandiose self through splitting. In individuals with narcissistic personality traits, the exaggerated narcissistic part is openly displayed, while the "needy" part remains hidden. Throughout their development, individuals unconsciously attempt to suppress or externalize the needy part of their personality, as it represents a vulnerable dependence, anger, envy, or disappointment. Considering the various manifestations of exaggerated narcissism, it is important to remain open to some degree of flexibility when determining what can be classified as pathological and what cannot be classified as pathological.

German psychoanalyst Gabriele Ast and Vamık Volkan (1994) discovered that the narcissistic personality disorder can be viewed as a range, going from "successful" to "malignant." The successful people are capable of reaching a point in life where their excessive self-love and belief of being better than others is confirmed by the admiration of many individuals. These people might become popular icons, leaders of organizations, or influential political figures. They possess intelligence, unconscious desires of being a savior, and are able to direct their desires in a positive way. They are able to maintain a balance between their psychological need for adoration, entitlement, and greatness and the responses they receive from the external world. On the other side of the range, there are people who feel compelled to repeatedly achieve aggressive victories over others, as a means to feel special, powerful, entitled, and defensively all-powerful. Their narcissism is tainted with suspicious expectations. These people show destructive narcissistic behaviors.

The defensive grandiose self is unstable since the feeling of specialness at its core is ephemeral. It must be perpetually renewed, or the narcissistic person will begin to feel as if they will no longer exist. Hence the constant need for attention and admiration becomes the central feature of the narcissistic personality. The feeding of the grandiose self with admiration and attention to maintain its sense of specialness is a life-or-death issue for the person with pathological narcissism. The grandiose self also wards off feelings from dissociated unintegrated object representations that are experienced as devalued and inferior. These are tinged with aggression and often projected externally, accounting for the narcissist's need to devalue and disparage certain groups of people.

Malignant Narcissism

If the grandiose self is dominated by libido (pleasure seeking) then the narcissist will function better and will be less likely to manifest aggression toward others. If, on the other hand, the grandiose self is governed by aggression, this will be directed towards the devalued objects which are projected externally onto individuals or groups of people. This has been labeled as *malignant* narcissism. In this case the narcissistic person will experience admiration and attention from others by having them seek out the people in the external world who represent the devalued objects and destroy them (Kernberg, 1975, 2014; V. D. Volkan, 2010). Unfortunately, this happens literally. The malignant narcissist has many traits in common with the psychopath, including ambition, lack of conscience, lack of remorse, paranoia, and power seeking. It is often difficult to distinguish whether narcissism or psychopathy predominates, and a differential diagnosis can be difficult. However, the underlying motivation of the malignant narcissist is different than the psychopath. The malignant narcissist is motivated to maintain and defend the grandiose self and will experience annihilation if the grandiose self becomes starved of attention. The psychopath is motivated primarily by gaining what is desired and the gratification of emotional impulses.

Pathological narcissists often will literalize their intense need to defend the grandiose self. This manifests in dreams of bunkers, walls, barricades, and as mentioned, bubbles. Some pathological narcissists can maintain relatively good social functioning and control of impulses. This allows the pathological narcissist the ability to develop, in some cases, some real capacity, allowing him or her to realize admiration for "greatness." Pathological narcissists often appear to have the ability to tolerate anxiety. Unlike someone with healthy personality organization, the narcissist is able to tolerate anxiety by increasing their narcissistic fantasies and withdrawing into what Kernberg calls "splendid isolation" (Kernberg, 1975, p. 230).

This bunker mentality was described very well by the author Franz Kafka (1988/1924) in *The Burrow* (Der Bau) which was an unfinished story. In this story, an anthropomorphic mole spends his life burrowing a vast underground bunker-like labyrinth. The story was written six months before Kafka's death and the ending, which was destroyed, allegedly details a struggle with a beast who seeks to invade the burrow. Kafka's story presents many of the unconscious defensive dynamics of bunker mentality including a withdrawal into isolated stillness. As Kafka puts it:

> *"But the most beautiful thing about my burrow is the stillness. Of course, that is deceptive. At any moment it may be shattered and then all will be over. For the time being, however, the silence is still with me."* (p. 356)

This seeking of anxiety-reducing defensive isolation may be why so many narcissistic leaders create, and at times retreat to bunkers or cower behind walls. For some narcissists this defensive barrier may be symbolic, manifesting in dream imagery. Vamık Volkan (2010) outlines the successful analysis of a narcissistic woman who has recurring dreams of a daisy in a glass bubble:

> *"It was a protective barrier under which she could replace her grandiose part and through which she could watch outside of her private and solitary kingdom to constantly observe who or what was threatening and who or what supported her being number one"* (2011, p. 225).

Over the course of her analysis the bubble imagery becomes more permeable to the outside and eventually fades. This woman, while having narcissistic personality organization, was not a malignant narcissist. As might be expected, the malignant narcissist, who defends against more aggressive impulses would have more formidable defenses. This may manifest in the literal creation of bunkers and walls.

When the external world doesn't cooperate with the narcissist's need for inflation, he or she becomes anxious, and the need to defend the grandiose self becomes paramount. In the situation where there is withdrawal of attention and admiration and/or the lack of persecution of those representing the projected devalued objects, the narcissist feels anxiety at the prospect that they will no longer exist. This motivates a return to a safe defended place where the external world cannot impinge. The bunker, especially those underground, may be a symbolic representation of this. Unsurprisingly we find that some pathological narcissists have what can almost be called an obsession with bunkers. When the narcissist can no longer see themselves as being at home in the world, they instead regress to a state of "narcissism-as-home" (Durban, 2019). When the pathological grandiose self is threatened, retreating to a bunker is possibly an attempt to return to the safe, undifferentiated body of the mother where the outside world doesn't exist.

There are many examples of pathologically narcissistic leaders who have bunkers. From elaborate structures like Muammar Gaddafi's "Splendid Gate" compound with miles of reinforced concrete walls protected by machine gun posts every 50 meters, to Saddam Hussein's "spider's hole" (Glancey, 2011). North Korea could be considered a bunker country. Its ruler Kim Jong Un not only has his own huge personal bunker buried in a mountain but has also riddled his country with so many bunkers that the US and South Korea are building up their arsenal of bunker busting bombs in case of an outbreak of hostilities (Ji, 2016; McGrath, 2020). While these leaders and others with bunkers are deserving of psychoanalytic analysis, we will focus on two examples here; Adolf Hitler, and Enver Hoxha, who exemplify the relationship between pathological narcissism and bunker mentality.

Hitler and Bunkers Under the Nazis

Adolf Hitler presents an example of malignant narcissism. Several works touch on aspects how Hitler's narcissism manifested during the Nazi rule over Germany. Two works from a psychoanalytic viewpoint (Bromberg & Small, 1984; Waite, 1978) and one non-psychoanalytic work (Haycock, 2019) illuminate some of Hitler's narcissistic traits. Hitler had an intense need for admiration and attention and developed extraordinary oratorical skill which brought him attention from masses of people. Hitler also projected the devalued aspects of his personality externally onto various groups, primarily the Jewish people. Through the development of the Nazi party and eventually coming to power in Germany, Hitler demonstrated his malignant narcissism by having his followers express their admiration for him by annihilating those who were the receptables of the projection of the devalued aspects of his personality. The enthrallment of the German people and the Holocaust can be seen as direct manifestations of Hitler's malignant narcissism.

While Nazi Germany expanded and conquered it was concerned

with building what has been called "intentional monuments," which are structures that give an impression of achieving goals and mastering power (Hatton, 2000). In his memoir, Albert Speer describes many scenes where he and Hitler plan vast and grandiose buildings and cities (Speer, 1997). Building these grandiose structures can be a precursor to building of bunkers and other protective structures. As will be discussed below, the building of monuments is intimately related to bunker mentality. After reversals on the Russian front in 1943, the Nazis turn more and more to building bunkers. These bunkers were defensive, created by a regime moving towards collapse. As Mao Zedong observed:

> *"If Hitler is obliged to resort to strategic defense, fascism is over and done with; indeed, a state like the Third Reich has from its inception founded its military and political life on the offensive. Put a stop to the offensive, and its existence ends."* (Virilio, 1994, p. 28)

Mao's observations fit well with Hitler's psychology. The Nazi regime, following the *Führerprinzip*, built bunkers in enormous quantities. Bunkers were built primarily as air raid shelters, U-boat and V2 bunkers, littoral protection (Atlantic seawall), and bunker dwelling/command centers like Hitler's infamous Wolf's Lair as well as the Berlin *Führerbunker* (Baxter, 2016; Foedrowitz, 2002; G. Forty, Marriott, & S. Forty, 2016; Karl-Heinz, 1999; Philpott, 2016; Tzalmona, 2011).

Virilio (1994), writing shortly after the end of WWII, commenting on the Atlantic seawall bunkers built by the Nazis says, "The immensity of this project is what defies common sense; total war was revealed here in its mythic dimensions" (p. 12).

There were around 12,000 *Atlantikwall* bunkers, built by slave labor along the Western European coastline (Tzalmona, 2011). There are more examples. The German *Bundesanstalt fur Immobilienaufgaben*, until recently held 150 bunkers in Germany, which they have been trying to sell off. Most of these bunkers, plus 70 others, date from the Nazi era. Some of the bunkers were built on the site of former synagogues, and some above ground bunkers have been in continuous use until they were finally decommissioned in 2007 (Torry, 2013). The city of Hamburg had more than 600 bunkers which were primarily used as air raid shelters (Rueb, 2019).

Armaments Minister Albert Speer was successful in moving a great deal of war production and "wonder weapon" bases underground before the end of the war. These facilities, which were often huge concrete structures, can also be considered bunkers. One example was the huge bunker built to house v2 rockets and liquid oxygen rocket fuel; code named *Kraftwerk Nord West* (Northwest Power Plant). This bunker was situated in the north of France in order to launch V2 rockets to the south coast of England. Construction commenced between 1943-1944 and the bunker was intended to house 100 rockets. The walls were up to 23 feet thick while the concrete roof alone weighed 37000 tons and was 16 feet thick. Allied bombing disrupted its completion (Foedrowitz, 2002; Henshall, 1985; Huzel, 1962; Ordway & Sharpe, 2008; Zaloga, 2008).

One of the most mysterious projects attempted by Speer was called *Project Riese* (giant) which was massive underground complex with seven underground structures in Lower Silesia. Speer claimed that when completed the structures of *Project Riese* could house 20,000 people. The purpose of *Project Riese* is unknown. It is possible that it was designed to be the last holdout for Hitler and other top Nazis. It has also been speculated that it was a secret test site for anti-gravity wonder weapons and time machines. A persistent rumor is that there is Nazi train filled with gold still buried inside. We do know that Hitler was anxious for it to be completed because he turned the project over to a construction firm when he felt Speer's progress was too slow. Nevertheless, even with the addition of concentration camp slave labor, *Project Riese* was never completed (Halpern, 2016; Rosen, 2016).

Much has been written about the *Führerbunker*, where Hitler spent his last days. Historian Hugh Trevor-Roper was one of the first to visit the Hitler's bunker and write about it directly after the war (Trevor-Roper, 2013). It was initially assumed that Hitler had escaped from the bunker. But consistent with Hitler's psychology, there could be no escape. For Hitler, the bunker would be the place of last resort. Leaving the bunker would be like death to someone with Hitler's personality makeup.

In 2002, the Soviets opened their archives providing more details about Hitler's last days in the bunker. Using this information German writer Joachim Fest wrote another book about what it was like to be in the bunker with Hitler as the Nazi regime collapsed. Fest documents Hitler's delusional selfish state, his lashing out at loyal followers, and his shambling decline (Fest, 2005). This is bunker psychology at its purest and viewing the film Downfall (*Der Untergang* - Hirschbiegel, 2004), derived in large part from Fest's book, conveys something of the experience of closely watching a pathological narcissist like Hitler suffer a deadly collapse in a bunker.

Enver Hoxha's bunkers

Enver Hoxha who was the dictator of Albania from 1944 until his death in 1985 provides a good example of bunker mentality. The Hoxhaist government fortified Albania by building more than 750,000 bunkers (Albanian: *bunkerët*). Vamık Volkan visited Albania in the 1990s and witnessed

these bunkers in person. He witnessed vast numbers of pillbox-shaped bunkers of various sizes scattered across the landscape. These were constructed on Hoxha's orders following his break with the Soviets in 1961. Even though Hoxha was ostensibly a communist he fell out of favor with Moscow for remaining loyal to Stalinist ideas even as the Soviet Union moved away from Stalin's legacy. In 1968, the Soviets invaded Czechoslovakia giving Hoxha valid reasons to be wary of the Soviets, to the point of paranoia. Hoxha, according to archeologist Nancy Wilkie,

> *"... thought of himself as a modern Skanderbeg, the fifteenth-century Albanian hero who resisted the Ottoman Turks, winning 25 of the 28 battles he fought against them. That the past has played an important role in the formulation of the modern state of Albania is evident in the claim that Albanians are direct descendants of the ancient Illyrians who some scholars maintain developed their language and culture in the region during the first or second millennium B.C. The power of the past, especially the remote,*

> *prehistoric past, is perhaps stronger here than anywhere else.*" (1999, p. 1)

Hoxha harbored delusions of a nuclear attack or an imminent invasion by foreign adversaries, and he fantasized about leading his soldiers and followers to seek refuge in the bunkers where they would defend their land. By the time Vamık Volkan visited Albania, over a decade after Hoxha's demise, the bunkers remained empty and dilapidated, serving as symbols of the deceased leader's paranoia. The Albanian bunkerët were almost all made from poured concrete, making dismantling them extremely difficult. Therefore, even as Albania developed its villages and towns, the bunkers remained. Vamık Volkan writing in his book *Blind Trust* describes his encounter with the bunkers in Albania:

> "*Seeing them for the first time was eerie, especially as none of the many books, papers, and reports on Albania I had read in preparation had mentioned the bunkers. Further, the contrast with the countryside we were driving through was extreme. Hoxha and his people, we were told, had learned to build terraced hillsides from the Chinese, and such terraces were everywhere, creating a soothing atmosphere. But these huge, ugly concrete mushrooms spoiled that beauty. Imagine the face of a person with smooth skin, and then imagine that person developing a dermatological problem that leaves the skin full of unsightly bumps. Having lived with these pillboxes for so long, Albanians did not seem to notice their existence. And, realistically speaking, post-Hoxha Albanian governments did not have funds to destroy them. Yet, perversely, these bunkers had actually become symbols of Albanians' large-group identity. In the handful of stores that sold souvenirs in Tirana in early 1998—when we were there we saw no foreign tourists; all foreigners were there for some kind of political or other business—we saw little bunkers, made of marble or wood, for sale alongside the Albanian flags that show a two-headed black eagle image superimposed on a dark red background. In fact, Albanians were still carriers of a "bunker mentality" in early 1998.*" (Volkan 2004, p. 241)

As with Nazi-built bunkers, the Albanians are trying to find new uses for their bunkers and well as come to grips with their past bunker mentality. Only a few bunkers have been turned into homes because of their association with the Hoxha regime when lovers risked death by using the bunkers for trysts. At least one bunker has been turned into a restaurant and a play titled "Kolonel Bunker"a fictionalized account of the military officer who designed the bunkers has been performed (Pope, 1999).

Bunker-like structures do not confer psychological protection on their own; they need concurrent social structures as well. It is not surprising to find that bunker-like structures also contain followers who serve to insulate narcissistic leaders, forming a psychosocial barrier to a menacing outside world.

Monuments

Bunkers, like those found in Nazi Germany, and Albania have an important corollary in monuments. Joost Meerloo (1954) claims that monuments are motivated by the expression of aggression, oedipal guilt, and a delusion of being important forever. Monuments free a person from feelings of sorrow and guilt, and represent the fulfillment of unconscious wishes, especially to escape death. In this sense, they can be seen as part of bunker mentality which serves many of the same functions. Monuments can be seen as the inverse of bunkers. Simply put, the bunker is defensive, while the monument is aggressive.

Like the intentional monuments of Nazi Germany, monument building may be more likely when the narcissistic leader's power is expanding. Conversely, building bunkers may be more likely when the leader's power is on the wane. Bunker structures represent an internalized good object, they envelope and protect like a mother. The monument on the other hand, represents a good object that has been projected into a powerful (usually) phallic structure to endure for all time. The bunker protects the good inside, the monument asserts the good externally. For the narcissist the bunker provides an interior place to experience the adulation needed to fuel the grandiose self while it is defended against bad objects on the outside. The monument, usually composed of impregnable and hard stone or metal, exists in the external world, phallically aggressive and seemingly invulnerable. In the presence of the monument the feeding of the narcissistic self becomes a public ritual. The narcissist receives adulation *in vivo* in the bunker, while the monument stands in place of the narcissist and receives adulation *in situ* for eternity. Monuments may be cast in the likeness of the narcissistic leader or not.

Hitler, interestingly, did not like the idea of his likeness memorialized in large monuments (Oltermann, 2020). He instead preferred imposing public buildings and having things named after him. Of course, this distinction is not absolute. Hitler did permit small busts to made of his likeness and liked to distribute pictures of himself. Bunkers, and monuments both serve as a bulwark against the pathological narcissist's fear of annihilation, just in different ways. For Hitler, the impending destruction of Berlin and its monument structures may have attended his realization that there was no possible path to a Nazi victory.

Large-Group Mourning and Monuments

It is important to make a distinction between monuments that serve as a projection of a narcissistic leader's grandiose self and those which function as linking objects helping people to mourn. A leader creating a bust or a monument to him- or herself should be distinguished from busts and monuments erected because of a large group's wish to honor the memory of a leader or mourn a collective loss. In the United States, for example, there are many monuments of George Washington as well as schools, cities, a state, and streets are named after him. In Türkiye one notices busts and monuments of Kemal Atatürk, the founder of the Turkish Republic after the collapse of the Ottoman Empire. An example of a monument that serves as a linking object would be the Vietnam Memorial in Washington, DC, which contains the names of those soldiers who died in the Vietnam war. When we analyze large, traumatized groups, we can see that these groups, who have experienced substantial losses and feelings of powerlessness and embarrassment, display behaviors akin to those of perpetual mourners. The memorials that are created to commemorate a collective trauma and honor their deceased members, lost territories, and a loss of status, can function as shared artifacts that bring people together. As architect Jeffrey Karl Ochsner (1997) states: "We choose to erect grave markers and monuments to commemorate the lives of the dead; we usually do not intend to build linking objects, although objects we do make clearly can serve us in this way" (p. 166). As we mentioned earlier the linking object serves as the meeting point between the mental representation of a lost person or thing and the corresponding image in the mind of the adult mourner. Certain adults, whom we call "perennial mourners," develop these linking objects because of their complicated mourning. Examples of linking objects include personal items owned by the deceased for instance a watch, or a shirt that the person wore on a regular basis. Gifts that the deceased gave before dying or a battlefield letter also serve as linking objects. In recent years we have begun to see large numbers of memorial tattoos that commemorate lost loved ones. This may be due to the popularity of tattoo-themed television shows such as LA Ink (2007), Miami Ink, (2005), and Ink Master (2012) which have to some degree made tattoos more acceptable to mainstream society. Tattoos as linking objects have the added property of an attempt to incorporate the deceased person in a concrete way – "under the skin" so to speak. We could not find any works on tattoos as linking objects in the psychoanalytic literature though a tattoo in a case history presented by Simone Wiener (2001) could be understood as to function this way.

Vamık Volkan has commented on what he termed "last minute objects." These are things that were present when the mourner first learned of a death, or saw the deceased body, of someone they were close to. These objects are connected to the final moments when the deceased person was still thought of as alive. By investing in these linking objects, long-term mourners externalize the process of grief and mourning, placing it outside of themselves. They hold onto a persistent hope that the magic of the linking object will somehow bring the deceased back, while also maintaining the desire to fully complete the mourning process by letting go of the linking object. It is important to understand that these linking objects are densely packed symbols, carrying deep meaning that is intertwined with both conscious and unconscious emotions and connections that existed prior to the significant loss. It is crucial not to confuse them with transitional objects (as described by Winnicott 1953) or ordinary keepsakes.

Working closely with psychiatric patients who experienced perpetual mourning, Vamık Volkan viewed the existence of linking objects as a manifestation of mourners externalizing and "freezing" their grieving process. Eventually, however, he began to observe that when a perennial mourner possesses a linking object, it holds open the potential for their mourning to end. Among immigrants, refugees, and displaced individuals, there was a common trend of creating linking objects or phenomena (Volkan, 2006b, 2007a, b, 2014c). Some of these people become excessively preoccupied with these objects to the point where they had little energy left to devote to finding new ways of living. Yet, when immigrants, refugees, or those who have experienced trauma use a linking object in a creative manner, they establish a connection between the lost individuals, things, places, or culture and their efforts to mourn their losses in a mature way. The adaptive utilization of a linking object provides them with the time needed to confront their denial of what has been lost, accept the changes, and recognize the potential for new gains. Monuments as shared linking objects can play this adaptive role.

When a monument transforms into a shared connecting object, the functions assigned to it will differ based on the type of collective grief experienced by the group. Similar to an individual perennial mourner's connecting object, monument may serve as a shared connecting object linked to the desire to facilitate the mourning process of a large group and aid its members in accepting the reality of their losses. However, it is also associated with the desire to sustain mourning in the hopes of reclaiming what was lost, which can fuel feelings of vengeance. Both desires can coexist, with one being dominant for a particular monument while the other prevails for another. In certain cases, a monument functioning as a connecting object absorbs unresolved aspects of incomplete mourning, assisting the larger group in adapting to its present circumstances without reliving the impact of past trauma and its unsettling emotions.

For instance, the *Crying Father* monument was employed by South Ossetians not only to externalize the mourning process but also to stoke feelings of revenge. This monument was constructed as a tribute to the memory of South Ossetians who lost their lives during the Georgia–South Ossetia War in the early 1990s (V. D. Volkan, 2006a).

Bunkers, walls, and monuments can carry a deep psychological meaning. The symbolic protection of bunkers and walls, as well as the public display of the grandiose monuments (as opposed to linking object monuments) is important to the pathological, and especially, the malignant narcissistic leader, to preserve an identity that is built around a grandiose self. Anxiety over being overwhelmed by those who are symbolically identified with the leader's devalued objects can drive leaders with exaggerated narcissism to seek out the symbolic protection and public assertion of the good. This type of behavior was seen in the leader of Nazi Germany and the former dictator of Albania.

An emphasis on building bunkers, walls, and monuments may be a warning sign that a leader is exhibiting exaggerated narcissism. This can be understood in a few ways. Bunkers and protective barriers may initially be built to protect the general population as in the case of air raid shelters. However, over time these structures become more focused on protecting the narcissistic leader and as well as supporting his destructive fantasies. Monuments may originally serve to inspire people and connect them to a collective ideal, yet that ideal can be derailed into the worship of a leader who is seeking to nourish a grandiose narcissistic self. This was seen in Germany when the Nazis began to focus on *Führerbunkers* and V2 rocket sites instead of air raid shelters, and Hitler's elaborate plans for imposing public works, even while the country was facing defeat.

A propensity to build bunkers and other psychologically symbolic structures seems to be a hallmark of totalitarian or totalitarian-leaning regimes. It is also likely that many, if not all, totalitarian leaders suffer from some degree of pathological narcissism. Pathological narcissistic individuals do not suddenly become leaders. This process takes time during which the bunker psychology outlined here will be apparent in the narcissist's rhetoric. A potential leader's plans for bunkers, bunker-like structures, and grandiose monuments, as well as the devaluing and denigrating of specific groups of people, should be taken as early warning signs. Awareness of these warning signs could help prevent bringing pathological narcissists to power.

Conclusion

Despise a long history of attempts to introduce psychoanalysis into politics and diplomacy, including the efforts of Harold Lasswell (1930), many obstacles to collaboration still exist between psychoanalysts and those officially and non-officially involved in international peacemaking efforts. Since it was introduced by Ludwig von Rochau in 1853, the concept of *Realpolitik* in general has evolved to mean the rational evaluation and realistic assessment of options available to one's large group and its enemies without considering in-depth psychological processes. Realism dominated political thinking for the next century. During the Cold War years, Realpolitik gave birth to what became known, especially in the United States, as *Rational Actor* models of politics and diplomacy. According to these models, governments function like "rational" individuals. When the shortcomings of Rational Actor models were noticed in the late 1970s and early 1980s, some political scientists, decision makers, and unofficial peacemakers began to borrow concepts from cognitive psychology to explain "faulty" decision making (Volkan, et al., 1998). They did not, however, look to psychoanalysis for insights.

Edward Shapiro and A. Wesley Carr (2006) state that the attempt to understand society is a daunting prospect, and that it may be "a defense against the experience of despair about the world, a grandiose effort to manage the unmanageable" (p.256). We join them, however, in their suggestion that to make some efforts nonetheless is essential for societies' psychological well-being and even survival.

We are unable to argue with Sigmund Freud's basic pessimism about ridding the mankind of the menace of war. However, we do think that certain insights of applied psychoanalysis can be and should be utilized and be made public in understanding the conditions that lead to a war-like event and war itself. James Gilligan (2017) writes that psychoanalysis has a lot to offer regarding the understanding and prevention of human violence.

Psychoanalysis specializes in understanding irrational and self-defeating behaviors, providing a way to comprehend extreme forms of violence and terrorism. Psychoanalysis can apply clinical insights in the service of preventing violence on a large scale, akin to public health strategies for preventing disease outbreaks. Psychoanalysis offers a framework to explore the psychological foundations of individuals who engage in extreme forms of violence such as genocide, terrorism, and war, objectively examining the motivations behind violent actions. This is the case even when those perpetrating the violence don't exhibit typical signs of mental illness as individuals. Psychoanalytic thought can help us understand how modernity can erode traditional belief systems resulting psychological distress.

As we write this book Russian-Ukrainian and Israel Gaza wars continue. We do not think that diplomatic efforts from outside, such as UN and other countries closely involved in these wars will seriously focus on the psychological aspects of large-group aggression. However, when settlements are reached, there is the possibility of initiating psychoanalytically-informed long-lasting dialogues between influential representatives of opposing large groups. Psychodynamically-informed organizations, such as the International Dialogue Initiative, can be involved in conducting these dialogues.

In this book we studied shared aggression in human psychology. It is here to stay. But perhaps there is some hope. Robert Jastrow, internationally known space scientist and astronomer who died in 2008 gives us a wider perspective. In his book, *Until the Sun Dies,* he writes that the span of human existence on the earth thus far is infinitesimal in comparison to the billions of years that remain for the further evolution of intelligence on our planet. He acknowledges that human achievements have been great, "but the promise of his future is far greater; for, if we can trust our reading of history of life, the evolution of higher forms will continue and Homo sapiens, the Man of wisdom, will become the root stock out of which still more exalted beings must emerge, to surpass man's achievements as he has surpassed the achievements of his ancestors (Jastrow 1977, pp. 214-215).

Bibliography

Abbass, A. A., Kisely, S. R., Town, J. M., Leichsenring, F., Driessen, E., Maat, S. D., Gerber, A., Dekker, J., Rabung, S., Rusalovska, S., & Crowe, E. (2014). Short-term psychodynamic psychotherapies for common mental disorders. *Cochrane Database of Systematic Reviews, 7.*

Ainslie, R. C., & Solyom, A. E. (1986). The replacement of the fantasied oedipal child: A disruptive effect of sibling loss on the mother-infant relationship. *Psychoanalytic Psychology*, 3(3), 257–268.

Akhtar, S. (1992). *Broken Structures: Severe Personality Disorders and Their Treatment.* Northvale, NJ: Jason Aronson.

Akhtar, S. (1999). *Immigration and Identity: Turmoil, Treatment and Transformation.* London: Karnac.

Akhtar, S., Parens, H., Blum, H., Edelsohn, G., Fischer, R. M. S., Freeman, D. M. A., LaFarge, L., Moore, M., Stone, M., & Watson, C. (2009). *Lying, Cheating, and Carrying On: Developmental, Clinical, and Sociocultural Aspects of Dishonesty and Deceit.* Northvale, NJ: Jason Aronson.

Alam, H. A., and & Regan, H. (2023). UN mourns the deaths of more than 100 aid workers in Gaza, the highest number killed in any conflict in its history. November 14. *CNN.*

Alcaraz, R., Barreiro, A., Castillo, J. M., Escalante, F. M., Iglesias, J. M., Muñoz, M. C. N., Ortiz, R., Payno, M., Prieto, G., Ramírez, I., Saborío, N., Schiafino, F., Segura, F., Torrescano, P. M., Urquidi, F., & Ramsey, A. C. (1850). *The other side: Or, notes for the history of the war between Mexico and the United States.* Hoboken, NJ: John Wiley.

Alcaro, A., & Carta, S. (2019). The "instinct" of imagination. A neuro-ethological approach to the evolution of the reflective mind and its application to psychotherapy. *Frontiers in Human Neuroscience, 12.*

Alderdice, J. (2010). Off the couch and round the conference table. In: A. Lemma and M. Patrick (Eds.) *Contemporary Psychoanalytic Applications*, pp.15–32. London: Routledge.

Allcorn, S. (2022). Binaries: Psychodynamic insights in a world view split apart.

The Journal of Psychohistory, 50(1): 2–15.

Allen, S. A., Rich, J. D., Bux, R. C., Farbenblum, B., Berns, M., & Rubenstein, L. (2006). Deaths of detainees in the custody of US Forces in Iraq and Afghanistan from 2002 to 2005. *Medscape General Medicine, 8*(4): 46.

Alpatova, K., Israeli, N., Micheli, L. D., Palvarini, V., Solano,P., Vulkovic, I. S., Jahovich, S., Ogimoto, K., Vargiu, M., Zeitseva, K., Pankova, T., & Svetlana Yeresko, S. (Eds) (2024). *The Mind Under Siege: Notes and Testimonies About War*. Manziana, IT: Vecchierelli Editore.

Altman, N. (2006). Psychoanalysis and war. *Psychoanalysis, Culture & Society, 11*(3): 243–250.

Aly, A. M. S., Feldman, S., & Shikaki, K. (2022). *Arabs and Israelis: Conflict and Peacemaking in the Middle East*. New York: Bloomsbury Academic.

American Psychiatric Association. (2013). *Diagnostic and Statistical Manual of Mental Disorders* (5th ed.). American Psychiatric Publishing.

Amnesty International. (2023). Israeli attacks wipe out entire families in Gaza. October 20. https://www.amnesty.org/en/latest/news/2023/10/damning-evidence-of-war-crimes-as-israeli-attacks-wipe-out-entire-families-in-gaza/.

Andrade, V. M. (1976). Projective identification and death instinct. *Revista Brasileira de Psicanálise, 10*(4): 453–486.

Anti-Asian hate attacks are down in L.A. Why some are worried. (2023). July 17. *Los Angeles Times*. https://www.latimes.com/california/story/2023-07-17/anti-asian-hate-attacks-are-down-in-l-a-why-some-are-worried.

Apprey, M. (1998). Reinventing the self in the face of received transgenerational hatred in the African American community. *Mind and Human Interaction, 9*:30–37.

Apprey, M. (2023) *Transgenerational Haunting in Psychoanalysis: Toxic Errands*. W. F. Cornell. (Ed). New York: Routledge.

Archer, J. (2009). The nature of human aggression. *International Journal of Law and Psychiatry, 32*(4): 202–208.

Arlow, J. S. (1973). *Motivations for peace. In Psychological Basis of War*, H. Z. Winnick, R. Moses, & M. Ostow (Eds), pp.193-204. Jerusalem Academic Press.

Art, D. (2005). *The Politics of the Nazi Past in Germany and Austria*. Cambridge University Press.

Asma, S. T. (2017). *The Evolution of Imagination*. University of Chicago Press.

Athar, M. (2023). The syndrome of collective callous-unemotional traits: Reflections from large group dynamics. *International Journal of Applied Psychoanalytic Studies, 20*(1): 83–97.

Atkin, S. (1971). Notes on motivations for war. *Psychoanalytic Quarterly, 40*: 549-583.

Baker, P., & Glasser, S. (2005). *Kremlin Rising: Vladimir Putin's Russia and the End of Revolution*. New York, Scribner.

Bakó, T. & Zana, K. (2023). *Psychoanalysis, COVID and Mass Trauma: The Trauma of Reality*. New York: Routledge.

Barajas, F. P. (2012). *Curious Unions: Mexican American Workers and Resistance in Oxnard, California, 1898–1961*. University of Nebraska Press.

Barajas, F. P. (2021). *Mexican Americans with Moxie: A Transgenerational History of El Movimiento Chicano in Ventura County, California, 1945–1975*. University of Nebraska Press.

Barocas, H., & Barocas, C. (1979). Wounds of the fathers: The next generation of Holocaust victims. *International Review of Psychoanalysis, 6*: 331–340.

Baxter, I. (2016). *Wolf's Lair: Inside Hitler's East Prussian HQ*. Charleston, South Carolina: The History Press.

Beauvoir, S. (1971). *The Second Sex*. New York: Alfred A. Knopf.

Bejerot, N. (1974). The six day war in Stockholm. *New Scientist, 61*(886): 486–487.

Bekoff, M. (2016). Dogs Display Dominance: Deniers Offer No Credible Debate. July 7. *Psychology Today*.

Belton, C. (2020). *Putin's People: How the KGB Took Back Russia and Then Took on the West*. New York, Farrar, Straus and Giroux.

Benjamin, J. (1988). *The Bonds of Love*. New York: Pantheon.

Bernstein, A. (2001). A note on the passing of the latency period. *Modern Psychoanalysis, 26*: 293–287.

Bion, W. R. (1952). Group dynamics: A re-view. *International Journal of Psychoanalysis, 33*: 235–247.

Bion, W. R. (1961). *Experiences in Groups and Other Papers*. New York: Routledge.

Bird, J., & Clark, S. (1999). Racism, hatred, and discrimination through the lens of projective identification. *Psychoanalysis Culture and Society, 4*: 332–335.

Bjelić, D. (2010). Mad country, mad psychiatrists: Psychoanalysis and the Balkan genocide. In *Freud and Fundamentalism*, Gourgouris, S. (ed). New York: Fordham University Press.

Blair, R. J. R. (2001). Neurocognitive models of aggression, the antisocial personality disorders, and psychopathy. *Journal of Neurology, Neurosurgery & Psychiatry, 71*(6): 727–731.

Blechner, M. (2009). The role of prejudice in psychopathology and psychoanalytic history. *Contemporary Psychoanalysis, 45*: 239–251.

Bloom, P. (2010). *How Pleasure Works: The New Science of Why We Like What We Like*. New York: W. W. Norton.

Blos, P. (1962). *On Adolescence*. New York: Free Press.

Blos, P. (1967). The second individuation process of adolescence. *Psychoanalytic Study of the Child, 22*: 162–186.

Blum, H. (1985). Superego formation, adolescent transformation and the adult neurosis. *Journal of the American Psychoanalytic Association, 4*: 887-909.

Boesch, C., Crockford, C., Herbinger, I., Wittig, R., Moebius, Y., & Normand,

E. (2008). Intergroup conflicts among chimpanzees in Taï national park: Lethal violence and the female perspective. *American Journal of Primatology, 70*(6): 519–532.

Böhm, T. & Kaplan, S. (2011). *Revenge: On the Dynamics of a Frightening Urge and Its Taming*. London: Karnac.

Bolkvadze, N., Chachava, K., Ghvedashvili, G., Lange-Ionatamišvili, E., McMillan, J., Kalandarishvili, N., Keshelashvili, A., Kuprashvili, N., Sharashenidze, T., & Tsomaia, T. (2021). *Georgia's information environment through the lens of Russia's influence*. Riga, Latvia: NATO Strategic Communications Centre of Excellence. Retrieved from: https://Georgias-information-environment-through-the-lens-of-Russias-infulence.pdf (stratcomcoe.org). April 15.

Bollas, C. (2015). Psychoanalysis in the age of bewilderment: On the return of the oppressed. *International Journal of Psychoanalysis, 96*: 535–551.

Bombieri, G., Naves, J., Penteriani, V., Selva, N., Fernández-Gil, A., López-Bao, J. V., Ambarli, H., Bautista, C., Bespalova, T., Bobrov, V., Bolshakov, V., Bondarchuk, S., Camarra, J. J., Chiriac, S., Ciucci, P., Dutsov, A., Dykyy, I., Fedriani, J. M., García-Rodríguez, A., … Delgado, M. M. (2019). Brown bear attacks on humans: A worldwide perspective. Scientific Reports, 9(1), 8573. https://doi.org/10.1038/s41598-019-44341-w.

Bosworth, C. E. (2014). The Encyclopaedia Iranica, *AJAM, 7*: 700–701.

Bouchard, T. J. Jr. (2009). Authoritarianism, religiousness, and conservatism: Is "obedience to authority" the explanation for their clustering, universality and evolution? In *The Biological Evolution of Religious Mind and Behavior*, E. Voland & W. Schiefenhövel (Eds.). New York: Springer Science + Business Media.

Bowlby, J. (1988). *A Secure Base: Parent-Child Attachment and Healthy Human Development*. New York: Basic Books.

Boyer, L. B. (1986). One man's need to have enemies: A psychoanalytic perspective. *Journal of Psychoanalytic Anthropology, 9*: 101–120.

Brenner, I. (2002). Foreword. In: V. D. Volkan, G. Ast & W. Greer, *The Third Reich in the Unconscious: Transgenerational Transmission and its Consequences*, pp. xi–xvii. East Sussex, UK: Brunner-Routledge.

Brenner, I. (2014). *Dark Matters: Exploring the Realm of Psychic Devastation*. London: Karnac.

Brenner, I. (Ed.) (2019). *The Handbook of Psychoanalytic Holocaust Studies: International Perspectives.* New York: Routledge.

Brogan, J. (2021, August 13). Dogs live in a human-dominated world. And that's just fine with them. Washington Post. https://www.washingtonpost.com/science/2021/08/10/behavior-dogs-dominance/.

Bromberg, N., & Small, V. V. (1984). *Hitler's Psychopathology*. International Universities Press.

Brown, M. (2005). "Setting the conditions" for Abu Ghraib: The prison nation abroad. *American Quarterly, 57*(3): 973–997.

Browning, C. R. (1992). *Ordinary Men: Reserve Police Battalion 101 and the Final Solution in Poland*. New York: HarperCollins.

Burns, J. M. (1984). *The power to lead: The crisis of the American presidency*. New York: Simon and Schuster.

Byles, J. M. (2003). Psychoanalysis and war: The superego and projective identification. *Journal for the Psychoanalysis of Culture & Society, 8*(2): 208–213.

Byman, D. (2022). *Spreading Hate: The Global Rise of White Supremacist Terrorism*. Oxford University Press.

Byrd, W. M., & Clayton, L. A. (2001). Race, medicine, and health care in the United States: A historical survey. *Journal of the National Medical Association, 93*(3 Suppl): 11S-34S.

Cantor, C., & Price, J. (2007). Traumatic entrapment, appeasement and complex post-traumatic stress disorder: Evolutionary perspectives of hostage reactions, domestic abuse and the Stockholm syndrome. *Australian and New Zealand Journal of Psychiatry, 41*(5): 377–384.

Caplan, N. (2019). *The Israel-Palestine Conflict: Contested Histories*. Hoboken, NJ: Wiley-Blackwell.

Carhart-Harris, R. L., & Friston, K. J. (2010). The default-mode, ego-functions and free-energy: A neurobiological account of Freudian ideas. *Brain, 133*(4): 1265–1283.

Caron, B. (Director). (2006, January 4). *Derren Brown: The Heist* [Reality-TV]. Objective Productions.

Carotenuto, A. (Ed.). (1986). Tagebuch einer hemlichen Symmetrie: Sabina Spielrein zwischen Jung und Freud. Kore.

Casoni, D., & Brunet, L. (2007). The psychodynamics that lead to violence: Part 2: The case of "ordinary" people involved in mass violence. *Canadian Journal of Psychoanalysis, 15*: 261–280.

Castillo, E. (n.d.). California Indian History. – *California Native American Heritage Commission*. Retrieved January 19, 2024, from https://nahc.ca.gov/native-americans/california-indian-history/.

CBS News (2023). Israel kibbutz the scene of a Hamas "massacre," first responders say: "The depravity of it is haunting." October 11. https://www.cbsnews.com/news/israel-babies-killed-hamas-terror-attack-kibbutz-kfar-aza-first-responders-say/.

Çevik, S. B. (2023). Grandiose dreams, mega projects: Ottoman nostalgia in "new Turkey." *International Journal of Applied Psychoanalytic Studies*. 1–14.

Chalk, F. & Jonassohn, P. K. (1990). *The History and Sociology of Genocide: Analyses and Case Studies*. New Haven CT: Yale University Press.

Charles River Editors (2019). *The Internment of Japanese-Americans and German-Americans during World War II: The History and Legacy of the Federal Gov-*

ernment's Most Controversial Wartime Policy. Ann Arbor, MI: Charles River Editors.

Charny, I. (1994). *Towards a generic definition of genocide. In Genocide: Conceptual and Historical Dimensions*. Andreopoulos, G.J. (Ed). pp. 64-94. University of Pennsylvania Press.

Chasseguet-Smirgel, J. (1984). *The Ego Ideal*. New York: W. W. Norton.

Chasseguet-Smirgel, J. (1990). Reflections of a psychoanalyst upon the Nazi biocracy and genocide. *International Review of Psychoanalysis, 17*: 167–176.

Cheng, L., Lucchesi, S., Mundry, R., Samuni, L., Deschner, T. & Surbeck, M. (2021). Variation in aggression rates and urinary cortisol levels indicates intergroup competition in wild bonobos. *Hormones and Behavior, 128*: 104914.

Chinese Exclusion Act (1882). (2021, September 8). National Archives. https://www.archives.gov/milestone-documents/chinese-exclusion-act.

Clover, C. (2016). *Black Wind, White Snow: The Rise of Russia's New Nationalism*. New Haven: Yale University Press.

Cockerham, W. C., Hamby, B. W., & Oates, G. R. (2017). The Social determinants of chronic disease. *American Journal of Preventive Medicine, 52* (1 Suppl 1): S5–S12.

Cohen, D. (2012). *Escape of Sigmund Freud*. New York: Abrams Press.

Council on Foreign Relations. (n.d.). *Global Conflict Tracker*. Retrieved November 2, 2023, from https://www.cfr.org/global-conflict-tracker.

Covington, C. (2016). *Everyday Evils: A Psychoanalytic View of Evil and Morality*. New York: Routledge.

Crisis Group. (n.d.). *Crisis Group*. Retrieved November 2, 2023, from https://www.crisisgroup.org/.

Czárán, T., & Aanen, D. K. (2016). The early evolution of cooperation in humans on cheating, group identity and group size. *Behaviour, 153*(9–11): 1247–1266.

Davison, J., Pamuk, H., Siebold, S., & Pamuk, H. (2023). Israel releases images of slain children to rally support. October 13. *Reuters*. https://www.reuters.com/world/nato-ministers-shown-horrific-video-hamas-attack-2023-10-12/.

Daykin, J. B. (2006). "They themselves contribute to their misery by their sloth": The Justification of slavery in eighteenth-century French travel narratives. *European Legacy, 11*(6): 623–632.

deMause, L. (2006). The childhood origins of the Holocaust. *The Journal of Psychohistory, 33*(3): 204–222.

Deutsch, H. (1942) Some forms of emotional disturbance and their relationship to schizophrenia. *Psychoanalysis Quarterly, 11*: 301-321.

Diamond, J. (1992). *The Third Chimpanzee: The Evolution and Future of the Human Animal*. New York: HarperCollins.

Diamond, J. (2005). *Guns, Germs, and Steel: The Fates of Human Societies*. New York:

W. W. Norton & Company.

Dietrich, D., Fodor, G., Zucker, G., & Bruckner, D. (Eds.). (2009). Basics. In: Dietrich, D., Fodor, G., Zucker, G., Bruckner, D. (eds), *Simulating the Mind*, pp. 7–36. Hanover, PA: Springer.

Dikötter, F. (2010). *Mao's Great Famine: The History of China's Most Devastating Catastrophe, 1958-62*. London: Walker Books.

Dimkov, P. R. (2019). Large-scale brain networks and Freudian ego. *Psychological Thought, 12*(2).

Drummond-Clarke, R. C., Fryns, C., Stewart, F. A., & Piel, A. K. (2023). A case of intercommunity lethal aggression by chimpanzees in an open and dry landscape, Issa Valley, western Tanzania. *Primates, 64*(6): 599–608.

Duke, L. (2006). Rev'd up: Archbishop Desmond Tutu looks back, definitely not in anger. October 9. *Washington Post*, C1, C8.

Dumas, D., & Davies, C. (2023). British-Israeli survivor tells of horrific scenes after kibbutz attack. October 10. *The Guardian*.

Durban, J. (2019). Heimat, heimatlosigkeit und nirgendwosein in der frühen kindheit. *Psyche, 73*, 17–41.

DW Documentary (Director). (2022). Russia: A small town clings to its Soviet past. March 29. *DW Documentary*. https://www.youtube.com/watch?v=48DaLYiO-yk.

Eckel, M. (2019). Two Decades On, Smoldering Questions About the Russian President's Vault to Power. *Radio Free Europe / Radio Liberty*. https://www.rferl.org/a/putin-russia-president-1999-chechnya-apartment-bombings/30097551.html.

Eckstaedt, A. (1989). *Nationalsozialismus in der "zweiten Generation": Psyschoanalyse von Hörigkeitsverhältnissen*. Frankfurt: Suhrkamp.

Ehrenreich, B. (2017). *The Way to the Spring: Life and Death in Palestine*. New York: Penguin Books.

Elliott, M., Bishop, K. & Stokes, P. (2004). Societal PTSD? Historic shock in Northern Ireland. *Psychotherapy and Politics International, 2*: 1–16.

Elmalky, R., & Nasser, H. (2023). "Never seen such atrocities": Palestinian reporters recount war horrors. October 30. *Al Jazeera*. https://www.aljazeera.com/news/2023/10/30/never-seen-such-atrocities-palestinian-reporters-recount-war-horrors.

Elsass, P. (1997). *Treating Victims of Torture and Violence: Theoretical Cross-Cultural, and Clinical Implications*. New York: New York University Press.

Emde, R. (1991) Positive emotions for psychoanalytic theory: Surprises from infancy research and new directions. *Journal of the American Psychoanalytic Association (Supplement) 39*: 5–44.

Equal Justice Initiative. (2018). Banks Continue to Deny Home Loans to People of Color. February 19. *Equal Justice Initiative*. https://eji.org/news/banks-deny-home-loans-to-people-color/.

Erikson, E.H. (1950). *Childhood and Society*. New York: W. W. Norton.

Erikson, E. H. (1956). The problem of ego identity. *Journal of the American Psychoanalytic Association, 4*: 56–121.

Erikson, E. H. (1966). Ontogeny of ritualization. In *Psychoanalysis: A General Psychology*, ed. R. Loewenstein, pp. 601-621. New York: International Universities Press.

Erikson, E. H (1977). *Toys and Reasons: Stages of Ritualization of Experience*. New York: W. W. Norton.

Erlich, H. S. (2013). *The Couch in the Marketplace: Psychoanalysis and Social Reality*. London: Karnac.

Ettlin, M. (2003). Bion's legacy to median and large groups: In *Building on Bion: Branches - Contemporary developments and applications of Bion's contributions to theory and practice*. Lipgar, R. M., & Pines, M., (Ed) (pp. 29–69). London: Jessica Kingsley.

UN Women – Palestine Country Office (2024). Facts and estimates: Women and girls during the conflict in Palestine. n.d.. Retrieved September 1, 2024, from https://palestine.unwomen.org/en/what-we-do/peace-security-humanitarian-response/facts-and-figures/conflict-in-palestine.

Fadeyev, A. (2017). *Molodaya Gvardiya*. Moscow, RU: Azbuka.

Faimberg, H. (2005). *The Telescoping of Generations: Listening to the Narcissistic Links Between Generations*. United Kingdom: Routledge.

Falk, A. (1974). Border symbolism. *Psychoanalytic Quarterly, 43*: 650-660.

Federn, E. (1960). Some clinical remarks on the psychopathology of genocide. *Psychiatric Quarterly, 34*, 538–549.

Fest, J. (2005). *Inside Hitler's Bunker*. Toronto: Picador.

Fisher, K. A., & Stankowich, T. (2018). Antipredator strategies of striped skunks in response to cues of aerial and terrestrial predators. Animal Behaviour, 143, 25–34. https://doi.org/10.1016/j.anbehav.2018.06.023.

Foedrowitz, M. (2002). *Bunkerwelten—Luftschutzanlagen in Norddeutschland*. Ammersee, DE: Nebel Verlag GmbH.

Fornari, F. (1975). *The Psychoanalysis of War*. Bloomington, IN: Indiana University Press.

Forty, G., Marriott, L. & Forty, S (2016). *Hitler's Atlantic Wall: From Southern France to Northern Norway, Yesterday and Today.* Havertown PA: Casemate.

Foulkes, S. H. (1975). Problems of the large group from a group-analytic point of view. In L. Kreeger (Ed). *In The Large Group*. London, UK: Karnac.

Frankel, J. (2023, November 5). These numbers show the staggering toll of the Israel-Hamas war. AP News. https://apnews.com/article/israel-hamas-war-death-toll-numbers-injured-5c9dc40bec95a8408c83f3c2fb759da0.

Frederick, J. C. (2002). A blood test before marriage: "Limpieza de Sangre" in Spanish Louisiana. *Louisiana History: The Journal of the Louisiana Historical*

Association, 43(1): 75–85.

Freud, S. (1893) The Psychotherapy of Hysteria from Studies on Hysteria. *Standard Edition, 2*: 253-305.

Freud, S. (1901). Psychopathology of the everyday life. *Standard Edition, 6*. London: Hogarth Press.

Freud, S. (1911) Psycho-Analytic Notes on an Autobiographical Account of a Case of Paranoia (Dementia Paranoides). *Standard Edition, 12*: 1–82.

Freud, S. (1912) The Dynamics of Transference. *Standard Edition, 12*: 97–108

Freud, S. (1913). Totem and taboo. *Standard Edition, 13*: 1–165. London: Hogarth Press.

Freud, S. (1915). Thoughts For the Times on War and Death. *Standard Edition, 14*: 273–300. London: Hogarth.

Freud, S. (1919). 'A Child is Being Beaten' A Contribution to the Study of the Origin of Sexual Perversions. *Standard Edition, 17*: 175–204

Freud, S. (1921). Group Psychology and the Analysis of the Ego. *Standard Edition, 18*: 65–144. London: Hogarth.

Freud, S (1926). Inhibitions, symptoms, and anxiety. *Standard Edition, 20*: 77–174. London: Hogarth.

Freud, S. (1927). The future of an illusion. *Standard Edition, 21*: 5–56. London: Hogarth Press, 1961.

Freud, S. (1930). Civilization and its discontents. *Standard Edition, 21*: 59–145. London: Hogarth.

Freud, S. (1933). Why War? *Standard Edition, 22*: 197-215. London Hogarth.

Freud, S. (1939). Moses and monotheism, *Standard Edition, 23*: 1–137. London: Hogarth Press, 1964.

Fromm, M. G. (2012). *Lost in Transmission: Studies of Trauma Across Generations*. London: Karnac.

Fromm, M. G. (2022). *Traveling Through Time: How Trauma Plays Itself Out in Families, Organizations and Society*. London: Phoenix.

Frosh S. (2010). *Psychoanalysis Outside the Clinic: Interventions in Psychosocial Studies*. New York: Palgrave Macmillan.

Frosh, S. (2022). Mass psychology and psychosocial assemblies. *Group Analysis, 55*: 325–341.

Fuentes, A. (2020). The evolution of a human imagination. In A. Abraham (Ed.), *The Cambridge Handbook of the Imagination*. Cambridge University Press.

Gao, J., & Tomonaga, M. (2018). The body inversion effect in chimpanzees (Pan troglodytes). *PLoS ONE, 13*(10).

García, D. G. (2018). *Strategies of Segregation: Race, Residence, and the Struggle for Educational Equality*. Berkeley, CA: University of California Press.

Gaveriaux, L.-M. (2023, November 26). « Ils ont arrêté lorsqu'ils m'ont crue morte »: Le calvaire d'Esther, violée et mutilée par les terroristes du Hamas—Le Parisien. Le Parisien. https://www.leparisien.fr/international/israel/israel-le-calvaire-desther-violee-et-mutilee-par-les-terroristes-du-hamas-26-11-2023-MK5HBAQRRZHENBBFEFOI6NDVWI.php.

Genocide Watch. (n.d.). *Genocidewatch.Com.* Retrieved December 6, 2023, from https://www.genocidewatch.com/.

Gerasimov, S. (Director). (1948). *Molodaya Guardiya.* Kinostudiya imeni M. Gorkogo / International Historic Films, Inc.

Gerlach, M. T. S. Hooke, & S. Varvin. *Psychoanalysis in Asia: India, Japan, South Korea, Taiwan.* London: Karnac. Books. New York: Routledge.

Gilligan, J. (2017). Toward a psychoanalytic theory of violence, fundamentalism and terrorism. *International Forum of Psychoanalysis, 126*: 174–185.

Glancey, J. (2011). From Hitler to Gaddafi: Dictators and their bunkers. August 26. *The Guardian.*

Glass, J. M. (2008). Group phantasy: Its place in the psychology of genocide. *International Journal of Applied Psychoanalytic Studies, 5*: 211–221.

Glower, E. (1933). *War, Sadism, and Pacifism: Further Essays on Group Psychology and War.* London: Allen and Unwin.

Goldhagen, D. J. (1996). *Hitler's Willing Executioners: Ordinary Germans and the Holocaust.* New York: Knopf.

Goodman, N. (1985). How Buildings Mean. *Critical Inquiry, 11*(4): 642–653.

Gould, S. J. (2002). *The Structure of Evolutionary Theory.* New York: Belknap Press.

Gourgouris, S. (Ed.). *Freud and Fundamentalism: The Psychical Politics of Knowledge.* New York: Fordham University Press.

Graff, G. (2016). Post Civil War African American history: Brief periods of triumph, and then despair. *The Journal of Psychohistory, 43*(4): 247–261.

Green, M., & Solnit, A. J. (1964). Reactions to the threatened loss of a child: a vulnerable child syndrome. Pediatric management of the dying child, Part III. *Pediatrics*, 34, 58–66.

Greenacre, P. 1970. The transitional object and the fetish: With special reference to the role of illusion. *International Journal of Psycho-Analysis, 51*:447-456

Greenspan, S. (1989). *The Development of the Ego: Implications for Personality Theory, Psychopathology and Psychotherapeutic Process.* Madison, CT: International Universities Press.

Grene, M. (1971). Sartre and the Other. *Proceedings and Addresses of the American Philosophical Association, 45*, 22–41.

Grubrich-Simitis, I. (1979). Extremtraumatisierung als kumulatives Trauma. Psychoanalytische Studien über seelische Nachwirkungen der Konzentrationslagerhaft bei Überlebenden und ihren Kindern. *Psyche, 33*: 991–1023.

Gruenewald, M. M. (2005). *Looking Like the Enemy: My Story of Imprisonment in Japanese American Internment Camps (Illustrated edition).* Thousand Oaks, CA: New Sage Press.

Gutman, Y. (1998). Goldhagen: His critics and his contribution. *Yad-Vashem Stud-*

ies, 26, 329–364.

Gumilyov, l. (1990). *Ethnogenesis and the Biosphere*. Moscow: Progress Publishers.

Halpern, J. (2016). Searching for Nazi Gold. May 2. *The New Yorker*.

Hamburg, D. (2010). *Preventing Genocide – Practical Steps Toward Early Detection and Effective Action*. Boulder, CO: Paradigm Publishers.

Haney, C., Banks, C., & Zimbardo, P. (1973). A study of prisoners and guards in a simulated prison. *Naval Research Reviews, pp. 1–17*. Arlington, VA: Office of Naval Research.

Harari, Y. N. (2014). *Sapiens: A Brief History of Humankind*. Oxford, UK: Signal Books.

Hare, B., & Wrangham, R. W. (2017). Equal, similar, but different: Convergent bonobos and conserved chimpanzees. In M. N. Muller, R. W. Wrangham, & D. R. Pilbeam (Eds.), *Chimpanzees and Human Evolution*, pp. 142–173. New York: The Belknap Press.

Hare, B., Wobber, V., & Wrangham, R. (2012). The self-domestication hypothesis: Evolution of bonobo psychology is due to selection against aggression. *Animal Behaviour, 83*(3): 573–585.

Hatton, B. (2000). Strategic Architecture. *AA Files, 42*: 28–35.

Havel, V. (1994). Post-modernism. *Vital Speeches of the Day, 60* (20), 613.

Haycock, D. A. (2019). *Tyrannical Minds: Psychological Profiling, Narcissism, and Dictatorship*. New York: Pegasus Books.

Hegel, G. W. F. (1807). *Phänomenologie des Geistes*. Bamburg & Würzburg: Joseph Anton Goebhardt.

Heig, A. (2014). La limpieza de sangre bajo las reformas borbónicas y su impacto en el Caribe Neogranadino. *Boletín de historia y antigüedades, 101*(858): 143–181.

Henshall, P. (1985). *Hitler's Rocket Sites*. New York: St Martins Press.

Hersh, S. (2004). Chain of Command. May 9. *The New Yorker*.

Hill, R. P., & Kozup, J. C. (2007). Consumer experiences with predatory lending practices. *Journal of Consumer Affairs, 41*(1): 29–46.

Hinshelwood, R. (2006). Racism: Being ideal. *Psychoanalytic Psychotherapy, 20*: 84–96.

Hirschbiegel, O. (Director). (2004). *Der Untergang* [Biography, Drama, History, War]. Constantin Film, Sept. 16. Norddeutscher Rundfunk (NDR), Westdeutscher Rundfunk (WDR).

Hitchcock, W. (2004). *The Struggle for Europe. The Turbulent History of a Divided Continent 1945 to the Present*. Palatine, IL: Anchor

Hoggard, L. S., & Lutchman, M. T. (2023). Police-perpetrated racism and health in African American and black communities. Social and Personality Psychology Compass. October 31. *SIPRI*.

Hollander, N. (2010). *Uprooted Minds: Surviving the Political Terror in the Americas*. New York: Taylor & Francis.

Hoşgören-Alıcı, Y., Hasanlı, J., Özkarar, Gradwohl, G., Turnbull O. H., & Çakmak, E. (2023) Defense styles from the perspective of affective neuroscience. *Neuropsychoanalysis, 25*:2, 181–189.

Howell, E. F. (2014). Ferenczi's concept of identification with the aggressor: Understanding dissociative structure with interacting victim and abuser self-states. *The American Journal of Psychoanalysis, 74*(1), 48–59.

Human Rights Watch (2024). Gaza: Israelis Attacking Known Aid Worker Locations. May 14. https://www.hrw.org/news/2024/05/14/gaza-israelis-attacking-known-aid-worker-locations.

Husserl, E. (1962). *Ideas: General introduction to pure phenomenology*. New York: Collier Books.

Husserl, E. (1991). *Cartesian meditations: An introduction to phenomenology*. Dordrecht, NL: Kluwer Academic Publishers.

Huzel, D. (1962). *From Peenemündet to Canaveral.* Upper Saddle River, NJ: Prentice Hall.

Ihanus, J. (2022). Putin, Ukraine and fratricide. *Clio's Psyche, 23*(3): 300–311.

Ink Master. (2012, January 17). [Game-Show, Reality-TV]. Truly Original.

Jackson, M. (Director). (201). *Denial* [Biography, Drama]. Oct. 21. Denial Film, BBC Film, Cornerstone Films.

Jacobson, E. (1964). *The Self and the Object World.* New York: International Universities Press.

Jastrow, R. (1977). *Until the Sun Dies*. New York: Warner Books

Javakhishvili, J. D. (2023). Substitutive trauma: preparing grounds for the Russian attack on Ukraine. *Torture: Quarterly Journal on Rehabilitation of Torture Victims and Prevention of Torture. 33*(3): 94–108.

Ji, D. (2016). S. Korea to develop 200 "bunker buster" missiles with 500km range. December 14. *North Korea News*.

Johnson, D. D. P., & Toft, M. D. (2013). Grounds for War: The Evolution of Territorial Conflict. *International Security, 38*(3), 7–38.

Jones-Brown, D. D., Frazier, B. D., & Brooks, M. (Eds.). (2014). *African Americans and Criminal Justice: An Encyclopedia*. Westport, CT: Greenwood.

Jones, E. (1915). War and individual psychology. *In Essays in Applied Psychoanalysis, Vol. 1*. pp. 55-76. New York: International Psychoanalytic Press.

Jones, E. (1961). *The Life and Work of Sigmund Freud, Vol. 2*. New York: New York: Basic Books.

Jones, K. (2023). Journalist casualties in the Israel-Gaza war. December 17. *Committee to Protect Journalists*. https://cpj.org/2023/12/journalist-casualties-in-the-israel-gaza-conflict/.

Committee to Protect Journalists (2024). Journalist casualties in the Israel-Gaza war. August 30. https://cpj.org/2024/08/journalist-casualties-in-the-israel-gaza-conflict/.

Jung, C. G. (1963). *Memories, Dreams, Reflections*. New York: Pantheon.

Jurcević, S., & Urlić, I. (2002). Linking objects in the process of mourning for sons disappeared in war: Croatia 2001. *Croatian Medical Journal, 43*(2), 234–239.

Kafka, F. (1988). *The complete stories* (N. N. Glatzer, Trans.). New York: Schocken Books.

Kakar, S. (1996). *The Colors of Violence: Cultural Identities, Religion, and Conflict*. Chicago IL: University of Chicago Press.

Kalikow, T. J. (1983). Konrad Lorenz's Ethological Theory: Explanation and Ideology, 1938-1943. *Journal of the History of Biology, 16*(1), 39–73.

Karl-Heinz, S. (1999). *German U-Boat Bunkers*. Atglen, PA: Schiffer.

Kawai, N., & Matsuzawa, T. (2001). Reproductive memory processes in chimpanzees: Homologous approaches to research on human working memory. In T. Matsuzawa (Ed.), *Primate origins of human cognition and behavior*. New York: Springer-Verlag Publishing.

Keller, A. S. (2006). Torture in Abu Ghraib. *Perspectives in Biology and Medicine, 49*(4), 553–569.

Kernberg, O. F. (1975). *Borderline Conditions and Pathological Narcissism*. Northvale, NJ: Jason Aronson.

Kernberg, O. F. (1976). *Object Relations Theory and Clinical Psychoanalysis*. Northvale, NJ Jason Aronson.

Kernberg, O. F. (1984a). *Severe Personality Disorders: Psychotherapeutic Strategies*. Yale University Press.

Kernberg, O. F. (1984b). The couch at sea: Psychoanalytic studies of group and organizational leadership. International Journal of Group Psychotherapy, 34(1), 5–23.

Kernberg, O. F. (1986). *Internal World and External Reality: Object Relations Theory Applied*. Northvale, NJ: Jason Aronson.

Kernberg, O. F. (2003a). Sanctioned political violence: A psychoanalytic view – Part 1. *International Journal of Psychoanalysis, 84*: 683–698.

Kernberg, O. F. (2003b). Sanctioned political violence: A psychoanalytic view – Part 2. *International Journal of Psychoanalysis, 84*: 953–968.

Kernberg, O. F. (2014). An overview of the treatment of severe narcissistic pathology. The *International Journal of Psychoanalysis, 95*(5), 865–888.

Kernberg, O. F. (2022a). Discussion of the comments on my paper "Some implications of new developments in neurobiology for psychoanalytic object relations theory." *Neuropsychoanalysis, 24*(2), 127–132.

Kernberg, O. F. (2022b). Some implications of new developments in neurobiology for psychoanalytic object relations theory. *Neuropsychoanalysis, 24*(1), 3–12.

Kestenberg, J. S. 1982. A psychological assessment based on analysis of a survivor's child. In: M. S. Bergman and M. E. Jucovy (Eds.), *Generations of the Holocaust* (pp.158–177). New York: Columbia University Press.

Keyes, L., Small, E., & Nikolova, S. (2020). The complex relationship between colorism and poor health outcomes with African Americans: A systematic review. Analyses of Social Issues and *Public Policy, 20*(1), 676–697.

Klein, M. (1929) Personification in the Play of Children. *International Journal of Psychoanalysis, 10*: 193-204.

Klinkby, I. M. I., Hastrup, L. H., Bo, S., Storebø, O. J., Simonsen, E., & Kongerslev, M. T. (2023). Prevalence and incidence of personality disorders among children and adolescents in Danish mental health services: A nationwide register study. *European Child & Adolescent Psychiatry.* 10.1007/s00787-023-02274-w. Advance online publication.

Knapton, S. (201). Blue Planet II: Giant cannibalistic squid filmed hunting in packs for first time. November 3. *The Telegraph.*

Knipp, K. (2023, Nov 1). Hamas: Who are the Qassam Brigades? November 1. *DW.com.* https://www.dw.com/en/hamas-who-are-the-qassam-brigades/a-67276661.

Koenigsberg, R. (1999). Awakening from the nightmare of history: Psychoanalytic interpretation of war and genocide. *Journal for the Psychoanalysis of Culture & Society, 4*(2), 228–237.

Koenigsberg, R. A. (2009). *Nations Have the Right to Kill: Hitler, the Holocaust, and War.* New York: Library of Social Science.

Koenigsberg, R. A. (n.d.). *The Soldier as Sacrificial Victim.* Retrieved November 8, 2023, from https://www.libraryofsocialscience.com/essays/koenigsberg-the-soldier/index.html.

Kogan, I. (1995). *The Cry of Mute Children: A Psychoanalytic Perspective of the Second Generation of the Holocaust.* United Kingdom: Free Association Books.

Kohut, H (1966). Forms and transformations of narcissism. *Journal of the American Psychoanalytic Association,* 14: 243–272.

Kohut, H. (1971). *The Analysis of the Self: A Systematic Approach to the Psychoanalytic Treatment of Narcissistic Personality Organization.* New York: International Universities Press.

Kohut, H. (1973) Psychoanalysis in a Troubled World. *Annual of Psychoanalysis* 1, 3–25.

Kohut, H. (1973). Thoughts on narcissism and narcissistic rage. *The Psychoanalytic Study of the Child,* 27: 360–400. New York: Quadrangle.

Krämer, G. (2011). *A History of Palestine: From the Ottoman Conquest to the Founding of the State of Israel* (G. Harman, Trans.). Princeton, NJ: Princeton University Press.

Kret, M. E., Muramatsu, A., & Matsuzawa, T. (2018). Emotion processing across and within species: A comparison between humans (Homo sapiens) and chimpanzees (Pan troglodytes). *Journal of Comparative Psychology, 132*(4), 395–409.

Kudors, A. (2010). Russian World: Russia's soft power approach to compatriots' policy. Russian Analytical Digest, 81(10): 2–4.

Kunkle, S. (1999). The Ugly Jouissance of Genocide. *Psychoanalysis Culture and Society, 4*(1), 119–133.

Kurczap-Redlich, K. (2016). *Wowa, Wolodia, Wladimir. Tajemnice Rosji Putina.* Warszawa, PL: W.A.B.

Kuwert, P., & Freyberger, H. J. (2007). The unspoken secret: Sexual violence in World War II. *International Psychogeriatrics, 19*(4), 782–784.

LA Ink. (2007, August 7). [Documentary, Reality-TV]. Truly Original.

Landis, J. (Director). (1983). *Trading Places.* Paramount Pictures, Cinema Group Ventures.

Lansky, M. R. (2008). Beobachtungen zur dynamik der einschüchterung: Spaltung und projektive identifizierung als abwehrmanöver gegen scham. *Psyche: Zeitschrift Für Psychoanalyse Und Ihre Anwendungen, 62*(9–10), 929–961.

Laqueur, W. (2003). *A History of Zionism: From the French Revolution to the Establishment of the State of Israel.* New York: Knopf Doubleday.

Lasswell, H. D. (1930). *Psychopathology and Politics.* Chicago: University of Chicago Press.

Laub, D., & Auerhahn, N. C. (1993). Knowing and not knowing massive psychic trauma: Forms of traumatic memory. *The International Journal of Psychoanalysis, 74*(2), 287–302.

Lauro Grotto, R., Guazzini, A., & Bagnoli, F. (2014). Metastable structures and size effects in small group dynamics. *Frontiers in Psychology, 5.* https://doi.org/10.3389/fpsyg.2014.00699.

Lavalley, R., & Johnson, K. R. (2022). Occupation, injustice, and anti-Black racism in the United States of America. *Journal of Occupational Science, 29*(4): 487–499.

Lee, E. (2003). *At America's Gates: Chinese Immigration during the Exclusion Era, 1882–1943.* Chapel Hill, NC: The University of North Carolina Press.

Legg, C., Sherick, I. The replacement child—A developmental tragedy: Some preliminary comments. *Child Psychiatry & Human Development*, 7, 113–126.

Lehtonen, J. (2003). The dream between neuroscience and psychoanalysis: Has feeding an infant impact on brain function and the capacity to create dream images in infants? *Psychoanalysis in Europe, 57*: 175–182.

Leowald, H. W. (1978). *Psychoanalysis and the History of the Individual.* New Haven CT: Yale University Press.

Lew-Williams, B. (2018). *The Chinese Must Go: Violence, Exclusion, and the Making of the Alien in America.* Cambridge MA: Harvard University Press.

Lewontin, R. C. (1979). The spandrels of San Marco and the panglossian paradigm: A critique of the adaptationist programme. *Proceedings of the Royal Society of London, B*(205): 581–598.

Lipstadt, D. E. (2005). *History on Trial: My Day in Court with David Irving.* New York: Ecco.

Loewenberg, P. (1991). Uses of anxiety. *Partisan Review, 3*:514–525.

Lorenz, K. (1966). *On Aggression*. Boston, MA: Mariner Books.

Maariv. (2023). Israeli hostage recalls horrors of Hamas's sexual assaults. *The Jerusalem Post*. https://www.jpost.com/israel-hamas-war/article-777622.

Mack, J. (1979) "Foreword." In *Cyprus—War and Adaptation*, by Vamık D. Volkan, p. ix–xxi. Charlottesville, VA: University Press of Virginia.

Madley, B. (2017). *An American Genocide: The United States and the California Indian Catastrophe, 1846-1873*. New Haven CT: Yale University Press.

Mahfouz, A., Twemlow, S. & Scharff, D. E. (2007). *The Future of Prejudice: Psychoanalysis and the Prevention of Prejudice*. Northvale, NJ: Jason Aronson.

Mahler, M. S. (1968). *On Human Symbiosis and the Vicissitudes of Individuation*. New York: International Universities Press.

Mann, G. (2020). Perpetrators and victims: Can the self renounce its trauma? Psychoanalytic *Inquiry, 40*(7): 487–496.

Manning, M., Byrd, D., Lucas, T., & Zahodne, L. B. (2023). Complex effects of racism and discrimination on African Americans' health and well-being: Navigating the status quo. *Social Science & Medicine, 316*: 1–7.

Marihuan, R. P. & Aguado, T. B. (2019). El estatuto de limpieza de sangre y sus repercusiones en Vitoria en tiempos de Felipe II. *Hispania, 60*(205): 515–562.

Marler, P. (1991). In memoriam: Konrad Lorenz, 1903-1989. *The Auk, 108*(1): 164–165.

Martini, E. A. (2012). *Agent Orange: History, Science, and the Politics of Uncertainty*. Amherst, MA: University of Massachusetts Press.

Martyn, B. C. (1979). *Racism in the United States: A History of the Anti-miscegenation Legislation and Litigation*. University of Southern California.

Masler, E. G. (1969). The interpretation of projective identification in group psychotherapy. *International Journal of Group Psychotherapy, 19*(4), 441-=–447.

Matsuzawa, T. (2013). Evolution of the brain and social behavior in chimpanzees. *Current Opinion in Neurobiology, 23*(3): 443–449.

McGrath, C. (2020). US tests "bunker buster" bomb which could take out Kim's nukes. June 11. *Express*. https://www.express.co.uk/news/world/1294594/north-korea-news-bunker-buster-nuclear-bomb-test-donald-trump-kim-jong-un-world-war-3.

Meerloo, J. A. M. (1954). The monument as a delusional token. *American Imago, 11*(4): 363–374.

Meissner, W. W. (1990). The role of transitional conceptualization in religious thought. In *Psychoanalysis and Religion*, eds. J. H. Smith and S. A. Handelman, pp. 95-116. Baltimore MD: John Hopkins University Press.

Melamed, A., & Hoffman, M. (2022). *Inside the Middle East: Entering a New Era*. New York: Skyhorse.

Menninger, K. A. (1938). *Man Against Himself*. San Diego, CA: Harcourt Brace and Company.

Miami Ink. (2005, July 19). [Documentary, Reality-TV]. Truly Original.

Milgram, S. (1974). *Obedience to Authority. An Experimental View*. New York: Harper & Row.

Mitscherlich, A. (1971). Psychoanalysis and aggression of large groups. International Journal of *Psycho-Analysis, 52*: 161–167.

Mitscherlich, A. & Mitscherlich, M. (1975). *The Inability to Mourn: Principals of Collective Behavior*. Trans. B. R. Placzek. New York: Grove Press.

Moccia, L., Mazza, M., Nicola, M. D., & Janiri, L. (2018). The experience of pleasure: A perspective between neuroscience and psychoanalysis. *Frontiers in Human Neuroscience, 12*.

Modell, A. 1970. The transitional objects and the creative art. *Psychoanalytic Quarterly, 39*: 240–250.

Mogielnicki, C. (2023). Wartime forced sex as a male mating strategy. *Theory in Biosciences, 142*(1): 67–85.

Money-Kyrle, R. E. (1951). *Psychoanalysis and Politics: A contribution to the Psychology of Politics and Morals*. New York: W. W. Norton.

Morley, J. (2003). The texture of the real: Merleau-Ponty on imagination and psychopathology. In J. Phillips & J. Morley (Eds.), *Imagination and Its Pathologies*. Cambridge MA: Massachusetts Institute of Technology (MIT) Press.

Moses, R. (1982). The group-self and the Arab-Israeli Conflict. *International Review of Psychoanalysis, 9*:55–65.

Mucci, C. (2022). *Resilience and Survival: Understanding and Healing Intergenerational Trauma*. London: Confer Books.

Muñoz Zúñiga, J. F. (2017). EnRAGEd: Introductory notes on aggression in a case of orbitofrontal syndrome. *Neuropsychoanalysis, 19*(1): 77–86.

Murguia, E., & Saenz, R. (2002). An analysis of the Latin Americanization of race in the United States: A reconnaissance of color stratification among Mexicans. *Race and Society, 5*(1): 85–101.

Murphy, R. F. (1957). Ingroup hostility and social cohesion. *American Anthropologist, 59*:1018–1035.

Myers, S. L. (2015). *The New Tsar: The Rise and Reign of Vladimir Putin*. Alfred A. Knopf.

Nadler, R. D., & Miller, L. C. (1982). Influence of male aggression on mating of gorillas in the laboratory. *Folia Primatologica, 38*(3–4): 233–239.

Naimark, N. M. (2010). *Stalin's Genocides*. Princeton, NJ: Princeton University Press.

Nelsen, P. M. (2022). Putin stripped of martial arts honors. February 28. *Around the Rings*. https://www.infobae.com/aroundtherings/articles/2022/02/28/putin-stripped-of-martial-arts-honors/.

A new chapter in the migration crisis. (2023). *Economist*, 446(9335), 35–36.

Ng, L. (2013). Objectifying and de-objectifying the dead: The use of images in Chinese ancestor worship. In A. Gerlach, M. T. S. Hooke, & S. Varvin (Eds.), *Psychoanalysis in Asia: China*. New York: Routledge.

Niederland, W.G. (1964). Psychiatric disorders among persecution victims. *Journal of Nervous and Mental Disorders, 139*: 458-474.

Niederland, W.G. (1968). Clinical observations on the "survivor syndrome." International *Journal of Psychoanalysis, 49*:313-315.

Nikolaĭ, Z., Bromfield, A. (trans), France, R. (trans), & Hippisley, A. R. (trans). (2016). *Children of war: Diaries 1941-1945*. Moscow, RU: Argumenty i fakty: AIF Kind Heart Charitable Foundation.

Nikolova, Y. (2024). Bulgaria on three seas. *International Journal of Applied Psychoanalytic Studies* (in press).

OCHA. (2023). November 2. https://www.unocha.org/.

Ochsner, J. K. (1997). A Space of Loss: The Vietnam Veterans Memorial. *Journal of Architectural Education*, 50(3), 156–171.

Ohlmeier, D. (1991). The return of the repressed: Psychoanalytical reflections on the unification of Germany. Paper presented to the Sandor Ferenczi Society, Budapest, June 7.

Oltermann, P. (2020). Surfing on Hitler's show grounds: New plan for Berlin's Olympic Park. June 20. *The Guardian*. https://www.theguardian.com/world/2020/jun/20/surfing-on-hitlers-show-grounds-new-plan-for-berlins-olympic-park.

Ordway, F., & Sharpe, M. (2008). *The Rocket Team* (Pap/DVD edition). Burlington, Canada: Collector's Guide Publishing.

Oren, M. B. (2002). *Six Days of War: June 1967 and the Making of the Modern Middle East*. Oxford, UK: Oxford University Press.

Ortiz, S. Y., & Roscigno, V. J. (2009). Discrimination, women, and work: Processes and variations by race and class. *The Sociological Quarterly, 50*(2): 336–359.

Pao, P-N. (1979). *Schizophrenic Disorders: Theory and Treatment from a Psychodynamic Point of View*. New York: International Universities Press.

Park, J. (2023). Anti-Asian hate attacks are down in L.A. Why some are worried. July 17. *Los Angeles Times*.

Paulhus, D. L., & Williams, K. M. (2002). The Dark Triad of personality: Narcissism, Machiavellianism and psychopathy. *Journal of Research in Personality, 36*(6), 556–563.

Pavlenko, V. N. (2019). S. Milgram's experiment through the lens of historical psychology. *Social Psychology and Society, 10*(3): 5–18.

Perry, G. (2013). *Behind the Shock Machine: The Untold Story of the Notorious Milgram Psychology Experiments*. New York: The New Press.

Persaud, F. (2023). Guess how many migrants have entered the U.S. via the southwest border this year? *New York Amsterdam News, 114*(40), 14–14.

Pew Research Center, (2014). Turks Divided on Erdogan and the Country's Direction. July 30. *Pew Research Center's Global Attitudes Project*.

Phillips, U. B. (1918). *American Negro Slavery*. New York: D. Appleton and Company.

Philpott, C. (2016). *Relics of the Reich: The Buildings the Nazis Left Behind*. Barnsley, South Yorkshire, UK: Pen & Sword Military.

Pierce, J., & Bekoff, M. (2021). *A Dog's World: Imagining the Lives of Dogs in a World without Humans*. Princeton University Press.

Pines, M. (1975). Overview. In In Kreeger, L. (ed.). *The Large Group: Dynamics and Therapy* (pp. 291–311). Itasca, Il: F. E. Peacock.

Pope, H. (1999, May 10). Bunker Mentality: Albania's New Uses For Old Fortifications — Relics of Enver Hoxha's Reign, They Become Restaurants, Toilets, Even Love Motels. Wall Street Journal, Eastern Edition, A1.

Poznanski, E. O. (1972). The "replacement child": A saga of unresolved parental grief. *Journal of Pediatrics*, 81(6), 1190-1193.

Price, G. N. (2022). Incarceration risk, asset pricing, and Black-White wealth inequality. *Social Science Quarterly, 103*(5): 1306–1319.

Purhonen, M., Kilpeläinen-Lees, R., Valkonen-Korhonen, M., Karhu, J. and Lehtonen, J. (2005). Four-month-old infants process own mother`s voice faster than unfamiliar voices: Electrical signs of sensitization in infant brain. *Cognitive Brain Research 3*: 627–33.

Putin, V., Gevorkyan, N., Timakova, N., & Kolesnikov, (2000). *A First Person: An Astonishingly Frank Self-Portrait by Russia's President Vladimir Putin*. New York, PublicAffairs.

Putin, V. V., Shestakov, V., Levitsky, A., Russell, G., & Fukuda, K. (2004). *Judo: History, Theory, Practice*. Berkeley, CA: Blue Snake Books.

Putinery (Director). (2012, November 7). *Let's Learn Judo with Vladimir Putin* (2008). https://www.youtube.com/watch?v=f62myM2iPjE

Radice, O. (2023, October 9). Hamas terror attack: Girls "raped next to their dead friends" at rave massacre. The Jewish Chronicle. https://www.thejc.com/news/israel/girls-raped-next-to-their-dead-friends-at-rave-massacre-r6tufvnf.

Raine, A. (2014). *The Anatomy of Violence: The Biological Roots of Crime*. New York: Vintage.

Rangell, L (1980.) *The Mind of Watergate*. New York: Norton.

Rao, J. M. (2021). The lasting impact of colonial trauma in India: Links to Hindu nationalism. *International Journal of Applied Psychoanalytic Studies*, 18(4): 345–362.

Raped by the Red Army: Two million German women speak out. (2009, April 15). The Independent. https://www.independent.co.uk/news/world/europe/raped-by-the-red-army-two-million-german-women-speak-out-1669074.html

Read, D. W., Manrique, H. M., & Walker, M. J. (2022). On the working memory of humans and great apes: Strikingly similar or remarkably different?

Neuroscience and Biobehavioral Reviews, 134.

Rice, A. K. (1965). *Learning for Leadership*. London: Tavistock.

Rice, A. K. (1969). Individual, group, and intergroup processes. *Human Relations, 22*: 565–84.

Rice, A. K. (1975). The basis of conference design. In A. Colman and W. Bexton (eds). *In Group Relations Reader*. Portland, OR: A. K. Rice Institute.

Richards, A. K. (2018). The Death Instinct and its Vicissitudes. *Canadian Journal of Psychoanalysis, 26*: 121–134.

Richebächer, S. (2005). *Sabina Spielrein: Eine fast grausame Liebe zur Wissenschaft*. Vatican City: BTB.

Rochau, A.L. (1853). *Grundsätze der Realpolitik*. Frankfurt, DE: Ullstein.

Rooker, K., & Gavrilets, S. (2020). On the evolution of sexual receptivity in female primates. *Scientific Reports, 10*(1), Article 1.

Rosen, B. (2016). A "Nazi gold train" in Poland: Why does the search persist? August 16. *Christian Science Monitor*.

Rosenfeld, H. (2017). El narcisismo destructivo y el instinto de muerte. *Revista de Psicoanálisis de La Asociación Psicoanalítica de Madrid, 79*: 45–73.

Rosenthal, G. (1997). *Der Holocaust im Leben von drei Generationen: Familien von Überlebenden der Shoah und von Nazi-Tätern*. Gießen, DE: Psychosozial-Verlag.

Roxburgh, A. (2013). *The Strongman Vladimir Putin and the Struggle for Russia*. London: I.B. Tauris.

Rueb, E. S. (2019). New hotel planed in German bunker. October 13. *The New York Times*.

Russia Matters. (2024). The Russia-Ukraine War Report Card. July 16. https://www.russiamatters.org/news/russia-ukraine-war-report-card/russia-ukraine-war-report-card-july-16-2024.

Russian Gravediggers Defy Coronavirus to Throw Speed-Digging Contest. (2020). September 20. *The Moscow Times*. https://www.themoscowtimes.com/2020/09/10/russian-gravediggers-defy-coronavirus-to-throw-speed-digging-contest-a71406.

Sachar, H. M. (2007). *A History of Israel: From the Rise of Zionism to Our Time*. New York: Knopf.

Sahoo, N. (2020- August 18). Mounting majoritarianism and political polarization in India. In *Political polarization in South and Southeast Asia: Old Divisions, New Dangers*. Washington D.C.: Carnegie Endowment for International Peace.

Sandmeyer, E. C., & Daniels, R. (1991). *The Anti-Chinese Movement in California*. Champaign, Il: University of Illinois Press.

Schissler, H. (2001). *The Miracle Years: A Cultural History of West Germany, 1949-1968*. Princeton, NJ: Princeton University Press.

Schlosberg, J. (Director). (2007). May 3. *Battle at Kruger*. https://www.youtube.com/watch?v=LU8DDYz68kM.

Schmidt-Löw-Beer, C., Atria, M., & Davar, E. (2015). Communism and the trauma of its collapse revisited. *American Journal of Psychoanalysis*, 75(4), 394–415.

Schutzenberger, A.A. (1998). *The Ancestor Syndrome: Transgenerational Psychotherapy and the Hidden Links in the Family Tree*. New York: Routledge.

Śebek, M. (1994). Psychopathology of everyday life in the post-totalitarian society. *Mind and Human Interaction, 5*: 104–109.

Segal, H. (1993). On the clinical usefulness of the concept of death instinct. *The International Journal of Psychoanalysis, 74*(1): 55–61.

Shakespeare, W. (2002). *The Merchant of Venice*. Mowat. New York: Washington Square Press.

Shapiro, E. R. (2019). *Finding a Place to Stand: Developing Self-Reflective Institutions, Leaders and Citizens*. London: Phoenix.

Shapiro, E. R. & Carr, W. (2006). "Those people were some kind of solution": Can society in any sense be understood? *Organizational & Social Dynamics, 6*: 241-257

Shestakov, V., Levitsky, A., & Putin, V.V. (2000). *Учимся Дзюдо с Владимиром Путиным*. Moscow, RU: Abris/Olmas.

Siegel, R. (2001). Vladimir Putin: Transcript of Robert Siegel Interview [Interview]. *NPR News*. https://legacy.npr.org/news/specials/putin/nprinterview.html.

Sills, P. (2014). *Toxic War: The Story of Agent Orange*. Nashville, TN: Vanderbilt University Press.

Sklarew , B., Twemlow, S. W. & Wilkinson, S.M. (Eds.) (2014). *Analysts in the Trenches: Streets, Schools, War Zones*. New York: Routledge.

Skynner, A. C. R. (1975). The large group in training. In In Kreeger, L. (ed.) *The large group: Dynamics and Therapy*. (pp. 227–251). F. E. Peacock.

Smeulers, A., & Van Niekerk, S. (2009). Abu Ghraib and the wWar on Terror—A case against Donald Rumsfeld. *Crime, Law and Social Change, 51*(3–4): 327–349.

Smith, H. F. (2006). Invisible racism. *Psychoanalytic Quarterly, 75*, 3–19.

Smith, J. H. (1919). *The War with Mexico*. New York: Macmillan.

Solms, M. (2013). The Conscious id. *Neuropsychoanalysis, 15*(1): 5–19.

Solms, M. (2018). The Neurobiological underpinnings of psychoanalytic theory and therapy. *Frontiers in Behavioral Neuroscience, 12*.

Speer, A. (1997). *Inside the Third Reich* (Reissue edition). New York: Simon & Schuster.

Spielrein, S. (1912). Die Destruktion als Ursache des Werdens. *Jahrbuch Für Psychoanalytische Und Psychopathologische Forschung, 4*: 465–503.

Stanton, G. (1996a). The Eight Stages of Genocide. In *The Genocide Studies Reader*, Totten, S. & Bartrop, P.R. (Eds.) (pp. 127–129). New York: Routledge.

Stanton, G. (1996b). *The Seven Stages of Genocide*. http://www.genocide-watch.

com/images/8StagesBriefingpaper.pdf

Stanton, G. (2019). Teaching Ten Stages of Genocide. In *Teaching about Genocide, Volume 2*, Totten, S. (Ed). Washington, DC: Rowman & Littlefield.

Stanton, G. (2023). The Logic of the Ten Stages of Genocide [Genocidewatch. com]. *Genocide Watch.*

Statista. (2024). Ukraine Civilian War Casualties 2024. August 1. https://www.statista.com/statistics/1293492/ukraine-war-casualties/.

Stefkovics, A. (2021). A divided society: Exploring new political fractures in Hungary. (pp. 74-87). In *Hyphens (kötő-jelek)*. Budapest, HU: ELTE TáTK.

Stekel, W. (1922). *Sex and dreams: The language of dreams*. London: R. G. Badger.

Stern, D. N. (1985) *The Interpersonal World of the Infant: A View from Psychoanalysis and Developmental Psychology*. New York: Basic Books.

Stoute, B. J. (2021). Black rage: The psychic adaptation to the trauma of oppression. *Journal of the American Psychoanalytic Association, 69*(2): 259–290.

Strachey, A. (1957). *The Unconscious Motives of War: A Psychoanalytic Contribution.* New York: International Universities Press.

Streeck-Fischer, A. (1999). Naziskins in Germany: Traumatization in the past and present. *Mind and Human Interaction, 10*: 84–97.

Strozier, C. B., & Mart, D. (2017). La politique de l'humiliation construite: Perspectives psychanalytiques sur la guerre, le terrorisme et le génocide. *Recherches En Psychanalyse, 23*: 27–36.

Swartz, M. (1991). The Cheerleader Murder Plot. *Texas Monthly*. https://www.texasmonthly.com/arts-entertainment/the-cheerleader-murder-plot/.

Tähkä, V. (1984) Dealing with object loss. *Scandinavian Psychoanalytic Review, 7*:13-33.

Tanggaard, L., & Tateo, L. (2018). Unity of the real and the non-real: Imagination in action and talk. *Nordic Psychology, 70*(1): 85–94.

Texier, T. (2019). Debunking the Stanford Prison experiment. *American Psychologist, 74*(7): 823–839.

The Horrors of San Domingo: Chapter V: Introduction of Slavery. (1863). *Atlantic Monthly, 11*(65), 289–306.

The Impact of Structural Racism on Black Americans (Report). (n.d.). *Catalyst.* Retrieved November 10, 2023, from https://www.catalyst.org/research/structural-racism-black-americans/.

Thompson, E. C., & Smutkupt, S. (2016). From sex tourist to son-in-law emergent masculinities and transient subjectivities of Farang Men in Thailand. *Current Anthropology, 57*(1): 53–71.

Thomson, J. A. (with C. Aukofer) (2011). *Why We Believe in God(s): A Concise Guide to the Science of Faith.* Pitchstone Publishing.

Toksabay, E. & D. Şenkaya, D. (2023). Eclipsing Turkey's centenary, Erdogan tells pro-Palestinian rally: Israel is occupier. October 28. *Reuters*. https://www.reuters.com/world/middle-east/erdogan-address-pro-palestinian-rally-eve-turkeys-centenary-2023-10-28/

Toler, A., Willis, H., Mellen, R., Cardia, A., Reneau, N., Barnes, J. E., & Koettl, C. (2023). A Close Look at Some Key Evidence in the Gaza Hospital Blast. October 25. *The New York Times*.

Torry, H. (2013). German Agency Searches for New Uses for Bunkers. January 23. *Wall Street Journal*.

Treadwell, H. M. (2020). The pandemic, racism, and health disparities among African American men. *American Journal of Men's Health, 14*(4).

Trevor-Roper, H. (2013). *The Last Days of Hitler*. London: Pan Macmillan.

Turquet, P. (1975). Threats to identity in the large group. In: *The Large Group: Dynamics and Therapy*, ed. L. Kreeger, pp. 87-144. London: Constable.

Twain, M. (1882). *The Prince and the Pauper*. Boston, MA: James R. Osgood and Company.

Twemlow, S. W. & Sacco, F. C. (2011). *Preventing Bullying and School Violence*. Washington, DC: American Psychiatric Publication.

Twitter, Instagram, Email, & Facebook. (2023, July 17). Anti-Asian hate attacks are down in L.A. Why some are worried. Los Angeles Times. https://www.latimes.com/california/story/2023-07-17/anti-asian-hate-attacks-are-down-in-l-a-why-some-are-worried

Tzalmona, R. (2011). Traces of the Atlantikwall or the ruins that were built to Last.... *Third Text, 25*(6):775–786.

Tzu, S. (1910). *The Art of War*. Luzac.

United Nations. (1951). *Convention on the Prevention and Punishment of the Crime of Genocide*. Adopted by the General Assembly of the United Nations on 9 December 1948.

Unnikrishnan, D. (2022). Dramatic Story of Vladimir Putin's Mother's Rescue During WW2 Goes Viral. February 26. *BOOM*. https://www.boomlive.in/news/vladimir-putin-parents-leningrad-dead-hillary-clinton-russia-ukraine-16937

UNRWA (2024). UNRWA Situation Report #132 on the situation in the Gaza Strip and the West Bank, including East Jerusalem. August 28. https://www.unrwa.org/resources/reports/unrwa-situation-report-132-situation-gaza-strip-and-west-bank-including-east-Jerusalem.

Valasquez, G., Rasuli, S., Knowles, L., & Ramezani, A. (2018). Neuroanatomical and Neurocognitive Functions of the Structure of the Mind: Clinical and Teaching Implications. *Scientia Ricerca, 2*(6): 567-584

van der Borg, J.A.M., Schilder, M.B.H., Vinke, C.M., de Vries, H. (2015) Dominance in Domestic Dogs: A Quantitative Analysis of Its Behavioural Measures. *PLoS ONE 10*(8): e0133978.

Varvin, S. (1995). Genocide and ethnic cleansing: Psychoanalytic and social-psychological viewpoints. *The Scandinavian Psychoanalytic Review, 18*(2): 192–210.

Varvin, S. & Volkan, V. D. (Eds.) (2003). *Violence or Dialogue: Psychoanalytic Insights on Terror and Terrorism*. London: International Psychoanalytical Association.

Veltri, M. (2018). Is Benjamin Wittes Underestimating Vladimir Putin's Martial Arts Skills? February 23. *Lawfare*. https://www.lawfaremedia.org/article/benjamin-wittes-underestimating-vladimir-putins-martial-arts-skills.

Virilio, P. (1994). *Bunker Archaeology*. Princeton, NJ: Princeton University Press.

Vogels, S. (2014). The Milgram experiment: Its impact and interpretation. *Social Cosmos, 5*(1):15–21.

Volkan, K. (1994). Psychopathology, groups, and group leaders: A psychoanalytic perspective. *Vision/Action, 13*(1): 19–24.

Volkan, K. (2021). Bunkers, bubbles, monuments, and walls: Pathological narcissism, Nazi Germany, and Donald Trump. *European Journal of Psychoanalysis, 7*(2): 1–21.

Volkan, K., & Volkan, V. D. (2022). *Schizophrenia: Science, Psychoanalysis, and Culture*. Oxfordshire: Karnac.

Volkan, K., & Volkan, V. D. (2023). *How the Mind Works: Concepts and Cases in Psychoanalysis and Psychotherapy*. Karnac.

Volkan, V. D. (1981). *Linking Objects and Linking Phenomena*. International Universities Press.

Volkan, V. D. (1972). The linking objects of pathological mourners. *Archives of General Psychiatry*, 27, 215–221.

Volkan, V. D. (1976). *Primitive Internalized Object Relations: A Clinical Study of Schizophrenic, Borderline, and Narcissistic Patients*. New York: International Universities Press.

Volkan, V. D. (1979). *Cyprus-War and Adaptation: A Psychoanalytic History of two Ethnic Groups in Conflict*. Charlottesville, VA: University Press of Virginia.

Volkan, V. D. (1984). Complicated Mourning. *The Annual of Psychoanalysis, 12*, 323–348.

Volkan, V. D. (1987). *Six Steps in the Treatment of Borderline Personality Organization*. Jason Aronson, Inc.

Volkan, V. D. (1988). *The Need to Have Enemies & Allies: From Clinical Practice to International Relationships*. Northvale, NJ: Jason Aronson.

Volkan, V. D. (1992). Ethnonationalist rituals: An introduction. *Mind and Human Interaction, 4*: 3–19.

Volkan, V. D. (1995). Totem and taboo in Romania: A psychopolitical diagnosis. *Mind and Human Interaction, 6*: 66-83.

Volkan, V. D. (1997). *Bloodlines: From Ethnic Pride to Ethnic Terrorism*. New York: Farrar, Straus and Giroux.

Volkan, V. D. (1999). *Das Versagen der Diplomatie: Zur Psychoanalyse nationaler, ethnischer und religiöser Konflikte*. Gießen DE: Psychosozial-Verlag.

Volkan, V. D. (2004). *Blind Trust: Large Groups and Their Leaders in Times of Crisis and Terror*. Pitchstone Publishing.

Volkan, V. D. (2006a). *Killing in the Name of Identity: A Study of Bloody Conflicts*.

Pitchstone Publishing.

Volkan, V. D. (2006b). What some monuments tell us about mourning and forgiveness. In *Taking Wrongs Seriously: Apologies and Reconciliation*, eds. E. Barkan & A. Karn, pp. 115-131. Stanford University Press.

Volkan, V. D. (2007). Individuals and Societies as "Perennial Mourners": Their Linking Objects and Public Memorials. In *On Death and Endings: Psychoanalysts' Reflections on Finality, Transformations and New Beginnings*, (Eds.), Brent Willock, B., . Bohm, L.C. & Curtis, R. C. (Eds.), pp.42-59. Philadelphia: Routledge.

Volkan, V. D. (2010). *Psychoanalytic Technique Expanded: A Textbook on Psychoanalytic Treatment*. London: Oa Publishing.

Volkan, V. D. (2013a). *Enemies on the Couch: A Psychopolitical Journey Through War and Peace*. Pitchstone Publishing.

Volkan, V. D. (2013b) Large-Group Psychology in Its Own Right: Large-Group Identity and Peace-making. *International Journal of Applied Psychoanalytic Studies 10*: 210–246.

Volkan, V. D. (2020). *Large-Group Psychology: Racism, Societal Divisions, Narcissistic Leaders and Who We Are Now*. London: Phoenix.

Volkan, V. D (2023). Political leaders' personalities, socio-political processes and the invasion of Ukraine," in *Why War in Ukraine and in Europe. Psychoanalysis, Trauma, and Resiliency*, ed. Leo Giuseppe Leo, pp. 51-11. Lecce, Italy: Frenis Zero Publishing House.

Volkan, V. D. & Ast, G. (1994). *Spektrum des Narzißmus: Eine klinische Studie des gesunden Narzißmus, des narzißtisch-masochistischen Charakters, der narzißtischen Persönlichkeitsorganisation, des malignen Narzißmus und des erfolgreichen Narzißmus.*). Göttingen: Vandenhoeck & Ruprecht.

Volkan, V. D., & Ast, G. (1997). *Siblings in the unconscious and psychopathology: Womb fantasies, claustrophobias, fear of pregnancy, murderous rage, animal symbolism, Christmas and Easter neuroses, and twinnings or identifications with sisters and brothers*. New York: International Universities Press.

Volkan, V. D., & Itzkowitz, N. (1984). *The Immortal Atatürk: A Psychobiography*. Chicago: University of Chicago Press.

Volkan, V. D., & Itzkowitz, N. (1994). *Turks and Greeks: Neighbors in Conflict*. Tallahassee, Fl: Eothen Press.

Volkan, V. D., Akhtar, S., Dorn, R. M., Kafka, J. S., Kernberg, O. F., Olsson, P. A., Rogers, R. R., & Shanfield, S. (1998). The psychodynamics of leaders and decision-making. *Mind and Human Interaction, 9*: 129–181.

Volkan, V. D., Ast, G., and Greer, Jr., W. F. (2002). *Third Reich in the Unconscious Transgenerational Transmission and its Consequences*. New York: Brunner-Routledge.

Volkan, V. D., Itzkowitz, N., & Dod, A. (1997). *Richard Nixon: A Psychobiography*. New York: Columbia University Press.

Waelder, R. (1930). The principle of multiple function: Observations on over-determination. *Psychoanalytic Quarterly, 5*: 45–62.

Waelder, R. (1960). *Basic Theory of Psychoanalysis*. New York: International Universities Press.

Waite, R. G. L. (1978). *The Psycho-Pathic God Adolf Hitler*. New York: Signet Books.

Wakida, P., & Hohri, W. (2014). *Only What We Could Carry: The Japanese American Internment Experience*, ed. L. F. Inada. Berkeley, CA: Heyday.

Waller, J. (2002). Perpetrators of genocide: An explanatory model of extraordinary human evil. *Journal of Hate Studies, 1.*

Wangh, M. (1964). National socialism and the genocide of the Jews. *The International Journal of Psychoanalysis, 45*(2–3): 386–395.

Warring, J. (2018). *Implicit bias in the 21st century American legal system*. Ann Arbor, MI: Proquest Dissertation Publishing.

Waska, R. T. (2000). Hate, projective identification, and the psychotherapist's struggle. *Journal of Psychotherapy Practice & Research, 9*(1): 33–38.

Weigert, E. (1954). The importance of flexibility in psychoanalytic technique. *Journal of the American Psychoanalytic Association*, 2(4), 702-710.

Werman D. S. (1988). Freud's "narcissism of minor differences": A review and reassessment. *The Journal of the American Academy of Psychoanalysis*, 16(4), 451–459.

Werner, H., & Kaplan, B. (1963). *Symbol Formation: An Organismic Developmental Approach to Language and the Expression of Thought*. New York: Wiley.

White, R. S. (2023). An antisemitic transference and countertransference. *International Journal of Applied Psychoanalytic Studies, 20*(1): 55–69.

Whitley, J. S. (1975). The large group as a medium for sociotherapy. In In Kreeger, L. (ed.) *The large group: Dynamics and therapy* (pp. 193–211). F. E. Peacock.

Wiener, S. (2001). Le tatouage, de la griffe ordinaire à la marque subjective. *Essaim, 2*, 35–49.

Wilkie, N. C. (1999). Politics and the Past. *Archaeology, 52*(5), 6.

Wilson, M. L., & Glowacki, L. (2017). Violent cousins: Chimpanzees, humans, and the roots of war. In M. N. Muller, R. W. Wrangham, & D. R. Pilbeam (Eds.), *Chimpanzees and human evolution*. pp. 464–508. Cambridge, MA: The Belknap Press of Harvard University Press.

Wilson, M., & Wrangham, R. (2003). Intergroup Relations in Chimpanzees. *Annual Review of Anthropology, 32*, 363–392.

Winnicott, D. W. (1953). Transitional objects and transitional phenomena. A study of the first not-me possession. *International Journal of Psychoanalysis, 34*, 89–97.

Winnicott, D. W. (1962). The aims of psycho-analytical treatment. The Maturational Processes and the Facilitating Environment: *Studies in the Theory of Emotional Development, 64*:166–170.

Winnicott, D. W. (1971). Case XIII. "Ada" at 8 Years. *Therapeutic Consultations in Child Psychiatry, 87*: 220–238.

Wittes, B. (2015). I'll Fight Putin Any Time, Any Place He Can't Have Me Arrested. October 21. *Lawfare*. https://www.lawfaremedia.org/article/ill-fight-putin-any-time-any-place-he-cant-have-me-arrested.

Wong, K. (2014). Rise of the Human Predator. *Scientific American. 310*(4), p. 46.

Wrangham, R. W. (1993). The evolution of sexuality in chimpanzees and bonobos. *Human Nature, 4*(1), 47–79.

Zaloga, S. J. (2008). *German V-Weapon Sites 1943–45*. Oxford, UK: Osprey Publishing.

Zepf, S. (2015). Penisneid und weiblicher Ödipuskomplex: Ein Plädoyer für die Wiederaufnahme einer wirkungsvollen Debatte. *Zeitschrift für Psychoanalytische Theorie und Praxis, 30*(1), 65–92.

Zimbardo, P. (1973). On the ethics of intervention in human psychological research: With special reference to the Stanford prison experiment. *Cognition, 2*(2): 243–256.

Zimbardo, P. (1995). The psychology of evil: A situationist perspective on recruiting good people to engage in anti-social acts. *The Japanese Journal of Social Psychology, 11*(2): 125–133.

Zimbardo, P. (2007). *The Lucifer Effect: Understanding How Good People Turn Evil*. New York: Random House.

Name Index

Subject Index

About the Authors

Vamık D. Volkan, MD, is an Emeritus Professor of Psychiatry at the University of Virginia and an Emeritus Senior Erik Erikson Scholar at the Erikson Institute of the Austen Riggs Center. He is the Emeritus President of the International Dialogue Initiative and a former President of the Turkish-American Neuropsychiatric Society, the International Society of Political Psychology, the Virginia Psychoanalytic Society and the American College of Psychoanalysts. Dr. Volkan was a member of the International Negotiation Network under the directorship of former President Jimmy Carter; an Inaugural Yitzhak Rabin Fellow, Rabin Center for Israeli Studies, Tel Aviv, Israel; a visiting Professor of psychiatry at four universities in Turkey; a visiting Professor of Psychoanalysis at East-European Institute of Psychoanalysis, Saint Petersburg, Russia; a visiting Professor of Law, Harvard University, Cambridge, Massachusetts and a Fulbright/Sigmund Freud-Foundation Visiting Scholar of Psychoanalysis in Vienna, Austria. He is the author, coauthor, editor or coeditor of over sixty psychoanalytic and psychopolitical books.

Kevin Volkan, EdD, PhD, MPH, is Professor of Psychology at California State University Channel Islands. He is also Adjunct Professor in the Clinical Psychology Doctoral Program at California Lutheran University and adjunct faculty in the Clinical Psychology PhD Program at Pacifica Graduate Institute. He holds doctorates in clinical and quantitative psychology, is a graduate of the Harvard School of Public Health, and a former Harvard Medical School faculty member. Dr. Volkan has testified before the United States Senate, served as a forensic consultant to state and federal law enforcement agencies, and made numerous appearances on television, radio, and podcasts. His clinical training and experience are in psychoanalytic psychotherapy as well as a wide variety of other modalities. Dr. Volkan was awarded the Sustained Superior Accomplishment Award from the State of California for his clinical work. He is author of *Dancing Among the Maenads: The Psychology of Compulsive Drug Use, Schizophrenia: Science, Psychoanalysis, and Culture* and *How the Mind Works: Concepts and Cases in Psychoanalysis and Psychotherapy*.

www.ingramcontent.com/pod-product-compliance
Lightning Source LLC
Chambersburg PA
CBHW020114230726
48635CB00028B/157

* 9 7 8 1 6 3 4 3 1 2 6 8 4 *